THE
GARDENER'S
HANDBOOK

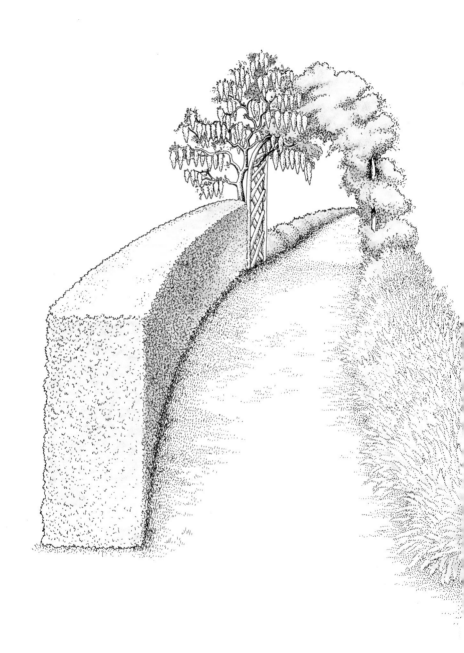

THE GARDENER'S HANDBOOK

THE ESSENTIAL GUIDE FOR SUCCESS WITH PLANTS

Tessa Paul and Nigel Chadwick

Consultant Editor
Dr Stefan Buczacki

GREENWICH EDITIONS

This edition published by GREENWICH EDITIONS in 1996
by arrangement with Marshall Editions Developments Limited
Greenwich Editions,
Bibliophile House,
10 Blenheim Court,
Brewery Road,
London N7 9NT

Reprinted in 1998

First published in the UK in 1993 by Pan Books Limited

ISBN 0-86288-105-6

Copyright © 1993 Marshall Editions Developments Limited

Editor	Gwen Rigby
Editorial Director	Ruth Binney
Art Director	Sara Kidd
DTP Editor	Mary Pickles
Picture Coordinator	Zilda Tandy
Production	Barry Baker
	Janice Storr

Film supplied by Dorchester Typesetting Group, UK
Origination by Scantrans, Singapore
Printed and bound in Portugal, by Printer Portuguesa

CONTENTS

INTRODUCTION

With so many new gardening books appearing each year, surely some justification is needed for yet another. In fact, there are relatively few reliable works aimed principally at newcomers to gardening, and it is to fill this need that we have created *The Gardener's Handbook*. And while this book is primarily directed at the inexperienced, many of those who are more practised in the horticultural arts will also find it an invaluable companion and memory jogger.

Here, in one volume, is a guide to the growing of ornamental plants that will, above all, enable those who have little or no experience in the subject to make their first decisions in a sensible manner. How much difference does my soil make to the plants

I want to grow; how do I choose and plant a tree; which fertilizer do I need; will I have to become an expert at pruning? To answer these and countless other potential queries, we have distilled a mass of facts and opinions and provided the best advice on offer. But it is one thing to collect the necessary information, quite another to write and present it in a readily palatable and very practical form. It is here, however, that the book really scores and why it is such a simple work to use. The information is set out logically in a sensible and readily accessible way and it is illustrated both usefully and attractively—far too many gardening books use pictures merely as embellishments. This one, to conjure up an expression I loathe but which is readily understood these days, is user friendly.

Every imaginable way of creating an attractive and enjoyable garden is covered and every necessary gardening technique carefully explained. There are lists of plants to succeed in particular places and step-by-step advice on mastering the tools of the trade. You will not be blinded with science or confused with technicalities. This is gardening in its basic, enjoyable essentials.

I spend much of my time answering gardeners' questions and helping to solve their problems. If all of them had started out their gardening lives equipped with *The Gardener's Handbook*, I'm sure that a considerable number of those questions and problems would never have arisen.

STEFAN BUCZACKI

Dr Stefan Buczacki is Britain's best-known gardening expert, familiar to millions through his contributions to BBC radio's Gardeners' Question Time, his television appearances, and his authorship of a prestigious list of gardening books.

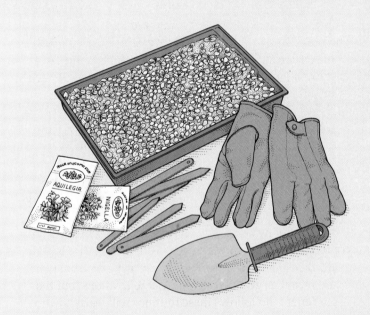

PRACTICAL GARDENING

The art of gardening has been described as the control and ordering of nature. Throughout the ages, gardeners have evolved tried and tested ways of creating an environment in which plants, many of which have crossed international boundaries, will flourish.

The first chapter of this book deals with the basic principles of soil care and maintenance and explains methods of improving its nutritional qualities through the addition of compost and fertilizers. Methods of soil preparation are outlined, followed by explanations of the different ways in which plants can be raised and propagated by sowing seed, division and layering. Planting routines are discussed in detail.

Some of the main garden problems which must be understood and controlled are then considered. Gardeners need to be able to recognize and remove weeds—the merits of hand weeding and chemical weed control are contrasted—and to identify various pests and diseases and guard their plants against them. The practices outlined here are meant as guidelines, not strict regulations, but the gardener who follows these routines will learn how to control the elements of the garden to create a rich, nutritious environment that will sustain healthy plant life.

PREPARING THE GROUND

If you observe the walls of a trench in your garden, you will see the "soil profile". This is revealed in a series of layers or "horizons", each with its own colour and texture. It is the top horizon, the topsoil, that is of interest to the gardener.

This horizon is of a darkish colour, caused by the activity of fungi, bacteria, insects and other organisms. A good topsoil must hold moisture, yet drain off surplus water. It must hold and circulate air, and it must feed the roots of plants.

A soil which breaks easily into round, porous crumbs is usually moist and well structured. However, if the soil is solid and compacted and does not break up easily, it is likely to be poorly aerated and low in humus.

To prepare the top-soil for cultivation, you must dig the earth to aerate it and prevent compaction; during this process, the humus already present in the top-soil should be supplemented by the addition of compost and, if necessary, of fertilizers to provide more nutrients. Annual weeds and plant remains can be dug in to create

THE IMPORTANCE OF HUMUS

Humus is decayed organic matter and has a fibrous appearance. It plays a vital role in the top-soil, for it introduces chemicals that are absorbed by the plant roots and supplies food for the teeming bacteria living in the soil. These, in turn, also make chemicals available to feed the roots.

Because humus is light and porous, it counteracts any compaction of the soil and so helps drain surplus water, keeping the soil open, airy and moist.

humus, but perennial weeds, with their long, tough roots, must be removed.

This type of digging, often termed single digging, is illustrated below. The ground should be dug roughly in the autumn when the soil is not wet: it should not stick to your spade. This digging will

At one end of the site, dig a trench the width and depth of a spade; move earth to other end of site.

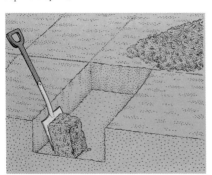

Fork the exposed earth at the bottom of the trench and add compost or well-rotted manure.

See also: Spring digging Pages 20–21
Nutrients and fertilizers Pages 28–29

Top-soil Fertile layer of earth which contains organisms, fungi and insects. This layer sustains plant life. Ideally it should be 3ft/1m deep, well aerated, well drained, and rich in nutrients.

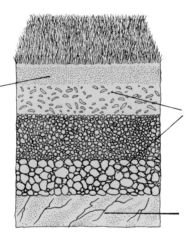

Sub-soil Bright in colour from traces of iron and other materials, with fragmented rock scattered throughout.

Bedrock or "origin"

open up the soil to the winter weather, when periods of cold and successive thaw will continue the process of aeration and decomposition of humus. By spring, the beds will be ready for final digging.

Some professional gardeners recommend that beds for annuals are double-dug every four years; by this, they mean dug to two spade's depth—which is extremely time-consuming and hard work. It is generally not practical to double-dig established herbaceous borders and shrubberies unless you are reorganizing the planting.

Dig a second trench. Put the earth from it into the first, mixing it with compost and manure.

Repeat the process throughout the site. Fill the last trench with the earth from the first one.

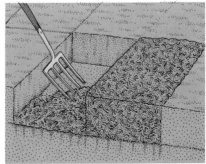

Weed identification and eradication Pages 36–39

SEEDS

Seed packets vary in the information they provide. Some are complex and scientific in their descriptions, others offer the most obvious tips about planting methods and little else. Since packeted seeds are produced and treated in different ways, it is helpful to understand some of the basic information you may encounter.

"F₁ hybrid" means that the plant is a variety that has been bred from a complicated ancestry and the seed company must repeat the breeding process to produce the variety again. It is an expensive method, but an F₁ hybrid will give uniformity of bloom and growth. It is not worth collecting the seeds of these plants, however, because they will not come true but will produce a hotch-potch of offspring.

Seeds of some plants are available coated with clay or similar material; these have been "pelleted", a process that suits very small, fine seeds, for the clay gives them some weight and size, making them easier to handle. However, the covering sometimes has an adverse effect on germination.

Partly because of economics and partly because they prefer them, many gardeners buy "open-pollinated seeds". These have not been specially treated in any way or hybridized. Such seeds are known as "standard" or "conventional", and seeds collected from the subsequent plants will generally prove reliable.

Many companies vacuum-pack their seeds, but there is also a system of packing germinated seed into waterproof sachets. These are known as "chitted seed" and must be sown immediately after purchase.

Faced with the rising cost of plants and seeds, the gardener may well groan at the expense of stocking a garden. The answer to this is to collect your own seeds or to save the surplus from any packets of commercially raised seeds you buy each season.

Prepare to collect seeds on the point of ripening but before they spill on the ground. This may need close observation of the seed heads. Most annuals have dry seeds, but should they be wet, remove the pulp, wash the seeds thoroughly to remove any chemicals and then spread them out to dry at room temperature.

Those plants with dry seeds, such as poppies and lupins, must have the flower heads cut off. Tie these together and put them upside down in a paper bag. Hang the bag in a warm, yet well-ventilated, dry place and shake it occasionally to collect the loose seed in the bottom.

When the seeds have dried out, or fallen, pack them in paper or cellophane envelopes. Never use plastic because, if the seeds have retained any moisture, fungus may grow in the bag.

STORING SEEDS

- Seeds can be stored in any cool dry place, but the best place is the refrigerator.
- Label paper or cellophane packets with the variety name and the date. It is important to keep track of the age of your seeds; some remain viable for only a year, others for much longer.
- Place the packets of seeds and a sachet of silica gel in a screw-top jar and put it in the fridge.
- Store surplus commercial seed in the same manner.

WHAT A SEED PACKET TELLS YOU

Name of plant
Snapdragon (common name), *Antirrhinum* (Latin name). A brief description may follow of the plant's habit—whether it is low, spreading, tall, free flowering—and the type of soil it prefers.

Hardening off How to prepare the seedlings for conditions outdoors through a gradual introduction to the weather.

Planting out When to transplant seedlings to a garden bed and advice on spacing.

Aftercare Outlines any special requirements, such as feeding, dead-heading or watering, that the plant needs.

Special note If the plant has any particular quality or can be cultivated under different conditions, the information will be given here.

Sowing time Will tell you the months or seasons in which to sow seeds.

Sowing Describes the method of sowing appropriate to the type of seed and suggestions for suitable compost.

Pricking out (sometimes called Growing on) Instructions for thinning out and spacing seedlings once they have grown their first leaves, or cotyledons.

See also: Propagation from seed Pages 14–15

PROPAGATION FROM SEED

Many of the familiar plants used in annual bedding schemes are native to warmer climates. In more temperate places, most of these plants need to be given warmth indoors before they will germinate.

Such plants are known as "half hardy annuals" although quite often, as with lobelias, they are actually perennials. You can sow these seeds in a pot or plastic seed tray. Because there is a risk that not all the seeds will germinate, you should sow roughly twice as many as the number of plants you will need.

• Find a proprietary brand of compost that is peat based or soil-less, or a type known as "universal".

• Do not try to re-use compost, but use a fresh batch for every seed tray.

• Do not allow the compost to dry out.

• Spread the compost on the tray, pressing it down loosely.

• Water gently, allowing 8fl oz/230ml for a standard seed tray.

• Do not cover the seeds with compost.

For larger seeds, draw "trenches" in the compost with the edge of a plastic card. The rows of trenches should be about 1in/2.5cm apart and, as you sow along each row, keep the seeds about ½in/1cm apart. Label the seed trays.

Cover seed trays with a rigid cover of plastic or glass; or clear plastic sheet draped over sticks if you are sowing in a pot. The seeds need warmth to germinate. An airing cupboard is ideal, but move the trays into the light as soon as the seedlings emerge, or put them on a window sill during the day, moving them to a warm room at night. If you are keen to grow your own plants from seed, it may be worth while to invest in a purpose-built propagator.

From the moment of sowing, the compost must be kept moist; use a child's watering can for this job. When the seedlings are sufficiently mature, prick them out.

Since hardy annuals are sown outdoors, some warming of the soil may be necessary. A week or so before sowing, place cloches

Fill a seed tray with compost. Firm the surface down with a board so that the compost is about ½in/1cm below the top of the tray.

Shake the seeds evenly from the packet. Sow more seeds than you require.

▼ See also: Seeds Pages 12–13
Pricking out Pages 16–17

or a plastic sheet over the seed bed, which should be prepared by digging as explained on Pages 10–11 and then raking.

Prepare drills in the bed—that is, make shallow grooves in the soil, using a cane or the back of a rake. Tiny seeds, weighted with brick dust, should be scattered along the drill. Other seeds should be planted approximately ½in/1cm deep and the same distance apart.

Use the back of the rake to push the earth gently over the drills. Firm the earth, gently patting it down with the back of the rake. Replace the cloches if you feel the seeds need extra warmth.

Do not water the seeds, the beds should be moist enough to make this unnecessary. For information on watering times and methods see Pages 34–35.

Seeds must be given close attention and the correct nutrients and watering if they are to flourish. Planting out also demands time from the gardener; care during these important initial stages will ensure that the garden will be filled with strong, healthy plants.

Sowing and planting your own seeds is a process that requires patience, but it is one of the most rewarding aspects of gardening. The true gardener will feel a great delight in growing, rather than buying, as many plants for the garden as possible.

A heated propagator serves as a mini-greenhouse for those without the real thing. It has a thermostatically controlled heating element and a plastic cover to create a closed environment.

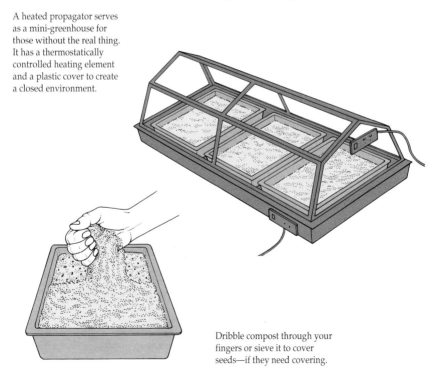

Dribble compost through your fingers or sieve it to cover seeds—if they need covering.

PRICKING OUT, HARDENING OFF

When your seeds germinate, the first thing you will see is the cotyledons, which are the initial pair of leaves on a seedling, emerging from the compost. At this stage you should open the vents on the propagator or ventilate the seed trays and pots by partially opening the covers.

Watch your seedlings straighten up and lengthen; as they grow stronger, all covers and protective ventilation can be removed. Throughout this growing process, you must keep the seedlings watered and protect them from too much strong sunlight.

As the seedlings grow, they will develop into a dense cluster of tiny plants. In such crowded conditions, they compete for water and nutrition. If all the seedlings are left, their growth will be spindly and they will be vulnerable to disease. So, to encourage vigorous growth and healthy development, these little plants must be thinned out and spaced—a process known as "pricking out". The weakest seedlings can be discarded.

Pricking out
- Prepare another clean seed tray.
- Fill it with universal compost, firming

HI-TECH SEED TRAYS
Small seed trays and pots made from peat impregnated with fertilizer can be purchased from shops and garden centres. Seedlings can be pricked out into these organic, biodegradable pots and hardened off. The whole pot can then be planted in the ground, where it will gradually decompose, causing minimal root disturbance to the plant.

---

and watering it just as you did when you were preparing the seed trays for sowing.
- With a pencil or "dibber" make holes in the compost about 2in/5cm apart. Their depth should be equal to the root length of the plants you are moving.
- A standard seed tray prepared in this way will carry approximately 35 seedlings.
- Do not try to separate very small seedlings, such as lobelia, or to lift them individually. Instead, using an old table fork, lever a clump from the compost of the first seed tray and move it to the second.
- Allow plenty of space around each clump so that the roots have room to spread. As the plants grow bigger, prick them out again if they become crowded.
- Stronger seedlings can be moved individually, but take care in handling them. If you lift the seedlings by their stems, be cautious, for they are easily damaged. You can hold the cotyledons, but perhaps the simplest method is to lift the plant out of the compost—again using a table fork—cup the small ball of compost and roots in your fingers and place it in a hole in the compost of the new seed tray.
- Firm the compost gently around each seedling or clump; remember, the roots, too, are very fragile at this stage.
- Gently water the replanted seedlings.

These little plants must now be prepared for their future in the flower bed. Because they have been reared indoors, in a warm environment, the seedlings have developed large, thin-walled cells which would collapse if they were to be exposed straight away to cold weather in the garden.

But this preparation for outdoor life, known as "hardening off", is not a harsh training and the weather should be

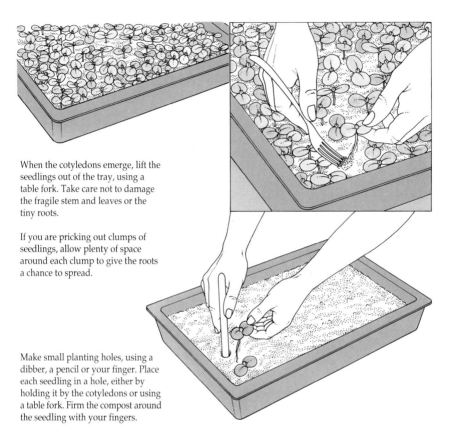

When the cotyledons emerge, lift the seedlings out of the tray, using a table fork. Take care not to damage the fragile stem and leaves or the tiny roots.

If you are pricking out clumps of seedlings, allow plenty of space around each clump to give the roots a chance to spread.

Make small planting holes, using a dibber, a pencil or your finger. Place each seedling in a hole, either by holding it by the cotyledons or using a table fork. Firm the compost around the seedling with your fingers.

springlike, with some warmth in the air, before you start upon it.

Hardening off

• The day after you prick out your seedlings, move the seed trays into a cold frame or unheated greenhouse.

• During the day, prop up the lid of the cold frame so that it is half open, and close it firmly at night.

• After a week, open the lid fully during the day and leave it half open at night. At the end of a week of this exposure, your seedlings should be ready for planting.

If you do not have a cold frame or greenhouse, move the seed trays and pots outdoors each day and bring them in every night for a fortnight. This is time-consuming and tedious, so if you have the space, it is worth acquiring a frame.

An extremely important element in all these procedures is the waterproof label. Your gardening life will be much easier if you keep track of the plants you are growing. Make a label for each packet of seeds and mark your plants at every stage: sowing, pricking out and planting.

See also: Planting Pages 20–21
Cold frames Pages 60–61

BUYING PLANTS

The selling of plants has spread from the traditional nursery into garden centres, market stalls, hardware shops, supermarkets and department stores. Mail-order shopping has also become popular. Before buying, become familiar with the soil and climate of your garden, and the kinds of plants suited to it. To avoid disappointment resulting from impulse buying, shop with a careful list and remember that with plants, as with most goods, you get what you pay for.

It is helpful to know some of the ways in which plants are sold. For instance, a container-grown tree or shrub has been raised as a seedling or from a cutting, then potted up in the container. The plant should not appear to have been dug up from the earth, then stuffed into it.

Grasp the plant firmly at the base of the stem; if it moves easily, do not buy it. Check that it is properly labelled, the soil is damp, the top growth vigorous and that no roots are emerging from the drainage holes. Many bedding plants come in trays

and must be checked in the same manner.

Certain, mainly deciduous, shrubs and trees are sometimes sold "bare-rooted": they have been dug up by the nursery and transported without soil. Because the roots must never dry out, they will usually be packed in peat or similar damp material and then in plastic or sacking. Such plants should be purchased only when dormant.

Pre-packed plants, wrapped in polythene, are often virtually bare-rooted, but have extra packaging. Hardware shops often stock pre-packaged plants, but these should be treated with caution; heating systems can dry out and damage them.

Evergreen shrubs, trees and conifers are frequently sold as "balled plants". This means that the nursery has dug up the plant, leaving the soil surrounding the roots intact. A hessian sack, nylon netting or polythene wrapping is then secured tightly around the roots and soil. Always lift balled plants at the base of the wrapping, which should not be torn or ragged. Neither should you be able to feel hard, twisted roots pressing against the wrapping. The plant should remain erect and fresh looking, with green foliage.

Mail-order buying from nurseries can be convenient, but plants will tend to be small and may not arrive in good condition or at the right time.

You should also be wary of "special offers" advertised in newspapers and magazines; when the plants arrive, check them for signs of unhealthy growth. Perfectly respectable mail-order companies advertise, but their offers tend to be at more realistic prices. The most economical buy is probably from market stalls, but beware—the stock is often inferior.

UNHEALTHY SIGNS
- Broken container; no label
- Dry compost or soil
- Weeds growing in containers
- Wilting stems
- Poor straggly top growth
- Yellowing leaves or damaged foliage, indicating attack by pests
- Premature budding or flowering
- Over-lush growth, rot
- Protruding or exposed roots in container plants
- Large exposed roots in balled plants

WHAT TO LOOK FOR WHEN BUYING PLANTS

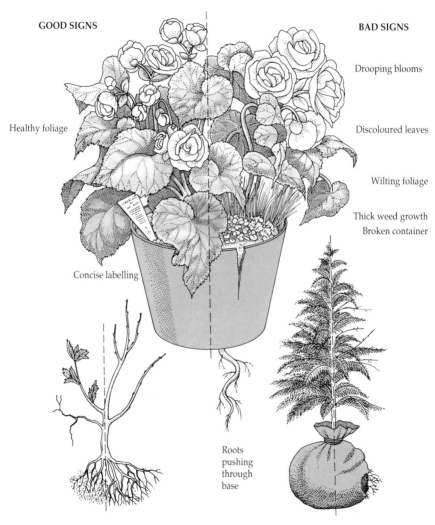

GOOD SIGNS

Healthy foliage

Concise labelling

BAD SIGNS

Drooping blooms

Discoloured leaves

Wilting foliage

Thick weed growth
Broken container

Roots
pushing
through
base

Bare-rooted plant The root system must be well developed and spreading. White, thin roots, shrivelled stems and early budding are all signs of poor health.

Balled plant Look for a strong, erect stem well clothed in fresh green foliage. Check that the soil is moist inside the sacking; the wrapping should be unbroken.

See also: Plant lists Pages 210–219

PLANTING

The health and beauty of a garden depends greatly on following correct planting methods. The plants referred to here are bedding plants. These used to consist of annuals, but because of modern breeding and gardening techniques many plants that are actually tender perennials are now treated as annuals.

The weather largely determines planting times. The soil must be neither frost bound nor saturated. A general guide is late spring for hardy annuals that have been raised indoors, and late summer or early autumn for some plants treated as annuals or biennials, such as pansies or wallflowers, which give a display in spring or early summer. Seedlings must be hardened off before planting.

At least six weeks before planting, the beds must be dug over again to break up clods that have formed. Do this with a fork, using the back of it to whack stubborn clods; remove weeds and fork in a general fertilizer or light dressing of compost.

One week before planting:
- Test the texture of the soil by crumbling a handful. It should form a fine tilth, that is, it should be light, crumbly and even-textured.
- Scatter a suitable fertilizer over the bed if this has not been done already.
- Smooth the surface of the bed by raking in one direction, then at 90 degrees to the first raking.
- Tread lightly over the bed to firm down the soil.
- Remove any new weeds.

A few hours before planting, water the seed beds, trays and containers. Rake the bed and weed it again.

Move the trays and containers out to the bed. With a hand trowel, dig a hole big

Tap the base of the pot to loosen the soil. With one hand over the top of the pot to hold the plant and the soil, turn the pot over. Fit the roots and soil ball into the planting hole. Replace dug earth and firm it gently around the base of the plant.

▼ See also: Digging Pages 10–11
Hardening off Pages 16–17

enough to give the plant's roots room to breathe and grow. Leave the soil that has been dug out on the edge of the hole.

Now, using a small hand fork or kitchen fork, carefully prise the plant from the tray. Try not to handle it, but use the fork to settle it in the hole. The ball of soil should sit in the space with the top roots just below the surface. Using your hands, firm the soil removed from the hole around the plant. Water it gently but thoroughly.

If the plant is pot-grown, tap the base to loosen the soil, place your hand over the the top of the container, taking care not to damage the leaves or, if possible, to touch the stem. Put the plant, with its roots and soil into the hole, firm it in and water it.

If you want to move an established plant, prepare the bed and dig the new hole. Mark a circle around the plant you wish to move, taking the root spread into account. Carefully, using the circle as a guide, dig with a garden fork, not a spade, around and under the roots so they are held in a

Water gently but thoroughly, using a watering can with a fine rose head or a child's watering can.

ball of soil. Ease sacking or plastic sheeting under this ball then tie it around the stem. Move the plant by dragging it on a sheet of plastic or, holding the base of the soil ball, put it in a wheelbarrow.

Follow the planting procedure described previously. Cut away the wrapping that surrounds the ball of soil and roots before you plant. And remember to water well.

Although a spade is the obvious tool for digging, do not be tempted to use it when handling plants. Use a garden fork whenever plants have to be moved or are lifted for overwintering. Moving any plant is likely to check its growth, but the tines of a fork will do less damage to the roots than a spade.

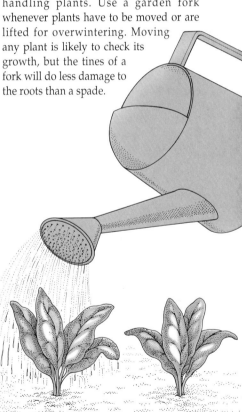

DIVIDING PLANTS

Most herbaceous perennials and many shrubs cannot easily be grown from seed. Many modern plants are hybrids, so either they do not produce seeds or, when they do, they will not grow like their parent but revert to their ancestral species.

But keen gardeners need not despair at the expense of stocking the garden with herbaceous perennials and shrubs. After an initial outlay, once a plant is established, you can have the pleasure of increasing stocks by the simple method of division.

During dormant, cold months many plants store food and raw materials in the roots and stems, and comparatively long-living plants such as herbaceous perennials and shrubs are able to regenerate growth through their roots and stems. Horticulturists make use of this process of storage and regeneration to propagate these plants and, through the division of roots and stems, to produce more plants from the parent.

The best time to undertake this division is when new growth from the dormant roots and stems is about to take place in spring, or as growth slows down in autumn.

Many herbaceous perennials, such as *Aster* (Michaelmas daisy), *Geum* and *Hosta*, form a dense clump, with stems and roots spreading out from a central core. This core, known as the crown, is well suited to division.

Plants have different growth patterns, but, generally, when the crown is about 6in/15cm in diameter, herbaceous perennials can be broken up or "divided" to provide up to 10 new plants. If the centre of the crown is old and bare, it can be discarded for it is unlikely to flourish; the young shoots on the perimeter can be

With a fork, lift the herbaceous perennial out of the soil in autumn. Drive two forks, back to back, into the crown of the plant. Gently lever them apart. Repeat if necessary before selecting divisions for planting. You may need to use a sharp spade or knife to divide solid clumps such as *Hosta*.

With smaller perennials, fork the plant out of the ground, then gently tease the crown apart by hand to make your divisions.

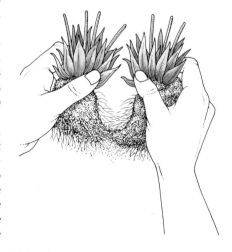

planted on to form new flowering clumps.

Those plants, such as some irises, which have a rhizome, or dahlias, which have a root tuber, can also be divided. Root tubers do not bear buds, and they should be divided so that each section contains part of the stem of the parent plant. A rhizome is, in fact, a fleshy underground stem and an iris can be split, or propagated, from this. Irises should be divided every four years, after flowering.

When rhizomes and tubers are lifted from the ground, they should be inspected carefully, for these fleshy organs are vulnerable to damage from various pests and diseases. For instance, some types of iris are subject to rhizome rot if they are growing in poorly drained soil.

If there are signs of damage on rhizomes and tubers, do not throw them away; they can often be saved if they are given the correct treatment. The rotting parts should be cut away and any wounds and exposed surfaces dusted with a dry copper fungicide such as Bordeaux powder.

Increasing the stock of plants is not the only benefit the gardener derives from dividing old crowns. It is also a rejuvenating process, for the young plants resulting from division, when replanted in well-prepared soil, will bloom more freely than the old, tired plant did. New foliage will flourish as elderly and unsightly stems and plants with bald centres are removed.

Gardeners often find they have surplus plants once they start dividing herbaceous perennials, but there are even advantages in this. Fellow gardeners will be pleased to grow the extra plants in their own gardens, and many a firm horticultural friendship has been forged in this way.

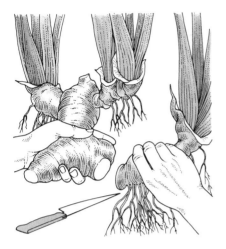

Lift irises every four years or so and divide the rhizomes by taking off small side shoots by hand and cutting the clump into pieces cleanly with a sharp knife. Discard the old centres.

Clumps of mature lilies may be lifted in autumn and carefully divided by hand. Otherwise, remove single scales and press them into seedling compost, tip uppermost; pot on when the first leaf appears. They should flower in 3–4 years.

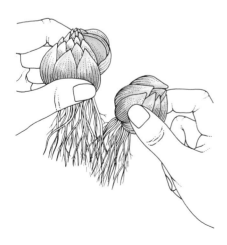

See also: Lifting and overwintering Pages 172–173

CUTTINGS

As the term suggests, "cuttings" are simply cut sections of a living plant. Many plants can be propagated from cuttings of one type or another. When these are put into suitable soil, they will eventually develop a root system and grow into plants. You can grow cut leaves, buds, stems or roots, depending on the type of plant. Annuals and hollow-stemmed plants are not usually propagated from cuttings, but most other plants are easily grown this way, which is particularly valuable with plants with double flowers or coloured or variegated foliage.

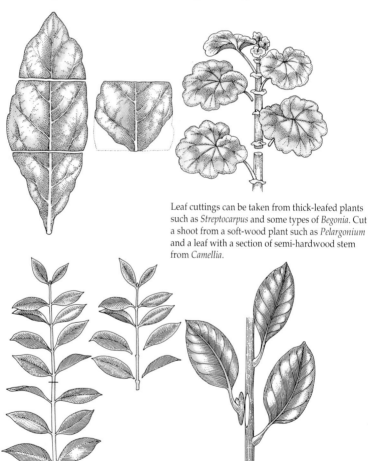

Leaf cuttings can be taken from thick-leafed plants such as *Streptocarpus* and some types of *Begonia*. Cut a shoot from a soft-wood plant such as *Pelargonium* and a leaf with a section of semi-hardwood stem from *Camellia*.

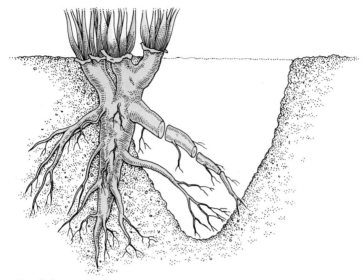

Cut roots from fleshy-rooted herbaceous perennials and shrubs. Each section must be 2–6in/5–15cm long and cut straight at the top, sloping at the base.

Bury the base and cover the top lightly with soil.

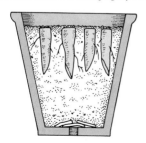

PROPAGATING CUTTINGS

Fill a seed tray two-thirds full with moist peat-based compost. Top with a shallow layer of horticultural sand so the tray is almost full.

• Moisten the tip of the cutting, dip it in rooting powder, shake off excess and plant so it is firm and its tip penetrates the compost.

• Put the tray into a propagator or under a cover to keep the cuttings moist. Mist frequently.

• When cuttings have rooted, transplant into individual pots. Do not plant outdoors until they have had time to consolidate.

See also: Planting out Pages 20–21

LAYERING AND GRAFTING

Two further ways of propagating plants are by layering and grafting. Layering is the term used to describe the rooting of a stem while it is still attached to its parent plant. It occurs naturally in a number of flowering and fruiting plants, although the group of plants that reproduces in this way is not large. Rambling Roses, rhododendrons, honeysuckle, magnolia, forsythia, clematis, jasmine and carnations can all be propagated in this way.

There are trees, too, that spread by layering: chestnut and beech are well-known examples. Their low, sweeping branches often rub against the earth, and this friction causes an "injury" to the bark. Eventually roots start to grow at the point of the wound which anchor the branch into the soil.

Layering is not a difficult task:
• Wait until after midsummer to choose a healthy plant.
• Strip all the leaves off a suitable branch except those at the tip.
• With a sharp knife, cut into the stem to about half its thickness, below a joint from which leaves have been removed.
• Bend the branch into a shallow trench so that the knife-cut will be buried.
• Pin the branch down in the trench with a small steel hoop.
• Turn the leafy tip up and stake it.
• Fill the trench with a mixture of soil and compost or peat.
• A supple and springy branch may need a weight, such as a rock, placed on top of the trench.
• Water the trench thoroughly.

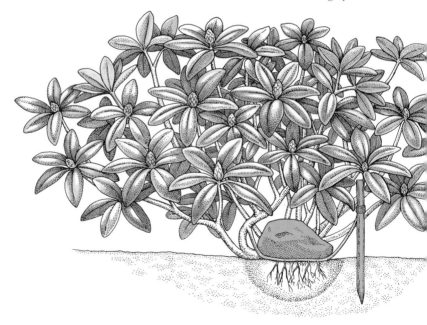

Layering requires a certain amount of patience, since it may be two years before the branch "takes". Watch for it to produce shoots. It is probably wise to mark the layered branch with a small bamboo stake, just to remind yourself where it is.

When the layered branch has formed roots, cut it away from the parent plant. You can leave the new plant a little longer in its position to give it time to establish itself, then carefully dig it up, using a garden fork, and replant it elsewhere.

With some smaller varieties of plant, it may be simpler to bend the branch into a pot. The pot, filled with compost and soil, is partially buried in the earth; when layering is completed, the new plant can be moved in the pot with little root disturbance.

You can also "grow" a better and stronger plant by grafting. The upper branch of one plant is joined to the lower stem and roots of another related plant and they are bound together so that they grow as one. The

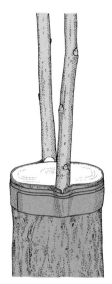

In crown grafting, the scions are cut in a wedge shape and fitted into vertical cuts in the bark at the top of the rootstock so that the exposed surfaces touch. They are then bound together until the shoots take.

The layered branch is weighted with a rock. When roots have formed, the branch is cut from its parent and the layered plant can be moved to its new position in the garden.

system, practised by fruit growers and many commercial rose growers, is tricky; it needs skill and patience, so it is not a means of propagation readily available to the average gardener.

Most roses from nurseries and garden centres are the product of grafting, and the union between parent stock and the grafted stem is revealed by a swelling where the secondary stem grows from the main stem (at the base of the stem, close to the roots, on Bush Roses and at the top of the stem on Standard Roses). This does not affect the domestic gardener's planting and growing routines.

Fruit growers experiment with grafting to improve the yield, taste and size of their commercial stock.

See also: Growing roses Pages 138–149

FEEDING

Plants are designed to absorb their food from the earth, and garden plants will survive without the addition of fertilizers to the soil, just as wild plants do. Gardeners give them extra nutrition because the soil is often poor in certain nutrients and also because they want larger, more showy flowers or fruits.

Fertilizers include the three essential plant nutrients—nitrogen, phosphates and potash—and are sold in two forms:
• Organic—those fertilizers derived from once-living organisms, hence, bonemeal, blood, fish and bone meal, dried blood, and seaweed extract.
• Artificial—fertilizers which are manufactured artificially from chemicals.

The differences in source material between these two forms are irrelevant to the plant. It will draw the nutrients it requires from either organic or chemical fertilizers.

The differences are, however, important to gardeners, who may want a fertilizer that releases nutrients quickly (many artificial forms do this efficiently) or may want a concentrated dose of, say, nitrogen for their plants. Whatever the particular need, gardeners will find a chemical fertilizer manufactured to fill it.

Artificial and organic fertilizers are sold in one of two forms:
• Solid—Powder or granules to sprinkle over the soil. These are usually economical and easy to use but take longer to work. They may be mixed with other materials, such as peat, sawdust or straw, to dilute the active ingredients and make them more convenient to handle and spread.
• Liquid—Concentrated liquid, or soluble powder to mix with water. These are convenient to use with indoor and container plants; although they act quickly, they require frequent application.

There is a further division into:
• "Straights"—usually containing a single active ingredient and used mostly to correct a particular deficiency or to promote a specific aspect of plant development such as flowering and fruiting.
• Compounds—usually containing a balanced mixture of the three principal ingredients: nitrogen, phosphate and potash. Fertilizer manufacturers are obliged by law to state the quantities of these ingredients on the packaging.

When using any fertilizer, always follow the instructions carefully and reserve a separate container for dispensing liquids or solids. Wear gloves to prevent skin contact with powdered fertilizers and avoid exposure to fertilizer dust.

It is important to feed plants correctly; this means applying the right sort of nutrition at the right time. If your soil is well supplied with humus or other organic matter, there may be only occasional need for additional fertilizers.

Slow-acting fertilizers, such as bonemeal, are generally applied at planting time or as a boost feed in late winter/early spring and later in the growing season. Soluble or liquid fertilizers, applied by watering, should normally be used regularly (about every two weeks) during the growing season. A convenient innovation for container gardeners is coated pellets, which are designed as a balanced fertilizer. They can be mixed into potting compost when planting and, depending on temperature, break down slowly, releasing nutrients throughout the plants' development.

See also: Seedlings Pages 16–17
Nutrient deficiencies Pages 32–33

TABLE OF ESSENTIAL GARDEN FERTILIZERS

COMPOSITION	APPLICATION
Balanced, general purpose solid fertilizer A typical artificial blend, which is granular, mixes 7% of each major nutrient: nitrogen (N) phosphates (P) and potash (K). This is shown as 7:7:7. The organic fertilizer mixes dried blood, fish meal and ground bonemeal with a chemical, sulphate of potash. The composition of N, P and K is variable.	Use on your plants at the start of the growing season.
General-purpose liquid fertilizer, with extra potassium Numerous proprietary brands are available. Comes in concentrated liquid, soluble crystal and powder form. Particularly suitable for use on peat-based compost of container-grown plants. The composition of nutrients varies between brands.	Use at the height of summer, when plants welcome both food and liquid.
Bonemeal (organic) or superphosphate (artificial) Both these fertilizers release phosphorus slowly into the soil.	Apply when planting trees, shrubs, herbaceous perennials and bulbs or, in winter, to feed established bulbs and plants. Use 5½oz: 1 sq yd/187g: 1 sq m.
John Innes Base This is particularly suitable for plants grown in containers.	Soil and compost cannot easily be completely changed in large containers; so instead of repotting, remove the top 1in/2.5cm of compost and replace with a mixture of peat and John Innes Base.
Rose fertilizer This contains a blend of all the major nutrients with special emphasis on potassium and added magnesium.	Apply not only to roses, but to all flowering plants in spring and midsummer at the rate of 1oz: 1 sq yd/ 34g: 1 sq m.

COMPOST

Although compost brings nutrition to the soil, it should not be thought of primarily as a plant food—it is humus, which improves the structure of the soil. Fertilizers are normally the main source of the nutrients gardeners add to the soil.

The humus you make in your compost bin is created from vegetable and animal waste. Much of this waste cannot be put as fresh material into the soil or on to flower beds because, until it has decomposed, it may actually take nitrogen out of the soil. The plants would, therefore, be temporarily deprived, not enriched.

When this organic waste is collected and stored correctly, however, it will break down into good humus, and a compost bin is the perfect storage system. In the confined space of the bin, refuse generates warmth that stimulates decomposition.

Other factors also contribute to creating good humus. Air is important, so the contents should not become packed solid, and bacteria must be encouraged, which means that the refuse must have a nitrogen

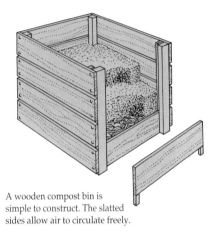

A wooden compost bin is simple to construct. The slatted sides allow air to circulate freely.

content. The third element a compost bin needs is water. There must be sufficient to keep it damp, but not so much that the compost becomes waterlogged.

Double bins are desirable, but not everyone has a large enough garden for these. Many garden stockists sell plastic barrels, pierced with holes, that serve as compost bins. These are suitable for small gardens but, if you have enough space, it is quite easy to construct a bin from wooden planks or bricks.

Site the bin in a shady spot that allows free circulation of air on all sides. You will have to water the compost periodically, using about 2 gallons/9 litres each time; to prevent waterlogging, place a layer of coarse rubble on the floor of the bin. As you fill it with refuse, cover it with sacking or plastic windbreak netting.

Nitrogen, in the form of a proprietary compost powder, will accelerate the composting process. Sandwich a thin layer of this powder between each 8-in/20cm layer of refuse. Fresh horse or poultry

A GOOD BIN
Think of your compost bin as a humus factory which needs to:
- Be constructed of sturdy and rust-proof materials
- Generate heat
- Offer a confined space in which to store organic waste
- Allow air to circulate: small blocks of wood screwed to the bottom of each plank will raise it off the one below
- Encourage the growth of bacteria
- Retain moisture without waterlogging

Use airbricks to build this type of bin, or lay ordinary bricks honeycomb fashion, to allow the passage of air. On this bin and the wooden one, *opposite*, one side can be removed, making it easier to fork out the compost.

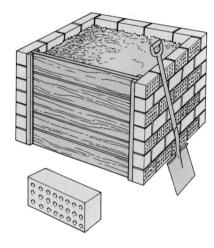

Trimmings and prunings make good compost, but only after they have been shredded to help speed decomposition. Fallen or rotten fruit is also welcome, but roughly chop up tough skins, using a spade. Weeds can be added, since they will not survive the heat in the centre of the bin, but make sure that seeds or perennial roots that will regrow are not included. Avoid using large quantities of lawn cuttings, for they can become slimy. The cuttings should never amount to more than a third of the total bulk of the compost.

Turn the compost over after about three weeks to help aeration and give the refuse on the outer edges a chance to benefit from the central warmth. The compost should be ready for use after about six months.

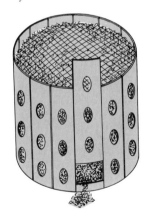

manure also produces nitrogen, so a layer of this could be used instead of an accelerator powder.

All types of kitchen and garden waste can be piled into the bin, to be returned to the land in its rich, decomposed form; but avoid the use of animal waste, such as chicken bones or bacon rind, which may attract vermin.

Do not put fallen leaves into the compost either; they decompose slowly and are better kept to create leaf mould. Non-organic material does not break down, so your compost bin will not give you the opportunity to recycle plastics, metals or minerals. Well-shredded newspaper can be included, but not the paper from glossy magazines.

A manufactured plastic bin and, *below*, plastic windbreak netting protect the compost from rain.

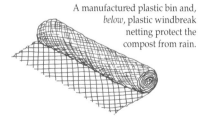

See also: Nutrient deficiencies Pages 32–33
Mulching and watering Pages 34–35

NUTRIENT DEFICIENCIES

Even if you apply fertilizers regularly, there may be deficiencies in your soil. Plants will soon reveal any shortages of the important minerals and trace elements they require by showing a range of symptoms, from leaf discolouration to poor growth or flowering. The average gardener does not need detailed scientific knowledge of the soil, but for a healthy and rewarding garden, it is important to be able to recognize signs which reveal a lack—or an excess—of the main nutrients that support the plants.

When you have identified these signs, you can look among the bewildering array of fertilizers to be found in nurseries and garden centres for the one that will supplement your soil most quickly with the nutrient it needs. The so-called complete fertilizers contain all the main nutrients.

Major nutrients
• Nitrogen (N) is essential for lush foliage and strong leaf colour. After applying a fertilizer rich in this nutrient, the gardener will see a rapid change in plants that were previously pale and weak. But it is important to follow the manufacturer's instructions, since too much nitrogen can cause soft leaf growth or even burn the foliage, and flowers and fruits will be sparse and inferior.

• Phosphate (P) promotes root development and the production of seeds. Lack of phosphates may lead to scorching of the leaf edges and plants may lose their leaves early. An ailing plant can often be revived by a judicious application of this nutrient. Dig up the soil around the plant, taking care not to disturb its roots. Mix the soil with a "superphosphate" fertilizer and replace it. But be patient—the effects will be seen only during the next growing season.

• Potash (K) hardens plants against fungal diseases and frost and helps them to fix nitrogen; wood ash is a rich source of potash, which also encourages flower and fruit development.

Intermediate nutrients
• Calcium (Ca)
• Magnesium (Mg)
• Sulphur (S)

The soil should contain moderate amounts of the intermediate nutrients. Acid soils can be lacking in calcium, sandy soils in magnesium and any type of soil may lack sulphur. Compound fertilizers often include these nutrients; check the packaging for details.

Trace elements
• Iron (Fe)
• Manganese (Mn)
• Molybdenum (Mo)
• Boron (B)
• Zinc (Zn)
• Copper (Cu)

Plants also require trace elements. These are rarely missing in soil that has sufficient humus, but sometimes peaty and acid or chalky soils may lack certain elements. If rhododendrons, azaleas and camellias in chalky areas show yellowing of their leaves, sequestered iron will help.

Because an acid soil changes the character of certain nutrients, some plants in such soil will struggle to find their essential foods and, unless you are growing only acid-loving plants, you will need to add lime. Dig it in thoroughly in the autumn, using a rotary cultivator if possible, and constantly check the pH of the soil to make sure that it has the right balance between alkaline and acid to feed your plants.

See also: Fertilizers Pages 28–29
pH testing Pages 70–71

SIGNS OF DEFICIENCY

Nitrogen deficiency: a chrysanthemum shows stunted growth, small pale leaves, and weak stems.

Phosphate deficiency: rose leaves are small, tinged with purple, stems and roots stunted.

Potash deficiency: leaf edges turn yellow, then brown; flowers are poor in colour.

Magnesium deficiency: young leaves drop off, older leaves are patched between veins with brown and yellow.

Lawn care Pages 86–87
Acid-loving shrubs Pages 118–119

Water is essential for plant life and a garden is unlikely to thrive on haphazard doses of it. The basic rule is to water plants when they need it most: at the crucial stages of growth.

Watering is especially important when seeds are sown, then as they germinate and develop. In dry weather, established plants, particularly annuals and herbaceous perennials, need occasional but thorough watering, especially as they are coming into bloom.

Though some varieties need more, or less, water than others, the standard amount is a 2-gal/9-litre can per large plant, applied slowly through the spout. If you are not sure whether plants are getting sufficient water, test the surrounding soil. It should be damp at least 3–4in/7–10cm below the surface. Try to water in the evening so that the soil remains damp overnight before the sun evaporates the moisture.

The watering of newly sown seeds and seedlings is described elsewhere. Small plants are generally best watered using a soft spray from a hosepipe or watering

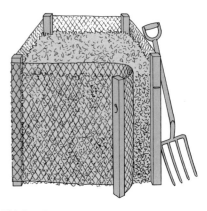

This "cage" is easy to make and is the best way to contain leaf mould. Water the leaves lightly now and again, and scatter compost accelerator powder over the growing pile occasionally.

can. Too forceful a stream of water can wash away precious soil or seedlings.

Flowerbeds can be watered with a watering can, but you will need some patience to plod around a shrubbery and lawn with a can; this is where a hose, with any one of the wide variety of spray fittings available, or a sprinkler system come into their own.

Weather conditions, too, will determine watering methods. Many gardeners are now faced with water shortages and charges for water supplies, as well as legal controls over the use of water—in the United Kingdom, for instance, gardeners are obliged by law to use a non-return valve on garden hoses. Consider these factors and if, as a result, you decide to grow fewer plants, choose those best suited to the particular conditions to be found in your garden.

Rainwater is best for plants generally and essential for calcifuges (lime-haters)

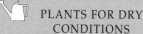
PLANTS FOR DRY CONDITIONS
Many plants will tolerate dry sunny conditions, among them are shrubs such as *Cistus* (Rock rose) and *Cytisus* (Broom), *Lavandula* (Lavender), *Santolina*, *Weigela* and *Rosmarinus* (Rosemary). Perennials include *Nepeta*, *Linaria*, *Artemisia*, *Aubrieta* and *Verbascum*. Some alpines and herbs will also do well.

such as rhododendrons. It is easily collected in rainwater butts connected to the downpipes from a roof gutter. Water from the domestic tap or water that has been used for washing can be used on the garden, unless it contains harmful chemicals or bleach.

To economise on watering, you can help to prevent the soil drying out by mulching the earth around plants. This means laying a "blanket" of organic matter over the earth which helps to retain moisture. It is obviously not sensible to apply this layer on top of dry soil, and mulching should be done during the wetter months of spring and autumn. A further advantage of mulching, especially in the spring, is that it helps suppress weeds by smothering them.

A mulch is usually laid around trees, shrubs and herbaceous perennials, rather than around short-lived annuals. Compost makes a good mulch, as does well-rotted farmyard manure, and spent hops, mushroom compost and ground tree bark are also highly efficient. Perhaps the best mulch of all, however, is leaf mould.

Leaf mould consists ideally of small leaves such as those of beech, hawthorn, and oak, which have rotted down to form a compost; tough leaves with strong veins may have to be chopped up first. Leaf mould is an excellent soil conditioner as well as mulch, especially on roses and other shrubs.

Chipped or composted bark makes an excellent, but expensive, mulch; use it to set off larger, more showy plants. It rots slowly but may need to be replaced by 50% of its volume each season.

Lay a "blanket" of compost or leaf mould by hand around smaller herbaceous plants to retain moisture and smother weeds around the roots.

See also: Watering seeds Pages 14–15

IDENTIFICATION OF WEEDS

There is a view that weeds need not always be eradicated but should sometimes be accommodated in the garden. Weeds, so the argument goes, are only wild flowers that have been given a bad name. But even if there is sympathy for this view, the plants we generally recognize as weeds are such vigorous growers, thriving naturally in their native soil, that they often make a mockery of the art of cultivation and grow wherever they wish, regardless of any aesthetic or food value.

Because weeds are so successful (they are extremely hardy and reproduce rapidly) they are more efficient than most of the cultivated plants in the garden at taking nutrients and water from the soil. These are good reasons for most gardeners to regard weeds with hostility. And if weather conditions have been poor for gardening, or there is a drought, weeds can become a positive menace.

Weeds can be divided into two broad categories. First there are the annuals that rise and fall in one year. This may not seem too threatening, but they shed their seeds, which germinate freely, so many generations of weeds can speedily establish themselves in your garden.

The second group of weeds is the perennials. These do not usually germinate with such speed, but they often have long, deep or creeping root systems and can renew their growth from these roots. This means that even if you hoe or pull up many types of perennial weed, the smallest piece of broken root left in the soil may well regenerate and grow.

There are many plants that can be regarded as weeds, but how much of a nuisance a weed is may depend on the area in which you live. Many weeds, however, are common to most gardens, and it is worth knowing about and learning to recognize them; some are illustrated here.

- *Aegopodium podagraria* (Ground elder) Extremely invasive perennial once established.
- *Agropyron repens* (Couch grass) A pernicious perennial whose rhizome can spread for 5ft/1.5m.
- *Convolvulus arvensis* (Field bindweed) Perennial with deep roots and a creeping habit; difficult to eradicate.
- *Cirsium arvense* (Creeping thistle) Perennial with vigorous growth; spreads rapidly through both roots and seed.
- *Equisetum arvense* (Common horsetail) Vigorous, persistent perennial.
- *Gallium aparine* (Cleavers) Annual with tiny white flower in summer.
- *Plantago major* (Greater plantain) Perennial reproducing by seed and by new growth from shoots at base.
- *Ranunculus repens* (Creeping buttercup) Perennial, spreads rapidly by runners and also by seed.
- *Rumex crispus* (Dock) Perennial with long tenacious tap root, also spreading by seed.
- *Senecio vulgaris* (Groundsel) Annual, having seeds with threadlike appendages, easily dispersed by the wind.
- *Sonchus arvensis* (Perennial sow thistle) Has a long underground root capable of sending up many shoots.
- *Taraxacum officinale* (Dandelion) Perennial with long, sturdy tap root. Seeds blown by the wind; common on turf.
- *Trifolium repens* (White clover) Creeping perennial that puts out roots along the entire length of its stems.

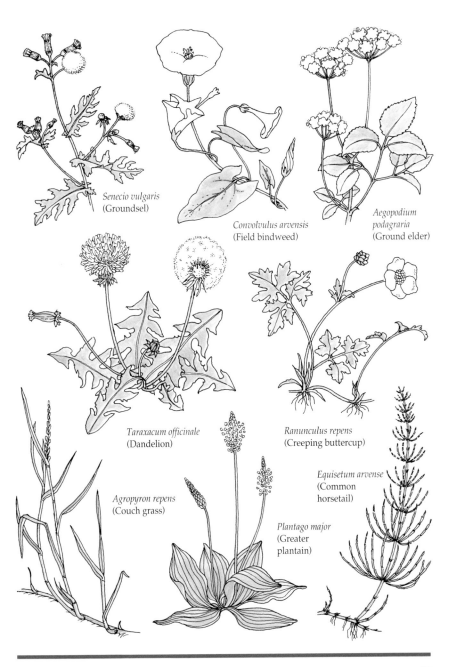

Senecio vulgaris
(Groundsel)

Convolvulus arvensis
(Field bindweed)

*Aegopodium
podagraria*
(Ground elder)

Taraxacum officinale
(Dandelion)

Ranunculus repens
(Creeping buttercup)

Agropyron repens
(Couch grass)

Equisetum arvense
(Common
horsetail)

Plantago major
(Greater
plantain)

See also: Mulching Pages 34–35
Eradication of weeds Pages 38–39

ERADICATION OF WEEDS

The best and most obvious way to get rid of weeds is to pull or dig them up, using a fork to make sure the whole root of each plant is removed. But many people do not have time for weeding by hand, it is, therefore, worth considering the alternatives in terms of cost and time.

• The seeds of many annual weeds will not germinate if they are buried too deeply. A 2-in/5-cm layer of mulch spread over cultivated beds will prevent most annual weeds developing prolifically. Bark mulch makes an excellent weed inhibitor.

• The same principle of smothering weeds can also be applied by growing ground cover plants or setting plants close together so that dense foliage prevents the weeds from getting sufficient light.

• Weeds can easily be sliced off at, or just below, ground level with a dutch hoe or similar tool; this will control most annuals.

• Neither mulching nor hoeing is reliable in controlling the most invasive perennial weeds, and many gardeners need to resort to weedkillers—easily the most efficient way of eradicating some of the worst types.

Contact/systemic weedkillers

These work only through the particular plant that is treated and do not harm the soil or plants that are not sprayed. Some brands are available in solution for painting directly on to individual plants.

Total/residual weedkillers

These work through the plant but also poison the soil and kill anything growing in it. Planting may not be possible for up to six months after an area has been treated so they are not suitable for small, closely planted or wildlife gardens and are usually used in areas overgrown with invasive weeds such as bramble.

When using chemical weedkiller, take care not to walk in it or spray it on your boots. You do not want to tread it over other parts of the garden.

When deciding on a weedkiller, read the package labels carefully so that you can determine what type you need to achieve your aim. Always follow the manufacturer's instructions to the letter.

Chemical weedkillers can be applied with a watering can or special sprayer. Whichever you use, be sure to rinse it out well. It is, in fact, preferable to keep a can or sprayer solely for applying weedkillers.

Growing concern about the effect of chemicals on the environment is making gardeners more cautious about using weedkillers. And it is certainly essential to consider the options carefully before resorting to total/residual weedkillers, which can also affect animal and insect life.

The ground should always be forked or hoed over after weeds have been removed and it will probably need feeding, for weeds can quickly rob the soil of nutrients. Non-woody, annual weeds, if they are not about to shed their seeds, can be added to the compost heap.

See also: Compost Pages 30–31
Mulching Pages 34–35

CHEMICAL WEEDKILLERS

CHEMICAL NAME	ACTIVITY	GARDEN USE/PLANTS KILLED
Alloxydim-sodium	translocated	selective (perennial grasses)
Aminotriazole/amitrole	translocated	total*
Atrazine	contact/residual	total*
Chloroxuron	residual	selective (principally moss)*
2,4-D	translocated	selective (broadleaved plants)*
Dalapon	translocated	selective (grasses)
Dicamba	translocated	selective (broadleaved plants)*
Dichlobenil	residual	selective (seedlings and young plants)
Dichlorophen	contact	selective (principally moss)
Dichlorprop	translocated	selective (broadleaved plants)*
Diquat	contact	total*
Diuron	residual	total*
Ferric sulphate	contact	selective (principally moss)*
Ferrous sulphate	contact	selective (principally moss)*
Glyphosate	translocated	total
MCPA	translocated	selective (broadleaved plants)*
Mecoprop	contact	selective (broadleaved plants)*
Paraquat	contact	total*
Propham	residual	selective (seeds/seedlings)
Simazine	residual	total**
Sodium chlorate	residual	total

* available in proprietary mixture with other weedkillers
**available alone or in proprietary mixture with other weedkillers

EFFECTS OF CHEMICAL WEEDKILLERS

• Total weedkillers kill all vegetation they contact.
• Selective weedkillers kill particular types of plant only.
• Residual weedkillers remain in the soil for some time, preventing the germination of weed seeds.
• Contact weedkillers are effective on surface green tissue.
• Translocated weedkillers are absorbed by the plant and destroy only certain parts of it.
• The effects of some chemical weedkillers persist; throw away or burn weeds shrivelled by them. Hand-pulled annual weeds not about to shed seeds may be added to compost.
• Most weedkillers begin to act in 3–14 days. Weeds with lengthy root systems may need more than one application.

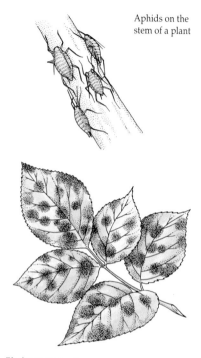

Aphids on the stem of a plant

 PEST OR DISEASE

ADELGIDS Insects related to aphids which suck the sap of plants, infesting conifers in the main.

APHIDS (Greenfly, blackfly) Insects which suck the sap of plants. Multiply rapidly, producing live young. Exude honeydew, which attracts sooty moulds; some virus diseases also are spread by aphids.

BARK BEETLES Insects

BEETLES Insects

BIRDS Troublesome species include blackbirds, tits, bullfinches, sparrows and pigeons.

BLACK SPOT Disease which attacks roses, particularly heavily pruned types such as Hybrid Tea Roses, around midsummer.

CABBAGE ROOT FLIES Insects whose larvae eat the roots of brassicas and related plants such as wallflowers.

CANKER Disease infecting trees and shrubs, especially older plants. Many fungi and bacteria are responsible.

Blackspot on rose leaves

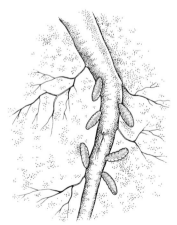

Cabbage root fly larvae

RECOGNITION	CONTROL MEASURE
Aphid-like in appearance. Colonies produce tufts of white waxy "wool" on needles in summer.	Spray in spring and again three weeks later with malathion. If galls appear, pull them off and burn them.
Swarms of tiny green, grey or black wingless insects on stems, leaves and buds, especially of roses.	Hose off with water or spray with a contact insecticide, such as malathion, pirimicarb or pyrethreum; vary the type, since aphids may develop a resistance to particular chemicals.
Holes tunnelled deep into wood, usually trunk and branches of ornamental trees.	Usually affect unhealthy trees, so pay attention to care of plants. Remove and burn damaged wood.
Pieces eaten from leaves, but check that beetles are present, since this can result from other pest activity too.	Not normally a problem, but if swarms appear, use a proprietary contact insecticide.
Buds, flowers or, more rarely, young shoots and leaves pecked and torn.	Use protective netting or bird scarers. Netting is unsightly, but all birds are protected by law so cannot be harmed. Try a bird repellant.
Black spots with surrounding yellow discolouration spread across leaves, which then drop off. The disease can spread to buds and stems.	Remove and burn diseased leaves. Spray weekly with a combined contact and systemic spray. Since disease is worst in weak bushes, spray with a foliar feed.
Although leaves seem healthy, the plant wilts; small white maggots can be seen at the bottom of the stem and on roots.	Protect plant with a matting disc placed around the base of the stem.
Diseased branch becomes cracked and sunken; bark swells and new tissue (a callus) forms over the wound.	Cut out and destroy affected branches.

See also: Pests and diseases of roses Pages 148–149

Caterpillar damage to leaves

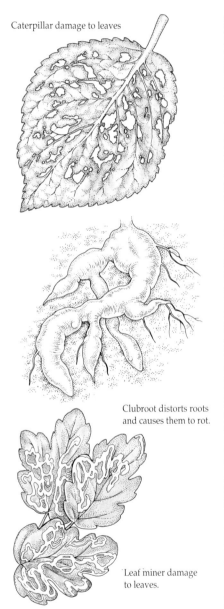

Clubroot distorts roots
and causes them to rot.

Leaf miner damage
to leaves.

 PEST OR DISEASE

CAPSID BUGS Insects. Several species of sap-sucking insects which attack a wide range of plants.

CATERPILLARS The larval stage of butterflies and moths. Adults lay eggs on plants and in the soil; the young feed on leaves, stems, buds, roots, bulbs, tubers.

CLUBROOT Soil-borne fungus disease which attacks the roots of wallflowers and brassicas.

CUCKOO-SPIT BUGS Insects. The young stages of a species of froghopper that feed on shoots of lavender, roses and other herbaceous plants.

EARWIGS Insects usually beneficial in the garden since they feed on aphids, but they can become a pest.

GREY MOULD (*Botrytis cinerea*)
Fungus disease affecting all types of plants. Spores present in the air; spreads also by contact.

HONEY FUNGUS (*Armillaria mellea*)
The most destructive tree fungus. Lives on dead trees, stumps and roots; spreads underground.

LEAF MINERS Insects. Name given to larvae of several insects, including moths and sawflies, which tunnel into leaves.

RECOGNITION	CONTROL MEASURE
Tiny greenish bugs, similar to aphids. Winged adults lay eggs on plants; feeding by young causes ragged, brown-spotted leaves, distorted growth of flowers.	Difficult to treat, since bugs have often moved on before symptoms are noticed; best tolerated.
Holes eaten into leaves or leaves chewed around the edges, bulbs and roots eaten. The pests or their dark droppings can often be seen.	Pick caterpillars off by hand or cut off affected stem. If infestation is severe, apply contact insecticide.
Leaves wilt and discolour. Roots are swollen and distorted and finally become a slimy mess from which millions of spores disperse into the soil.	Remove and destroy affected plants. Do not grow related plants on the site for five years; apply lime before planting the same type of plant again.
Blobs of white froth, like spittle, on stems and leaves of affected plants; made by small yellow insects which live inside.	None necessary, but plants can be hosed to remove froth.
Has a pair of pincers at the hind end. Ragged holes chewed in leaves and petals of chrysanthemums, dahlias and clematis.	Spray plants with a contact insecticide; search out hiding places and spray them; clean up garden debris.
Soft, rotting leaves, stems and flowers, which become covered with soft, downy, grey fungal growth.	Cut out and destroy affected parts; spray with systemic fungicide. Special control measures needed for certain plants.
Honey-coloured toadstools growing close to trees. Black bootlace fungal strands visible under the ground, white fanlike strands on trunk if bark peeled back.	Remove and burn all affected wood, including as much of the root system as possible. Change or sterilize the soil before replanting with resistant trees.
Maggots in meandering tunnels on discoloured leaves of woody plants.	Remove and destroy leaves of smaller plants; no treatment is possible for large trees.

See also: Pests and diseases of roses Pages 148–149

PESTS AND DISEASES/3

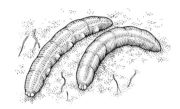

Leatherjackets: the larvae of craneflies

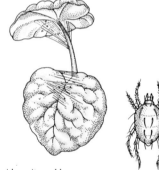

Red spider mite and leaves
showing cobwebs

Rust patches on leaves

PEST OR DISEASE

LEATHERJACKETS Insects. Larvae of craneflies which live in the soil and feed at night on roots of plants; particularly troublesome in grass.

MILDEW Disease. Name applied to both downy mildew (the less serious) and powdery mildew, fungal diseases that attack a wide range of plants.

RED SPIDER MITES Mites. One of many species of mite related to spiders. Feed on underside of leaves and can cause serious damage, especially in the greenhouse.

RHODODENDRON BUGS Insects. Shiny black-brown bugs, which suck the sap through the underside of leaves.

RUST Disease. Spore stages of a large group of fungal diseases that live as parasites on various plants.

SCALE INSECTS Insects, which suck the sap. Limpet-like females (the scales) remain inactive; the infestation is spread by young swarming over plants.

SILVER LEAF Disease. The airborne fungus lives on dead wood, entering trees and shrubs through wounds, produces a toxin that spreads through the sap.

RECOGNITION	CONTROL MEASURE
Large, dark grey grubs, wrinkled and leathery, legless and slow-moving. Stems of plants eaten through at or below soil level.	Cultivate affected soil to expose larvae to birds. Use a lawn-pest killer on lawns; chemical treatment is ineffective on other plants.
Downy mildew lives inside plant tissue, causing poor growth and yellowing of leaves. Powdery mildew lives on the plant surface, giving it a white, floury appearance.	Improve growing conditions of plants. In both cases, remove and destroy affected plants, then spray with a systemic fungicide or sulphur.
Bronze marks on leaves, which wither and fall; in severe infestations, fine white cobwebs are visible; mites can be seen under a lens.	No effective treatment for outdoor attack; regular watering and mulching can help. In the greenhouse, destroy affected plants and mist them regularly. The predatory mite *Phytoseiulus persimilis* will prey on red spider mites.
Leaf edges curl, leaves become wrinkled, with mottled rust-coloured discolouration on the undersides. Bugs can be seen.	Spray thoroughly with contact insecticide at first sign of trouble; repeat four weeks later. Pick bugs off by hand.
Bright orange, brown or black spots on leaves or needles.	Pick off and burn diseased leaves. Spray roses with myclobutanil fungicide, other ornamentals with propiconazole.
Leaves become sticky and sooty; brown, yellow or white waxy scales are visible on stems and leaves.	Spray ornamental plants with a systemic insecticide, shrubs and small trees with a tar-oil wash in winter.
Leaves look silver, caused by air forming under the upper surface; may become brown in severe cases. Shoots and branches die back.	Cut off and burn affected branches; if tree does not soon recover, and if silvering appears on suckers, tree must be destroyed.

See also: Pests and diseases of roses Pages 148–149

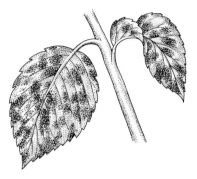

Mottling of leaves caused by virus infection

Vine weevil larvae

Whitefly infestation on plant leaves

PEST OR DISEASE

SLUGS AND SNAILS Slugs are more numerous and destructive than snails; all feed at night on leaves and stems.

TORTRIX MOTHS Insects. The caterpillars of these moths differ from many other caterpillars in that they spin a large cocoon inside which they eat the plants.

VINE WEEVILS Insects. Small, dark adult beetles attack foliage of evergreens, including rhododendron and camellia, at night; live in soil. Curled, white, legless larvae eat roots and bulbs.

VIRUSES Microscopic particles that enter plants through wounds, causing many types of disease; spread mainly by aphids, mites, whitefly, leafhoppers.

WHITEFLIES Insects related to aphids which look like tiny white moths. Nymphs feed on undersides of leaves, sucking sap and exuding honeydew.

WILT Disease caused by infection by various soil-borne fungi. Clematis specially badly affected.

WIREWORMS Insects. Soil-dwelling larvae of click beetles; horny, shiny yellow-brown and slow-moving. Eat roots of many plants, tubers, and stems.

RECOGNITION	CONTROL MEASURE
Shiny slime trails on plants, paths or walls. Clusters of white translucent eggs in the soil. Snails easily seen under leaves, stones.	Keep garden free of plant debris. Pick snails off by hand. Use proprietary poisonous pellets if infestation severe.
Leaves and shoots on trees and shrubs bound together by fine silken threads behind which caterpillars can be seen.	Pick off and destroy affected leaves; spray plant with fenitrothion.
Shoots and leaves show damage; bulbs and roots, particularly of pot plants such as begonia and cyclamen, are eaten away by larvae.	Adults difficult to eradicate; spray with fenitrothion after hoeing the soil. Eliminate grubs by treating compost with a soil insecticide; check bulbs carefully when repotting.
Irregular, different-coloured markings appear on leaves, stems, flowers; plant shows wilted, stunted or distorted growth; distortion of roots or tubers.	There is no treatment for plants infected by viruses. Ignore mild attacks, but destroy severely infected plants. Use only healthy stock for propagation.
Large numbers visible on young plants and young shoots of older plants. When disturbed, adults rise in clouds. Plants wilt and lack vigour.	No treatment possible outdoors. Spray house or greenhouse plants with contact insecticide or introduce a parasitic wasp, *Encarsia formosa*, to control pests in greenhouse in summer.
Shoots or whole plants collapse and die back rapidly; on clematis, leaf stalks go black.	Clematis: cut back to healthy tissue; other plants: destroy any severely affected. Do not grow the same type of plant in the same place for three years.
Visible in the soil when it is dug over; particularly severe in land recently converted from grassland. Often found in stems of chrysanthemums.	Cultivate soil often and thoroughly, and sprinkle with a proprietary soil insecticide. Treat seeds with insecticide before sowing.

V See also: Pests and diseases of roses Pages 148–149

METHODS OF SUPPORT

There are two main ways of supporting climbing or "wall" plants. You can trail them over rocks, other plants or natural supports, or you can build an artificial support system. If you intend to use a natural support such as a tree:
• Make sure the tree is strong enough to support the mature climber.
• Do not hammer nails into the trunk; use plastic or wire netting instead.
• Be cautious about using dead trees or old stumps. In time these may topple over or rot, and their presence in the garden can encourage pests and diseases.

There are many excellent artificial supports which can themselves add to the garden scheme. Arches and pergolas bring interest to the perspective as well as supporting attractive plants.You do not have to buy expensive materials. A dead tree can be sawn up to make an arbor (its rounded, rustic supports may well be more in keeping visually with the style of the garden than sawn and squared-off poles). This type of structure will easily support a climbing rose.

Whatever wood you use, it must be treated with a preservative. Make sure the poles are sturdy—at least 2½–3in/6–8cm in diameter. Bury each pole as deeply as you can and ram earth in around it; a good 3ft/1m depth will ensure that the pole stands firm without a concrete surround.

A pergola is an extended wooden frame on a large scale and can be used to mark a pathway or soften a paved courtyard or patio. Although it is tempting to grow many different climbers on such a large structure, it is best not to do so, since it may become merely a jumble of colour and foliage. Rather choose a smaller number of plants that between them provide an extended period of interest from flowers and foliage. A single large climber such as a mature wisteria is especially good on a pergola.

Most people think of fixing a trellis against a wall as a support for climbing plants, but it can be fixed between poles to make a free-standing screen, or added to the top of a fence to give extra height. If you are fixing trellis to a wall, first fix battens to it and attach the panels to them; this provides better support and

A wigwam of canes 8ft/2.4m tall allows air to circulate and gives plenty of room for the plants to spread. It is an ideal support for sweet peas.

▼ See also: Supporting plants Pages 50–51
Planting trees Pages 100–101

allows air to circulate behind the climber.

Moderately vigorous climbers, such as honeysuckle, with an irregular habit of growth can also be supported by a framework of wire strung between lead-headed nails or vine eyes secured to the wall. If necessary, train the plant up to the frame with canes or stakes and fasten it to the wire with plastic ties or clips.

If you want a free-standing trellis, fix it to a wooden framework firm enough to withstand wind. A trellis used in conjunction with a fence also needs a sturdy foundation. Make sure the fence is solid enough to support both trellis and plant.

Many herbaceous perennials with tall or floppy stems, including delphiniums, peonies, lupins and dahlias, need support. Bamboo canes, wooden stakes or large bunches of brushwood twigs are traditional supports for these plants, and plastic-coated support wires of various shapes and sizes are now available.

Young trees also need to be staked. Choose a good stake, about 5ft/1.5m long, and bury it to a depth of 24in/60cm. Then secure the sapling to the stake with two belt-style tree ties made from plastic, rubber or heavy webbing, one at ground level, the other where the branches begin. Tighten the ties against the stake, not the tree, and make sure the stake is on the windward side so that the plant is not blown against its support. Check ties yearly and replace as necessary: if they become too tight, they can cause irreparable scarring to the trunk.

Recent research has shown that a shorter stake angled across the trunk, providing stability for the base of the tree but allowing the top to move, gives the best type of support.

The square or rectangular design is generally more robust than the diamond-patterned trellis. Use whatever suits the growing habit of your climber.

The plant will twine itself through the framework of the trellis.

Trellises come in plastic and wood. The latter look more attractive.

A wooden trellis fixed to battens against a wall supports a clematis or similar climber.

Supporting climbers Pages 150–151
Types of climbers Pages 154–155

STAKING PERENNIALS

I n the wild, tall herbaceous perennials support themselves by leaning on other plants, or they simply fall over at the end of the flowering season and spill their seed to promote new growth. Also, by their very nature, some "wild" species do not need the same amount of care and support as cultivated varieties of the same plant.

Horticulturists have selectively bred plants to grow very tall or to carry wonderfully large heads of flowers. But many gardeners do not want stems that flop untidily, nor are they keen to have unwanted seeds scattered in the garden, and these taller plants often need support to keep them orderly and visually pleasing.

Supports range from straightforward bamboo canes or sticks to carefully designed metal structures. The traditional

A metal framework supports a shorter plant without twine or tying. The stems are held in a fairly free fashion, allowing them to grow through the frame and bend but not flop.

See also: Methods of support Pages 48–49
Planting trees Pages 100–101

cane or wooden stake needs to be long enough to be pushed 10in/25cm into the ground and to stand 6–8in/15–20cm below the height of the mature plant; the growing plant is tied to it with soft twine or raffia. Early staking affords least disturbance to the plant's roots and may mean that foliage will help to disguise the support.

The stems of a plant do not have to be staked individually. A number of canes can be placed around a cluster of stems and twine bound from cane to cane to encircle and support the whole group. Another simple way of supporting multi-stemmed plants, such as taller peonies or geraniums, is with one of the wide range of wire frames available. The "legs" are pushed into the soil over the young plant, which grows through the frame.

If you prefer a more "natural" look, twigs pushed into the ground around a clump of stems are often strong enough to support a plant, even when in flower.

Because tall herbaceous perennials need this sort of attention, site them carefully.

• Do not plant a tall perennial where it will look isolated and unattractive; groups of at least three plants look best.

• Try to reduce the visual distraction of stakes. With large, leafy plants, such as dahlias, use three stakes, one at the back, one each side. Plan surrounding planting so it helps hide the stakes.

• Arrange your garden so that the height and density of the plants is varied and offers natural support for those plants that need it; do not clump all the tall plants together.

Finally, remove dead flowering stems promptly to reduce the likelihood of plants flopping over and self-seeding where they are not wanted.

A delphinum tied to a sturdy traditional stake, still a suitable support for these giant plants.

Another system to support drooping stems. This "cat's cradle" allows a variety of plants to grow together without the need for individual stakes.

BASIC PRUNING

Many a keen gardener is put off by the topic of pruning: it seems to imply a degree of technical knowledge and expertise which most amateur gardeners feel is beyond them. It is important to overcome this misleading impression since the basic principles of pruning are easily learnt and applying them will help to keep the living framework of the garden shaped and in good health.

Pruning is simply the removal of unwanted parts of a plant. First, diseased or dead material is cut out to keep the plant healthy; then other parts may be cut back to encourage the new growth that will give the plant its desired shape or increase its yield of flowers and fruit.

To achieve these aims, the gardener makes use of the plant's own natural chemistry. The shoot at the tip of every stem grows vigorously, but by doing so it inhibits the growth of the small shoots farther down the stem. If this terminal bud is removed, the dormant buds on the stem spring to life, producing more leafy shoots which change the plant's shape.

This holds good for all forms of pruning, from pinching out the soft shoot tips of non-woody plants by hand to cutting out the leading shoot on trees and shrubs. Some plants require pruning annually, others only now and then or hardly at all.

A great deal of pruning in later years can be avoided by careful initial siting of large shrubs and trees so that they have room to grow to their full size. If you do have to tackle an unruly or misshapen plant, you are unlikely to do any damage by trimming it to shape. But, before you start:

• Be sure it is the right time of the year to prune the particular plant—and that it will

When pruning, make a clean cut a little above and sloping away from the bud that you want to sprout.

Too close to bud   Too far from bud   Ragged cut

Wrong slope   Correct cut

Cut shrubs that flower on the current year's shoots back to strong main stems in early spring. Some established shrubs, such as *Buddleia davidii*, should be cut back to about 12in/30cm from the ground.

See also: Pruning trees Pages 103–104
Pruning shrubs Pages 128–129

WHEN TO PRUNE

Broadleaved evergreens—Prune in late summer/early autumn only if neccessary.
Conifers—Among common types, hard prune only *Taxus* and *Thuja*. Lightly trim only green growth on other varieties in late spring/late summer.
Shrubs flowering on previous year's growth—Prune lightly after flowering; thin out by removing several shoots from the base of the plant.
Shrubs flowering on current season's growth—Cut back in early spring to strong stems or, with some established shrubs, to 12in/30cm from the ground.
Bush, Climbing, Standard and Miniature Roses—Prune in early spring. Dead-head throughout the flowering season to encourage further blooming.

Rambler Roses—Prune as soon as flowering is over.
Formal hedges—Trim closely initially to encourage bushy growth; thereafter, clip frequently to maintain shape.
Informal hedges—Trim once or twice a year; cut out crossing stems and weak growth. Timing as with type of shrub above.
Deciduous climbers—Little pruning needed except to limit size. Prune flowering climbers as similar types of flowering shrubs.
Evergreen climbers—Cut out dead wood and any crossed shoots in late winter/early spring.
Plants with variegated leaves—Cut out stems reverting to green as noticed.

respond by sprouting new growth (a number of conifers will not do this).

• Check that your tools (pruning knife, secateurs, pruning saw) are sharp.

• Examine the plant carefully, taking time to consider the effect you wish to achieve and how best to achieve it.

When pruning:

• Always make a clean cut, sloping away from the bud.

• Cut away unwanted growth flush with the stem. Do not leave short pieces of branch (snags), for they will either make ugly clusters of shoots or die back, which may affect the rest of the plant.

For larger plants, particularly deciduous shrubs, the early years are the formative ones, for pruning while the shrub or deciduous tree is young establishes the shape of the mature plant. Remove all weak shoots. New growth will take place only from buds, so you should cut back the side shoots to an outward-facing bud. Once the desired shape has been established, you need prune only to maintain the plant's size and health.

Evergreen trees and shrubs generally need little pruning. Young conifers may fork; if so, cut out the weaker shoot and, if necessary, stake the remaining shoot to guide it upright. Later pruning is then only a matter of removing weak and untidy growth. Pruning tall trees is best left to the professional gardener or tree surgeon.

Flowering evergreens, such as heathers and rhododendrons, should be dead-headed, and selected stems can be shortened at the same time.

PROTECTING PLANTS

Protecting young or tender plants against winter cold requires a certain amount of work and preparation. Most gardeners, however, will feel that the time and effort involved is worth while to achieve a healthy garden, free from unsightly gaps caused by winter damage or losses. The first requirement is to understand how and where frost will affect your garden and its plants.

• Try to establish if your garden lies in, or contains, a "frost pocket". These occur in the low-lying dips where dense, cold air lingers long after the sun has risen.

• A too-rapid thawing of frost causes more damage to plants than frost itself. Generally speaking, a spell of days warm enough to thaw frozen ground, which then refreezes at night, causes more damage than continuous cold followed by a general thaw.

With these points in mind you can choose those sites that are most suitable for tender plants. Place them on higher ground and, if possible, in a spot that is shaded from the early morning sun so that the thawing process is more gradual. *Camellia*, for instance, benefits from this kind of gentle thawing out.

• Many slightly tender perennials or sub-shrubs, such as *Ceratostigma* or tarragon, can be protected from frost with a mulch of leaf mould or a layer of straw packed around the base and stems of the plant as soon as cold weather threatens.

Heavy mulches should be removed sufficiently early in spring for the plants to be able to make unimpeded new growth after the danger of frost has passed. It is a good idea to remove the mulch in two stages so that shoots do not immediately have to withstand strong spring sunshine after winter darkness, but have a period of "half-light" in between. And, should there be an unexpectedly late frost, the plants will still have some protection.

PLANTS NEEDING PROTECTION

In prolonged periods of severe cold, some normally hardy plants may need protection.

• Late frosts can damage flowers of Japanese maple, pieris and magnolia.

• Cover crowns of acanthus, anchusa, hollyhock, delphinium, lupin, nepeta, thalictrum, tropaeolum and some ferns and grasses.

• Protect slightly tender plants, shrubs and bulbs, including diascia, cordyline, nerine, osteospermum, phormium and schizostylis.

Bamboo canes erected in a wigwam shape are covered with straw. Inside, a yucca is given protection against frost.

• Straw (hay or wheat chaff) is another useful material for frost protection. It can be laid around the base of plants, tied around stems or leaves that persist after autumn, or woven around bamboo canes to form a protective "tent".

It may be sensible to delay the main pruning and tidying up until early spring so that stems provide support for insulating materials, or large dead leaves can be used to protect the crowns. Old matting or polythene sheet will provide good makeshift protection in unexpected cold spells.

• Protect young trees and shrubs with a screen made from hessian or synthetic wind-proof material.

• The cloche is a handy item of garden equipment which has several uses. Basically it is a cover made of glass or (less efficiently) of plastic, which keeps cold air off the soil, thus retaining any warmth within it. By placing a cloche over a plant in autumn, you may be able to enjoy its flowers, foliage or even its fruit for far longer than the weather would normally permit. Do not use a plastic cloche very early or very late in the season; the air may be colder underneath it than outside.

Cloches are also useful in spring, since the soil underneath will warm up more quickly than exposed earth does. You can plant out seedlings earlier than the conventional time if you increase the temperature of the soil in this way for a week to ten days beforehand.

If you are sowing seeds, use a cloche, or even polythene sheet laid on the earth, to warm the ground first. Otherwise you run the risk of seeds sitting in cold, possibly wet, ground, a prey to pests and fungal diseases, until the spring sun has warmed it enough for germination to take place.

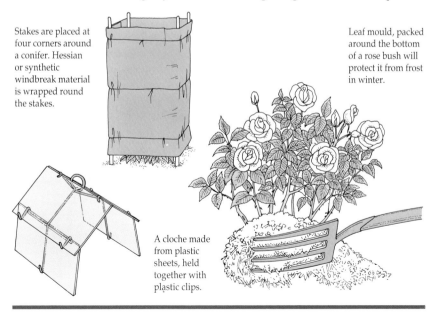

Stakes are placed at four corners around a conifer. Hessian or synthetic windbreak material is wrapped round the stakes.

Leaf mould, packed around the bottom of a rose bush will protect it from frost in winter.

A cloche made from plastic sheets, held together with plastic clips.

See also: Mulching Pages 34–35

GREENHOUSES

Many gardeners long for a greenhouse only to find, on buying one, that the benefits do not always match expectations. This is generally because people have not adequately considered the fundamental conditions needed for a serviceable greenhouse. The site needs to be:

• Preferably close to mains electricity and water supplies.

• Level, open yet sheltered, and not over-shadowed by trees.

• Ideally, orientated so the long axis can lie east–west to optimize the use of light.

The design and materials of a greenhouse need practical as well as aesthetic consideration. There are some quaint and interesting designs on the market, but many of these are expensive to maintain. Often they do not hold heat well, or cost a lot to warm up. "Glass to ground" designs have both these faults. You will have a more efficient greenhouse if it has walls from the ground to the level of the staging.

Aluminium is a common fabric in greenhouse building. It does not need regular maintenance as wood does, but wood has some advantages: it retains heat efficiently; insulation and other attachments are easily fixed to it; and it is resilient in high wind. Wood is also more attractive than aluminium and blends better with the colour and foliage of the garden.

A greenhouse floor should be gravel over a firmed soil base, or concrete with

A half-boarded lean-to takes up less room in the garden, but obviously requires plenty of wall space. Windows that open are important for ventilation.

Heating bills can be reduced by using wooden frames, since these are more heat retentive than aluminium. Brick or wooden walls to the level of the staging will also help to retain heat.

drainage channels. Both these allow free drainage and can be disinfected quite easily, which helps to keep pests at bay.

You may be tempted to use plastic instead of glass in the windows, because initially this is inexpensive. But plastic does not last long; it attracts dust and tears, so it needs to be replaced regularly. Glass, once installed, is easy to clean, is a good transmitter of light and lasts a lifetime.

Ventilation is important in greenhouse gardening, so make sure there are windows that open on the sides and in the roof. The best vents allow ventilation to be controlled.

If you have a small garden, you can buy or construct a lean-to or half-greenhouse; this simply means that one wall is an outside wall of the house or garage. Make sure it faces the sun and paint it white to optimize the light.

A greenhouse will extend your gardening activities and allow you to grow plants that might otherwise be impossible. You can use it to:
• Produce half hardy perennials or bedding annuals grown from seed both during sowing and pricking out.
• Protect tender plants and bulbs during the winter months.
• Grow "hobby plants", such as chrysanthemums, fuchsias or exotic orchids.
• Cultivate indoor pot plants.
• Cultivate alpine species.

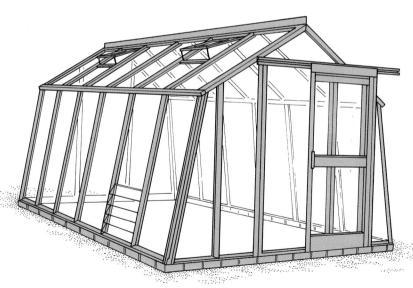

Aluminium greenhouses are often less sympathetic than wooden ones to the overall appearance of the garden, but are cheap to make, easy to install and excellent transmitters of light.

Louvred vents help in controlling ventilation, but "Glass to ground" greenhouses are very inefficient at heat retention and it is difficult to regulate and maintain the temperature inside them.

See also: Heating a greenhouse Pages 58–59

HEATING A GREENHOUSE

To enjoy the full potential of your greenhouse, you need a source of heat, if only to maintain the temperature above freezing in winter so as to be able to store tender plants. For general gardening purposes, it is best to maintain a minimum temperature of 45°F/7°C, for this will prevent pot plants from becoming chilled and also enable you to raise early bedding plants. If you wish to raise crops all year round or keep tropical plants, you will obviously need to keep the temperature much higher, but these more specialized requirements fall outside the scope of most gardeners.

There are several different types of greenhouse heater; before deciding which one to install, check with the manufacturer's specifications and make sure that it will produce sufficient heat for your locality, the size of your greenhouse and the plants you intend to grow.

Electric heaters

A thermostatically controlled electric fan heater is a simple solution, and it is easy to regulate. A radiant electric heater will give more uniform heat than a fan. Both are fairly expensive to run, but they have the advantage of needing minimal attention.

If your greenhouse is too far from the mains supply to install either of these, a low-voltage propagator or a heating mat, which can be laid on a bench in the greenhouse, can quite easily be connected to a transformer. They are usually sold as kits with the transformer.

Paraffin heaters

Paraffin burners are a cheap source of heat in the greenhouse, but they do need regular filling and the wicks require frequent attention.

Gas heaters

This type of heating is usually the most expensive to install, but running costs are low and it needs little attention.

It is no good heating the greenhouse unless there is adequate insulation during the winter months. Double-skin bubble polythene sheeting is the easiest to install and is highly efficient, since it can cut heat loss by around 40 per cent.

Any additional insulation must be removed in the spring; then you will have to protect plants from the heat of the sun shining through the glass. A whitewash type of shade paint will lower the transmission of infra-red radiation by 20–30 per cent. It is not washed off by rain, yet can quite easily be wiped off in autumn, when the sun is not so fierce.

Shading can also be provided by roller blinds made up of wooden or cane slats, or by automatic blinds controlled by photoelectric cells, though these are more expensive.

Greenhouse hygiene

A greenhouse should be disinfected once a year. The best time to do this job is in late autumn or in spring. All the plants must be removed from the greenhouse, and this is the time when they will suffer least from the disturbance. Scrub down the framework and benches, and all pots and seed trays, with a mild proprietary garden disinfectant. Clean the glass and spray against pests and diseases.

Good greenhouse hygiene may seem tiresome, but it is important in helping to control the pests that readily proliferate in this warm environment.

There are several pests that can be a particular nuisance in the greenhouse.

A GOOD GREENHOUSE

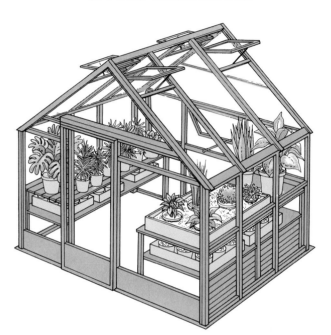

To ensure the circulation of air, the greenhouse should have skylights or a window that opens; some also have louvres at the bottom which can be opened in hot weather. A sliding door takes up little space and can also be left slightly open.

Staging equipment needs some thought. You should have wide, shallow metal trays, filled with gravel or pebbles to retain moisture, in which to set pots and also slatted shelves on which to stand plants that need free drainage.

Among the most prevalent are:
• **Red spider mites.** These live on foliage, feeding on plant tissues. The leaves become mottled and yellow, then dry up; when infestation is severe, fine white threads may be seen on the plant. Infestation is most likely to occur in hot, dry conditions, so minimize the possibility of attack by maintaining adequate humidity (regular misting) in the summer. Red spider mites can also be biologically controlled by purchasing a "starter" colony of another mite, *Phytoseiulus persimilis*, which preys on them and dies out when they are eliminated.
• **Whitefly.** This is not a fly at all, but a sap-sucking insect closely related to aphids. Regular spraying with insecticides such as permethrin or resmethrin will control the adults but leave the immature stages unaffected, so spraying or smoke treatments must be carried out each week to catch each generation of adults as they hatch out.

See also: Pests and diseases Pages 40–47

COLD FRAMES AND SHEDS

For hardening-off young plants before planting them out in the garden, you need a cold frame. This is a simple, box-type enclosure, usually made of wood, with a removable cover panelled in glass. This helps to raise the temperature within the frame higher than the outside temperature during the day and traps some warmth for the protection of the plants at night. Many half hardy plants will react badly to sudden drops in temperature such as those experienced in late spring; 45–50°F/7–10°C is the ideal minimum range for these plants.

In mild weather, the cold frame cover should be propped open during the day, or removed, to expose the seedlings directly to air and sunlight, but it should be shut at night until there is no longer any likelihood of frost. After two to three weeks, the plants should be strong enough to plant out.

Another indispensable item in the garden is a good shed. As with greenhouses, there is a wide variety available, and many models now come in pre-cut packs which are assembled on site. Generally speaking, you should aim to buy, or build, the largest and sturdiest shed you can afford.

Most purchased sheds will be made of wood; when buying, check that:
• Timber is pressure treated with preservative that is not soluble in water.
• Key joints are made with rust-proof screws and not nailed.
• Floor boarding is tongued and grooved and supported by a fully braced framework of joists.
• Walls are fully framed, with diagonal bracing. Wall planks overlap completely or are properly butted up to each other.
• Door is fully framed, with diagonal bracing, and is lockable, either with a key or padlocked hasp and staple.
• Windows are fully framed, glazed and will open.
• Roof has an adequate slope—if it is not pitched—and that it is fully felted, with all joints and edges well overlapped.

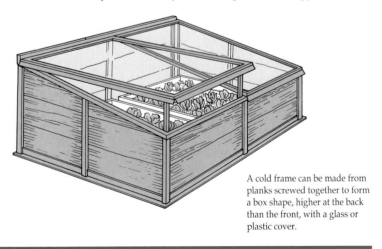

A cold frame can be made from planks screwed together to form a box shape, higher at the back than the front, with a glass or plastic cover.

See also: Pricking out, hardening off Pages 16–17
Protecting plants Pages 54–55

CLOCHES

Originally bell-shaped glass domes (from the French word for bell), cloches today take many forms and can be made of plastic or glass, but their function is the same.

Placed over plants in winter, they will protect them from bad weather. In spring they can be used to warm the earth before sowing, allowing early-sown seeds to germinate more quickly, and they will shelter tender young plants. In the autumn they can be used to prolong the growing season of plants.

The shed should stand on a solid concrete base and, if possible, the window should catch some sun. Once the shed is in place, add hooks on which to hang tools and shelves to hold flower pots and seed trays. A bench along the window wall will be useful for potting up plants, standing trays of germinating seeds in spring and overwintering plants such as geraniums.

Make sure that insecticides, fungicides and weed killers are locked in a cupboard. Indeed, old cupboards or chests of drawers are useful for housing secateurs, twine, gloves and gardening notes.

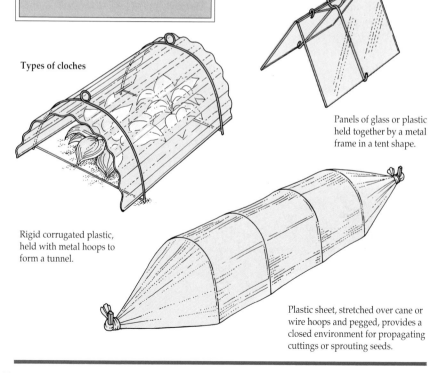

Types of cloches

Panels of glass or plastic held together by a metal frame in a tent shape.

Rigid corrugated plastic, held with metal hoops to form a tunnel.

Plastic sheet, stretched over cane or wire hoops and pegged, provides a closed environment for propagating cuttings or sprouting seeds.

ESSENTIAL TOOLS

With the bewilderingly large range of tools and gardening equipment now available, it is important to consider carefully what particular tasks tools are need for, and to balance factors such as price and convenience with safety measures, especially if there are children to consider.

The features of a garden will, to some extent, dictate the tools that are needed. There will also be decisions about what type of tool will suit both you and the job, since some of the popular tools, such as forks, spades and shears, come in a range of sizes and weights suited to the particular height and strength of individuals. It is worth taking the trouble before purchasing tools to ensure that each item not only represents good value but is also convenient and comfortable to handle.

> ## ESSENTIAL TOOLS
> Basic handtools for the average small to medium-sized garden would be:
> - Garden fork and handfork
> - Garden spade
> - Garden and/or spring-tine rake.
> - Dutch hoe
> - Trowel
> - Watering can
> - Hosepipe and sprinkler
> - Secateurs
>
> Depending on the features of your garden, you may need:
> - Lawnmower
> - Lawn-edging shears
> - Shears, if there is a hedge
> - Sprayer
> - Wheelbarrow

HANDLE SHAPES

D-shape—this was formerly a popular shape for wooden hilts.

T-shape—generally used with wooden shafts but is now old-fashioned.

YD-shape—considered the strongest, most convenient handle for modern tools.

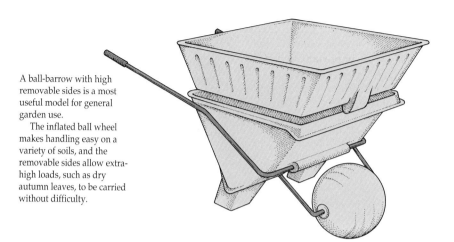

A ball-barrow with high removable sides is a most useful model for general garden use.

The inflated ball wheel makes handling easy on a variety of soils, and the removable sides allow extra-high loads, such as dry autumn leaves, to be carried without difficulty.

Spades and forks

These are available with shafts of different lengths and bases of different sizes. The types of handles, too, have varied, but most modern tools made of steel or reinforced plastic now have the YD-shape.

A border, or "lady's", spade (and fork) is smaller, shorter and lighter than the standard form and is intended for light digging or edging work. There are also models available with longer-than-normal shafts, which are more comfortable for taller people or for deep digging. Some makes of spade have a flattened metal surface, or tread, on the upper edge of the blade, which makes digging less hard on the sole of the foot.

Forks and spades of polished stainless steel are expensive, but they are easy to clean, pleasant to handle and long lasting.

Rakes and hoes

The standard garden rake is used mainly for breaking down the soil and producing a level surface, while the spring-tine rake with its long, slightly flexible, metal or plastic teeth is specially suited to assembling piles of leaves, grass or other garden refuse or to de-thatching lawns.

The most useful hoe for general garden purposes is the horizontal-bladed type, known as the dutch hoe, which is good for slicing off small weeds at the root and for breaking up compacted soil surfaces.

Secateurs and shears

Whether you choose the popular cross-blade or anvil type of secateurs, it is essential to ensure that they are adequate for the job and are not put under strain. A general-purpose model 8–10in/20–25cm long will deal with stems up to about ½in/1cm in diameter. Thicker branches may need a long-handled pruner or pruning saw. Shears are handy for trimming hedges, long grass or herbaceous plants.

Good tools may seem expensive, but they are likely prove inadequate or short-lived at the cheaper end of the range. It is sensible, therefore, to look at a variety of models and buy the best and most long-lasting tools you can afford.

See also: Looking after tools Pages 64–65
Mowers Pages 86–87

MODERN TOOLS

Multiple head tools

A useful development has been the integrated systems of garden tools recently produced by leading manufacturers. They provide a choice of parts which can be detached and reassembled on handles of different types and lengths. This means that a wide range of tool heads can be clipped or twisted on to make tools to suit the individual gardener.

Power tools

An increasing range of tools, particularly larger items for more specialized work, has become available in mechanical form. Driven by petrol or electricity, these are generally known as power tools. While some types of power tools, such as hedge cutters and grass trimmers and mowers, have become almost standard items of garden equipment, other larger tools— chainsaws, cultivators, shredders and powered rakes—are better hired from shops or garden centres.

Looking after tools

Safety precautions are essential. All tools should be stored out of reach of young children in a dry, secure place, such as a shed or garage, which should be lockable. Wear appropriate footwear and gloves when using potentially dangerous tools. Properly used and cared for, many tools will last indefinitely, some a lifetime.

- Clean and dry tools after use and wipe them occasionally with an oily rag.
- If possible, keep tools off the floor, preferably hung against a wall.
- Regularly sharpen tools which have cutting edges.
- Check all tools frequently for mechanical soundness, applying oil or a rust inhibitor if necessary.

POWER TOOL SAFETY

Power tools can be dangerous unless they are working properly and are used carefully.

- Always keep tools in good working order and follow any instructions and warnings supplied with them. (Hire shops should make regulations available and should offer demonstrations to customers.)
- Keep small children and pets away from the area in which you are working.
- Wear suitable protective clothing (including goggles, gloves and heavy footwear) when necessary.
- Use a residual current device (a power breaker) with any electric power cable. These are available from electrical shops, hardware shops and garden centres.
- Do not use electric tools in wet conditions.
- Never attempt to examine or clean an electric tool without switching off the power.
- Keep any cable untangled and running behind you.
- Switch off at the mains immediately if you cut the cable or leave the machine unattended.
- Keep any petrol cans or petrol-driven machines away from flames or cigarettes and avoid spilling petrol when filling the tank.

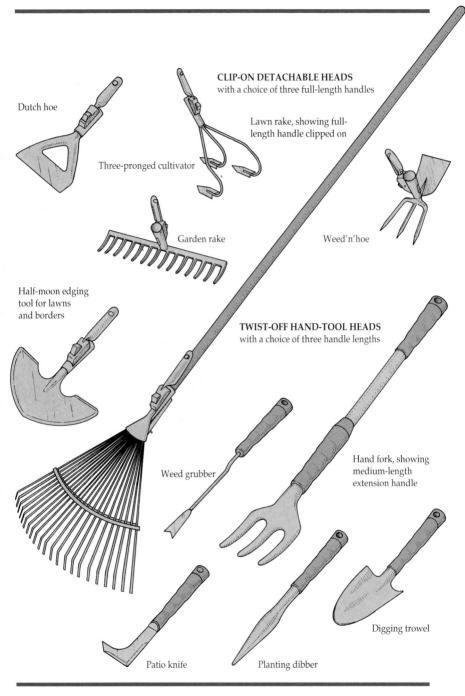

Dutch hoe

CLIP-ON DETACHABLE HEADS
with a choice of three full-length handles

Three-pronged cultivator

Lawn rake, showing full-
length handle clipped on

Garden rake

Weed'n'hoe

Half-moon edging
tool for lawns
and borders

TWIST-OFF HAND-TOOL HEADS
with a choice of three handle lengths

Weed grubber

Hand fork, showing
medium-length
extension handle

Patio knife

Planting dibber

Digging trowel

GARDEN
BASICS

For the beginner, gardening can seem a confusing
occupation. There are few fixed rules to help the novice;
nature is not predictable and a gardener needs to learn
something of its variety as well as its patterns before even a
small plot of land can become productive or agreeable.
This chapter deals with the important elements
of a new site, including its micro-climate, that must be
considered before any dreams of creative design can be
realized and explains the implications for the gardener,
offering advice on such basic procedures as
soil testing and improving poor soil.
It also suggests solutions to a variety of problems which will,
at some time or another, engage anyone who is interested in
creating or improving a garden. These range from growing
choice plants if the garden soil is unsuitable to dealing with
pests and diseases; the best place to site a path or patio;
which materials to use; and how to reconcile the sometimes
apparently conflicting requirements of taste and practicality.
But part of the pleasure of a garden comes from
meeting challenges, and this information will help keen
gardeners with the painstaking but rewarding task of
bridging the gap between the raw reality of the unimproved
site and the achievement of the garden of their dreams.

ELEMENTS OF THE SOIL

Before you start planning your garden, it is essential to understand the broad categories of soil types. Look first at the plants, wild and cultivated, that thrive in your area; they will give you a good indication of the type of soil you are likely to find in your garden. Then make a simple analysis of your garden soil. In this way you will avoid the frustration of trying to grow plants that are unsuitable and will not waste money buying them.

The main soil types are:

• **Clay**—rich in plant food, but cold and tends to become waterlogged. Drain, dig and add humus.

• **Sand**—short of plant food and water-retentive material, but warm and well drained. Add humus and fertilizer.

• **Chalk**—suits many shrubs and herbaceous plants, but too alkaline for others. Add humus and fertilizer.

• **Peat**—moisture retentive, but too acidic for a number of garden plants. May need to be fertilized and limed.

Most garden soils are, in fact, a mixture of these types.

Testing the soil

To simplest way to test your garden soil is to shake up a sample in a jar of water. When it settles, you can see the amounts of sand (which settles on the bottom) and clay (the upper layer) that it contains; humus usually floats on top of the water.

Another simple test to determine soil type is to squeeze a ball of it in your hands. If it holds together, is sticky and looks shiny, it is clay. If it does not hold together, even when damp, it is sand. If it forms a loose, firm ball and feels even textured yet crumbly, it is the best mix for gardening.

Well-cultivated, even-textured, crumbly

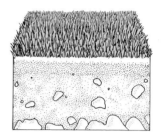

The ideal garden soil, or loam, is a mixture of sand, clay and humus. The darker its colour, the more humus it contains.

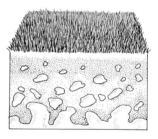

Chalky soil can be difficult to cultivate. It drains freely and the top-soil is shallow and low in nutrients. Peat or humus improves the texture and reduces alkalinity.

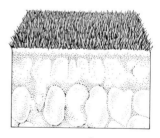

Clay is sticky and easily becomes waterlogged. It is rich, but must be drained and lightened by thorough digging and the addition of compost.

SOIL PROFILES

Loam—a mixture of sand, clay and humus, the best soil for gardening. Ideal for most plants. If acidic, it is also good for ericaceous plants such as *Arbutus, Camellia, Pieris, Rhododendron* and *Trillium* (Trinity flower).

Chalk—tends to be dry and deficient in some minerals but is also free draining and alkaline. Suits *Althaea* (Hollyhock), *Buddleia, Cistus, Cytisus, Fagus* (Beech), *Dianthus, Gypsophila*, Bearded iris, *Juniperus, Lavandula, Papaver* (Oriental poppy), *Philadelphus, Scabious* and *Taxus*.

Clay—rich in nutrients but can, unless improved, be heavy and waterlogged in wet weather. Its moisture-retentive qualities suit *Alnus* (Alder), *Anemone* x *hybrida, Cornus* (Dogwood), *Bergenia, Fraxinus* (Ash), *Helleborus, Populus* (Poplar), *Salix* (Willow), *Sambucus* (Elder), *Trollius* (Globeflower) and, of course, roses.

soil is referred to as loam, and it is important to have a high proportion of it if plants are to grow to their best advantage. Poor growth is not always attributable to pests and diseases but may be due to poor soil. It is usually not enough merely to analyse the soil then treat it once to achieve a good structure; it needs regular maintenance and improvement. To provide the right conditions for the plants to thrive, compost must be regularly dug into garden beds, and manure and fertilizers applied to replenish the nutrients in the soil that are leached out by water and depleted by the growing plants.

Compost and humus

Compost is decomposed organic matter; humus is a rich form of it which never completely decomposes since it decays so slowly. Together they are the chief natural source of nitrogen, a vital plant nutrient, which also serves to feed bacteria and the many other miniscule life forms teeming within the soil. These organisms in turn help to produce an improved, granulated soil structure. Adding compost to a heavy clay soil can be make the clay lighter, while a sandy soil will become bulkier and more water retentive.

Aerating the soil

Compost and humus also help to aerate the soil. Another important agent assisting with aeration is the earthworm. This creature can be irritating in a lawn because it leaves small mounds of earth, or casts, at the entrance to its burrow. But earthworms eat decaying organic matter and at the same time ingest soil, so helping to aerate it. They also draw organic matter down into their burrows, where it decays more rapidly than on the surface.

See also: Preparing the ground Pages 10–11
The pH content of soil Pages 70–71

TESTING YOUR SOIL

Soil is an extremely complex material, constantly changing as various substances within it react to each other to modify its chemical elements.

• A very high alkaline content will reduce the availability of the major nutrients—Nitrogen, Phosphorus and Potassium (N, P, K)—and minor elements such as iron will also be much reduced.

• An excess of acid in the soil also reduces the major nutrients, as well as the quantity of calcium. The acidity may lead to a surplus of iron, manganese and aluminium, which can produce toxic symptoms in the soil.

Obviously the acid–alkaline balance in the soil is fundamentally important to the health and vigour of plants because it affects the availability of the nutrients they require for survival. This balance is ascertained by a chemical scale known as "pH"; the pH reading shows the acid or alkaline content of the soil.

• The pH scale ranges from 0 to 14. A reading of 7 is considered "neutral". Over 7 indicates alkalinity; for example, a reading of 8.5 would probably come from a very thin soil overlying chalk. Below 7 indicates acidity; a reading as low as 3 would come from an area of acid peat.

• The ideal level is between 5.7 and 6.7; at this level, most nutrients are held in a soluble state and are, therefore, available to the plant.

There are a number of popular ornamental plants that prefer an acid soil; rhododendrons, camellias, hydrangeas, azaleas and many in the *Erica* family ideally need a soil that shows a pH reading of 4.5 to 5.5. Many other plants, including lawn grass, will not thrive at this level of acidity, and for them the soil may need the addition of lime to improve the chemical balance.

The natural amount of lime in the soil is steadily depleted by rain, but the amount you add will be determined by the pH reading of your soil. Lime should not be added to alkaline soil.

• Add lime in the autumn, turning it into the soil with a rotary cultivator if the area is large.

• Leave an interval of at least a month between adding lime and applying animal manure or other fertilizers. The combination can cause a reaction which releases ammonia, a harmful agent.

• Seeds can also be sown a month after liming.

• Test the pH reading of your soil nine months after applying lime and act accordingly.

Lime also serves other purposes in the soil. Mixed in humus it helps to liberate essential nutrients and introduces calcium, and it discourages some pests, although it can encourage others.

It is rather more difficult to alter highly alkaline soil. Iron deficiency can be somewhat modified by adding sequestrene, and sulphur will counteract the alkalinity to a certain extent, but it is simply not practical to add large amounts of either of these substances to large areas of soil in your garden.

You will be a happier gardener if you grow the plants suited to your type of soil and, if necessary, put those that prefer acid soil into containers. Numerous alpines succeed in alkaline soil, as do carnations, wallflowers, some heathers, and many shrubs.

Soil-testing kits vary. With this one, water and soil in a ratio of 5:1 are shaken up in a jam jar and allowed to settle; a clear, coloured liquid results after about 30 minutes. The appropriate colour-coded tester for the level of the pH, nitrogen, phosphorus or potash and the type of plant is selected. The cap of the tester and the colour-coded capsules it contains are removed.

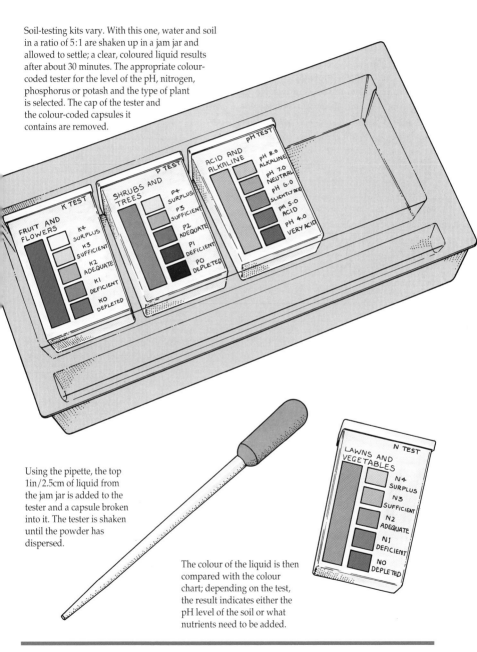

Using the pipette, the top 1in/2.5cm of liquid from the jam jar is added to the tester and a capsule broken into it. The tester is shaken until the powder has dispersed.

The colour of the liquid is then compared with the colour chart; depending on the test, the result indicates either the pH level of the soil or what nutrients need to be added.

See also: Nutrient deficiencies Pages 32-33
Elements of the soil Pages 68–69

CLIMATE ZONES

In North America, a system of zone ratings is used to indicate the average minimum temperature a plant will tolerate; the same system is sometimes used in Europe. But factors such as altitude, exposure, soil type and water content, can all make a plant more or less hardy than the average minimum temperatures would suggest. Dry, free-draining soils tend to promote a plant's hardiness in winter, damp soil to decrease it. Heat and dryness are also crucial. As a result of these complex factors, a number of the indicator plants listed as hardy in North America would not be considered so in Europe. Many of the plants listed for one zone will also grow in succeeding zones.

Zone 1: below -50°F/-45°C.
Betula glandulosa, Populus tremuloides, Rhododendron lapponicum, Salix reticulata

Zone 2: -50°F/-45°C to -40°F/-40°C.
Acer saccharum, Betula papyrifera, Cornus canadensis, Larix laricina, Picea glauca

Zone 3: -40°F/-40°C to -30°F/-34°C.
Berberis thunbergii, Eleagnus commutata Juniperus communis, Thuja occidentalis

Zone 4: -30°F/-34°C to -20°F/-29°C.
Hydrangea paniculata, Juniperus chinensis, Quercus coccinea, Spiraea x vanhouttei

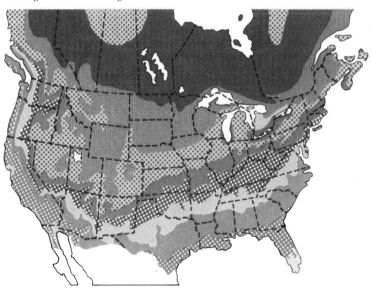

Zone 5:-20°F/-29°C to -10°F/-23°C.
*Cornus florida, Deutzia gracilis,
Ligustrum vulgare, Parthenocissus
tricuspidata, Rosa multiflora ,
Taxus cuspidata*

 Zone 8: 10°F/-12°C to 20°F/-7°C.
*Arbutus unedo, Ceanothus impressus,
Choisya, Pittosporum tobira, Prunus
laurocerasus, Rhododendron* var.,
Viburnum tinus

 Zone 6: -10°F/-23°C to 0°F/-18°C.
*Acer palmatum, Buxus sempervirens,
Euonymus fortunei, Hedera helix,
Ilex opaca, Ligustrum ovalifolium,
Prunus yedoensis*

 Zone 9: 20°F/-7°C to 30°F/-1°C.
*Camellia reticulata, Casuarina,
Eucalpytus* var., *Fuchsia* hybrids,
*Grevillea robusta, Olea europaea,
Nerium oleander, Schinus*

 Zone 7: 0°F/-18°C to 10°F/-12°C.
*Acer macrophyllum, Cedrus atlantica,
Cotoneaster microphylla, Ilex aquifolium,
Lagerstroemia indica, Taxus baccata*

 Zone 10: 30°F/-1°C to 40°F/4°C
*Bougainvillea, Cassia, Euphorbia
pulcherrima, Ficus elastica, Hibiscus
rosa-sinensis, Jacaranda, Musa ensete,
Phoenix canariensis*

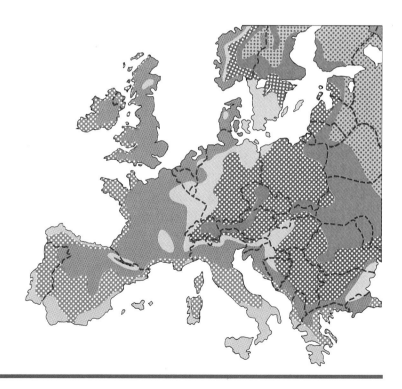

See also: Making the most of your site Pages 74–75

MAKING THE MOST OF YOUR SITE

If you are keen to develop a garden on a new site, begin by taking stock of the existing conditions and features, since these will create microclimates within the garden: areas which are especially warm or cool, dry or damp, shady or exposed. Understanding these microclimates will help you plant the garden effectively by creating features and choosing plants best suited to each area. In particular, consider:

• The position of the house and garden in relation to the sun. Note the areas of maximum and minimum exposure and features, such as walls, which will absorb and reflect the sun's heat.

• Shady areas, and the times of the day and year at which these occur: a wall that is only partly shaded in summer can be entirely sunless in winter. Areas of continuous dry or windy shade make interesting planting difficult but may prove suitable for sheds or compost bins. Remember, you

Little sun reaches the front of this house. *Thuja*, some dwarf conifers, a hardy birch tree and low-growing vinca and ivies tolerate such conditions and will give colour and interest all year round.

The low hollow walls provide an open, well-drained position for growing alpines.

The terrace gets sun all year round, and heat reflected off the walls and paving stones makes it ideal for such plants as pelargoniums and succulents, which enjoy hot conditions. In summer, climbers on the pergola provide dappled shade.

Scented plants along the edge of the terrace, add to the pleasure of sitting out.

can create shade with trees and pergolas.

• The slope of the ground. This, in relation to such factors as sun, rainfall, soil type, will help to determine what plants or features are suited to a particular area. For instance, a terrace with Mediterranean-type plants on a higher, well-drained area. And while hollows may seem ideal sites for ponds or sheltered beds, they can also create frost pockets, making them unsuitable for tender or late-flowering plants.

• Any unwanted features or eyesores that may have to be screened out, such as ugly walls or buildings. Conversely, removing part of a hedge, wall or shrubbery could open up an attractive view.

• The prevailing winds and areas exposed to them. Wind can quickly desiccate plants as well as damage stems and flowers. Solid walls and fences often create damaging eddies and down-draughts of wind, which a hedge will filter more effectively.

On the perimeter of the lawn, a border with a sunny aspect allows a mixture of herbaceous plants and deciduous shrubs to thrive. Any wind is filtered by thick hedges and plants will not suffer unduly.

A border which gets some sun in summer but little in winter is good for deciduous and some evergreen shrubs, and ideal for clematis, which likes shade at the roots and its head in the sun.

The pond is in an open position, away from overhanging trees, for most water plants will not thrive in the shade.

Hidden by a sweep of hedge and a large, leafy tree, the shed and compost bin are sited out of view of the terrace, but in an uncrowded and convenient positon.

See also: Climate zones Pages 72–73
Designing a garden Pages 76–77

DESIGNING A NEW GARDEN

It is useful to think of a garden in terms of a house—of which it can considered an extention. Hard landscaping (the solid, constructed items) is the equivalent of the structure itself; soft landscaping (plants and ornamental features) is the furnishing and decoration which make it habitable. After surveying your site, think about the changes you might want to make. Visit garden centres, landscape suppliers and other gardens or browse through garden design books for ideas. Make a note of the features you want to change or introduce. Now you are ready to begin a "do-it-yourself" design.

• Take the measurements of the garden (metric is the easiest), including all boundaries, house walls and other permanent structures.

• Decide on your scale eg. 1:50 (1cm= 0.5m) for smaller gardens, 1:100 (1cm=1m) for larger ones. Use a large sheet of paper marked in 1-cm squares to help you draw an outline scale plan of the garden viewed from above. Mark in fixed or permanent features as accurately as you can.

• Using a different pen or pencil, sketch in the new features you want (see list below). Check on the site that measurements are realistic and adequate, especially for trees, lawns, paths and outdoor living areas.

• Make the shapes of your plan attractive as well as practical. Paths, lawns and beds with curving lines create appealing vistas

THE PLAN

Utilitarian features such as greenhouse, compost areas and surrounding hard surface are sited away from living area and are softened by the attractive curve of the path and the screening hedge.

The right planting in key areas adjacent to paths and patios is important in small gardens

A border of trees or taller shrubs can provide privacy and shelter, as well as screening from unsightly structures.

Aim to include an attractive focal point—here, an ornamental tree to give year-round interest.

Patios or outdoor living areas are usually sited in sunny spots adjacent to the house.

and are often more restful and pleasing than straight ones. If you find it hard to imagine a plan three-dimensionally, visit mature gardens to look at good design and interesting planting which can give a clear idea of overall effects.

• Tackle the essential hard landscaping items first since these are the most expensive and can affect subsequent planting. A qualified landscaper will be able to provide the detailed measurements and specifications of materials which will be needed if you do not want to do this yourself.

• The soft landscaping, or planting, is usually the last stage. Try to gauge the size of trees and other major ornamental plants in several years' time and to site them correctly. Remember that successful growth will be in proportion to the time and costs allowed for good soil preparation and careful planting.

Checklist of garden design features

Hard landscaping items: barbecue or paved areas, paths, ponds or pools, pergolas or arches, walls, fences, trellises or screens, conservatories, greenhouses, sheds or bins.

Soft landscaping items: new planting areas—rockeries, beds, borders, etc, all plants including trees and hedges, containers, statuary, seats and other ornamental items.

THE GARDEN

This three-dimensional image shows the features in proportion to one another. A good design will take into account the foreshortening effect which seems to bring the back of the garden closer to the house.

Because taller objects such as trees and buildings draw the eye, they are best sited away from the house toward the end of the garden.

The curving lines of path and lawn soften the overall design and create a soothing effect.

Interesting containers and low foliage plants are good for setting off paths and patios.

See also: Making the most of your site Pages 74–75

IMPROVING YOUR GARDEN

Most people moving house and inheriting a boring garden will want to modify or alter it rather than create a completely new one. Allow time to "live with" the new garden and take careful stock of it, making a note of what changes you might want to make. When considering what to keep, be cautious, at least initially, about removing trees or shrubs, which may provide necessary shade or privacy.

Think next about what changes are desirable. You may want to move a shed which is in the wrong place or create a vegetable plot or patio extension. It is probably easiest to make your plan by using the same graph paper method recommended for designing a new garden.

Having decided on necessary changes, think what features could add interest to your garden. These might include:

• Raised beds (or a rock garden)—sited near a house or patio, both can provide an attractive setting for interesting or scented perennial plants or alpines.

• Improving existing shapes or materials— a gently curving path or planted border is often more interesting than a straight one. Paths or patios with dull surfaces could be

BEFORE

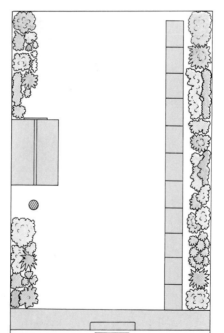

The squared shapes and dreary expanse of lawn add up to a boring garden, ripe for improvement.

Straight lines of planting along the boundaries may provide some screening but make for a very dull layout.

A garden shed, obtrusively placed half-way down the garden and without the convenience of a path obviously needs to be moved.

The path's rigidly geometric lines, unsoftened by planting or any ornamental features, add to the general tedium.

replaced with more colourful or attractive materials.

• Vistas or focal points—clearing and opening out a cluttered lawn or lengthening a border can give the opportunity for a striking plant or specimen tree to provide the focal point of a view.

• Divisions—unbroken or undifferentiated areas of grass or shrubs can be monotonous. Use screens, low hedging or different types of planting to create discrete areas or smaller garden "rooms", which lead the eye on and arouse a sense of curiosity.

• Ornaments—these can range from an elaborate garden pool or pergola to the simpler device of a garden bench, piece of statuary or just a handsome pot.

• New plants—even a few, well-placed and really interesting plants from the enormous range now available can make a big difference to a garden. Do not forget trees or shrubs, which will give year-round interest, particularly in the autumn and winter months.

The illustrations will give you some idea of what can be done, without much effort or expense, to turn even a small, boring "back yard" into a charming garden.

AFTER

The main shrub planting has been broken up to create different areas and a more interesting overall layout.

Shaped stepping stones, set in pleasing curves, lead to the re-sited garden shed, now largely concealed by a screening of shrubs and climbers.

The patio has been reconstructed and extended to produce a practical and attractive outdoor living space.

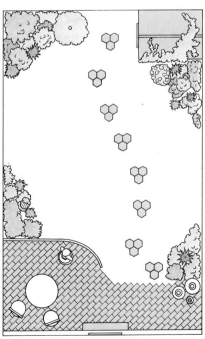

Suitable shrubs for shady areas and for screening include : *Eleagnus, Ilex, Pyracantha, Cotoneaster, Spiraea, Mahonia, Philadelphus, Sambucus, Taxus;* for ornamental interest: *Cupressus* var., *Cytisus, Kerria, Viburnum, Syringa, Acer, Lavatera.*

Scented or bold-foliage plants such as *Daphne, Lilies, Bamboo, Fatsia, Hosta, Lavender* and *New Zealand Flax,* augmented in summer by container plants, enliven the patio.

PATIOS

The Spanish word "patio" originally meant the open inner courtyard of a house; today, the term refers to any paved outdoor area near or adjoining the house. Combining the practicality of a surfaced path with the luxury of a leisure area, patios have become an essential feature of many homes.

If you are putting in a patio, there are a number of points to consider:

• Proximity to a house door—or a garage or shed for easy access to storage.

• Sun and shelter—you can provide shade if necessary.

• Privacy—most patios are situated away from the street and front door.

• Views—a patio may form, or lead to, a terrace with a pleasant view.

• Main functions—the way in which a patio is to be used may affect its final position, size or shape.

• Existing buildings and garden furniture—these may guide your choice of design and the materials you use.

Having decided on the position and design of a patio, you need next to consider what materials to use. Most patios require the same basic foundation—a 1–2in/2.5–5cm layer of sand or sand and cement on a firm, level base. There is, however, a considerable choice of paving materials available from garden centres, building merchants and DIY stores.

Stone slabs—the well-known York stone is a beautiful material especially for old properties with matured gardens, but at around £70 per slab it is expensive.

Pre-cast concrete or composite (stone/sand/cement) slabs—these are avaible in a wide range of textures, colours, sizes and prices from inexpensive plain concrete to dearer riven slabs with the appearance of natural stone. A pattern of two or more colours and shapes can be very attractive.

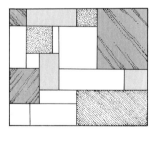

Slabs or bricks of different colours can be used to make attractive patterns.

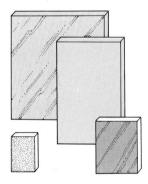

Paving materials are available in different sizes as well as types or styles. Use a "mix and match" method to build up an effective surface design.

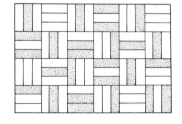

See also: Designing a new garden Pages 76–77
Improving your garden Pages 78–79

Allow sufficient space for furniture and practical items such as a rubbish bin.

An edging of bricks, laid on edge, provides a neat finish to the patio.

Scented or eye-catching plants bordering the patio are an essential feature.

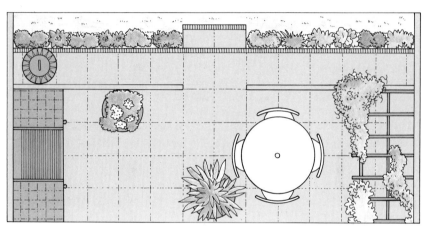

A built-in barbecue can be a useful and attractive feature.

Dappled shade can be provided by a creeper-clad pergola.

Paviours or bricks—paviours are heavy-duty composite bricks available in a few natural-looking colours and especially suitable for areas which may be used by cars or subjected to heavy wear. Old bricks look attractive but are expensive and their worn, uneven surface can be impractical.
Sets—small concrete or granite blocks suitable for building into patterns.
Laid concrete—cheap and rather dull, but if used with other materials can look acceptable when weathered.
Gravel or shingle—a cheap but practical and pleasing alternative, particularly if used with paving slabs as stepping stones.
    Other factors you need to consider are:
• Edging—this can be of a different material and need not be in a straight line.

Remember that paved surfaces should be slightly below the level of a lawn (and two brick-widths below a damp course) and must not block drains or soakaways.
• Levels—surfaces should slope slightly away from buildings to allow water to drain off. Changes of level add character, but steps should be low and any supporting walls need a concrete foundation.
• Barbecues or built-in seats—need to be planned as part of a practical, overall design, with materials that tie in with the rest of the patio.
• Plants—scented or low-foliage and flowering plants grown between slabs, in containers or among small beds of washed river stones will soften the appearance of large paved areas.

PATHS

Because their main function is to provide a convenient walking surface, particularly in winter, paths tend to be thought of merely as practical items in an overall garden design. There is, however, plenty of scope, both in the materials available and the possible shapes of paths, to make them attractive, as well as functional.

When deciding on the position of a path, try to balance the practical need for a direct route with aesthetic design considerations. It may seem convenient—or sometimes be appropriate—for a path to run the shortest possible distance and in a straight line. But stepped or curved lines can complement and enhance other features such as lawns and borders.

The width of a path is a further crucial factor. Routes across a lawn or through a border or shrubbery may be reduced to the simple, but effective, device of round or square paving slabs set in the ground. More elaborate types of path must be wide enough to allow comfortable walking, as well as the passage of bicycles and mowers or wheelbarrows.

When the size and route of a path have been decided, the next important matter is the materials for construction. The choice is similar to that for patios, although there are some additional materials available. The following ideas should also be considered:

• Set slabs diagonally instead of laying them square with the edge of the path.
• Leave gaps for planting or fill some squares with bricks or cobbles.
• Edge a stone or concrete path with different-coloured bricks or paviours laid edge on edge.

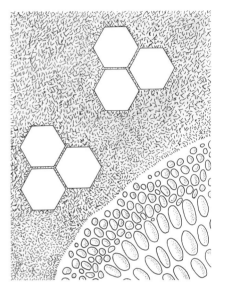

• Position plain or brick-patterned slabs with gravel surrounding them.
• Steps, raised planters or adjoining borders make good complementary features for paths.
• Soften the appearance of new paths by sympathetic planting along the edges with low-growing plants such as *Alchemilla mollis*. Make sure that large or badly sited plants do not cover or conceal the path.

Laying paths

If a path is to be long lasting, it is important not only to use good-quality materials but to lay it correctly.

• Proper foundations are essential. These may require some excavation and will normally consist of a layer of sand or mortar mix, if necessary over a base of hardcore or builder's rubble.
• A layer of cement, or blobs of mortar on the foundation, may be required if slabs or

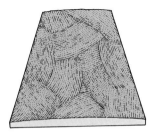

Brushing the surface with a stiff yard broom while it is still wet will produce a safer, more attractive concrete path.

Treated timber or old railway sleepers can be used to form a raised edge to gravel or brick paths or to make steps.

Gravel is a cheap and easily laid material which sets off plants very well, but weeds may grow in it and prove a problem.

bricks are being used for surfacing. The latter need to be tapped level gently with a piece of wood or mallet.
• Curved or irregularly shaped paths may require bricks, slabs or timber to be cut to size with special equipment.
• Gaps in paving can be filled with sand or pointed with a stiff mortar.

Maintenance of paths

As paths weather, they become more mellow and attractive in appearance, but they may also become weedy or covered in moss or algae, especially in damp shady places. Control weeds by hand weeding or using a systemic weedkiller. Moss or algae can become slippery and dangerous in winter. To prevent this, apply a proprietary fertilizer-free moss killer in spring or autumn. Gravel paths require little maintenance, but they may occasionally need topping up, firming down or raking.

> ## PAVING MATERIALS FOR PATHS
> • Concrete—cheap and dull but can be used with other materials.
> • Bricks or paviours—attractive appearance; expensive and fiddly to lay.
> • Tarmac—unattractively functional.
> • Gravel or stone chips—effective with plants but the loose surface needs containing with a raised edge.
> • Paving slabs—available in a range of styles and sizes. Can be laid plain or mixed and matched.
> • Wood—treated and stained timber sleepers or cross-trunk slabs; natural looking but slippery when wet.

See also: Patios Pages 80–81

ESTABLISHING A LAWN

One of the most important elements in the design of a garden is the lawn. A smooth, thick lawn, green, fresh-looking and neat, is not only a pleasing foundation to the garden plan but a practical feature, for nothing else controls the spread of weeds with such efficiency. A lawn is easy to establish and maintain, except in areas of deep shade under trees.

The site for a lawn must be thoroughly prepared; although it is a daunting task, double digging is best. Perennial weeds, such as couch grass, must be eradicated before planting. This can best be done by applying a systemic weedkiller. Annual weeds can usually be dealt with by hoeing.

Levelling the site

If the site is very irregular, you may have to grade it, but small humps and hollows can be levelled quite simply by making a grid across the area with pegs and string.
• Hammer in wooden pegs 6ft/2m apart to form a grid pattern.
• Lay a plank across adjacent pegs in turn, place a spirit level on the plank and hammer in pegs until all are level.
• Tie string between the pegs about ½in/1cm above the level at which you want the lawn.
• Fill up with top-soil until you reach the string; it will settle back to the correct level.
• Firm the soil, using the back of the head of a rake.

Preparing the site

The best time to make a lawn is in the spring or autumn, when there is no threat from frost and rain is likely.
• One month before sowing or laying turf, rake the surface of the ground with a spring-tined lawn rake. Remove weeds,

TURF VERSUS SEED
Turf
• Usually laid in autumn or spring.
• May have to be ordered.
• Costs much more than seed.
• Less choice in types of grass.
• Some ground preparation needed.
• Frequent watering until established.
• Lawn established in weeks.
Seed
• Best sown in autumn or spring.
• Seed mixtures widely available.
• Choice of grass types.
• Much cheaper than turf.
• Thorough preparation needed.
• Regular watering required initially.
• Lawn established after 2–3 months.

leaves and stones and break up any clods of earth.
• One week before sowing or laying, apply a lawn fertilizer. Whether working in spring or autumn, use a fertilizer with a low nitrogen and high phosphate content.
• Firm the area with the head of a rake or by treading; if possible, avoid using a roller, since this will compact heavy soils and may lead to drainage problems later.

Sowing seed

If you intend to produce a lawn from sown seed, choose the seed carefully. Seed for a fine lawn is made up mainly of fescues and bent grasses, but this mixture is not suitable for a lawn that will have heavy use. Instead, use a blend that contains hard-wearing rye grass or one of the modern hybrid grasses.
• Sow the seed as uniformly as possible, using 1oz:1sq yd/35g:1 sq m.

- Sieve a fine layer of soil over the seed, then cover the area with light-weight fruit-cage netting as protection against birds.
- Water with a fine lawn sprinkler. Seeds should germinate within a fortnight.

Laying turf

Turf will be delivered in heavy rolls, so have them dropped as near to the lawn site as you can and lay them within a week or the grass will turn yellow.

- Starting at one edge of the lawn area, lay the turves in straight rows, staggering the blocks. Do not stand directly on them, but use a plank.
- Firm the turves with the back of a rake, filling any gaps between them with soil or compost.
- Water with a fine lawn sprinkler and make sure the grass does not dry out over the next 10–14 days, by which time the roots will be established and you can walk on your lawn.

> **NON–GRASS LAWNS**
> Some low-growing plants make good "no mow" lawns in the right spot:
> - Ivy (*Hedera helix*)—variegated or plain, spreads to make a 6-in/15-cm high evergreen ground cover. Good for shady areas but cannot be walked on and needs to be trimmed.
> - Chamomile (*Anthemis nobilis*)— low (1in/2.5cm), feathery-leaved, scented herb, best in non-flowering form 'Treneague'. Use in small, sheltered areas; withstands some treading. Needs regular watering. and hand weeding. Useless in cold,wet sites.
> - Thyme (*Thymus* spp.)—mats of attractive flowers and minute scented leaves. Similar uses to chamomile; better for sunny, dry or chalky sites.

Stretch a string along one side of the lawn area and lay the first row of turves up to it. Stand or kneel on a plank and not on the grass. Stagger the turves like bricks in a wall when laying them.

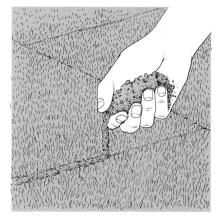

Tamp down the turves with the back of a rake; pour soil between the blocks and brush it in; trim the edges of the lawn with a turfing iron. Water thoroughly with a sprinkler.

See also: Lawn care Pages 86–87

LAWN CARE

A good lawn needs regular maintenance and feeding, but compared to other parts of the garden it is, nevertheless, relatively trouble free.

To keep your lawn springy and green it should receive a thorough soaking quite regularly. In the wetter climates of the northern hemisphere, keeping the lawn watered is not usually a major problem, but as a general rule, where there is inadequate rainfall, you should water the lawn every 10–14 days throughout spring and summer.

The easiest and best way to do this is to use a sprinkler, although gardeners in drier climates may prefer to install an irrigation system that is laid beneath the grass and has an automatic switching mechanism. Local regulations on the use of water in the garden must be considered when you are planning areas of lawn, and it would be wise to take these into account before deciding on a large expanse of grass.

Feeding

Nutrients are important in keeping grass thick and resilient, and lawns can be fed twice a year, in spring and autumn. For the spring feed, wait until the soil has warmed up and it is moist, then apply a powder formulated, combination lawn fertilizer and weedkiller (weed and feed). This application of weedkiller should prove adequate for the season, although you may find that small patches require localized treatment.

The spring feed should have a relatively high nitrogen content to promote growth, whereas the later, cold-season feed, which is also powder formulated, should have a relatively low nitrogen content. The autumn fertilizer is also suitable for use when sowing lawn seed or laying turf.

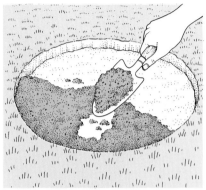

Bare patches in the lawn need special attention. Dig out the dead grass and soil and fill the hole with turf or compost with grass seed added to it. Fill any gaps between turves with top dressing.

Aerating the soil

Turf gradually forms a fibrous layer of dead blades, known as "thatch", between the roots and the foliage. This acts as a mulch, since it inhibits evaporation, but it can become so thick that its effect is adverse, and water and fertilizer may not be able to reach the roots. The soil then becomes clogged, it lacks drainage and air and must be aerated. Check particularly those areas which have become compacted through heavy usage; look for signs of poor drainage or patches where the lawn lacks vigour.

The best way to aerate the soil is by spiking it:
• Turn your garden fork so that it faces you and drive it vertically into the turf.
• The tines should penetrate to a depth of 4–6in/12–15cm.
• Ease the fork back and forth a few times before removing it, and repeat the process all over the affected area, spacing the sets of holes 6in/15cm apart.

Firm down and, with a plank, make sure that turves or seed mixture are level with the existing lawn. Cover seed mixture with plastic or fine netting until it sprouts, to protect it from the birds.

You may need a hollow-tined fork to deal with heavy compaction, but this is very hard work, and if your lawn needs widespread aeration the best idea is to hire a powered spiking machine.

If necessary, repeat the spiking every four or five weeks during the summer, or until the patch improves. In autumn, carry out a more general aeration, using a scarifying tool or long-tined rake and dragging it through the thatch before feeding the lawn. You may find that some areas need spiking even in the winter.

Mowing

Lawns must also be cut. Try to mow at least once a week from late spring to late summer. Set the blades fairly low, but not at their lowest—very closely cropped grass encourages the growth of moss. Mow only if necessary in winter, when the weather is mild. At this time, the blades need to be set high; if the grass is too short, the roots may be damaged by frost. Mow in straight lines in alternate directions.

LAWNMOWERS

Your choice of lawnmower will depend on the size of your lawn; the amount of wear it receives; the quality of finish you require; the amount of time you can give to the job and how much you can afford.

• If yours is a "tough" lawn, designed for family life, you will not be aiming for a fine finish. It will also probably contain rye grass. In these circumstances a rotary mower will be satisfactory. Use a wheeled rotary on a level lawn; a hover is ideal for mowing banks or around shrubs and trees.

• A fine lawn will be best mown by a cylinder mower. If it is small, a hand mower will probably do; if it is large, buy the best petrol-driven cylinder mower you can afford.

• Electric machines have well-designed safety features, but a trailing cord can be hazardous, and they are best in small gardens. Battery-powered mowers are heavy; so for a medium-sized or large lawn, use a petrol mower.

• Use a grass collector; cuttings left on the lawn tend to prevent the penetration of air and water.

• At a speed of 3mph/5kmph, with an overlap of 2in/5cm, the areas that can be cut are approximately:

Width of cut	Area mown in 1 hour
12in/30cm	1,470sq yds/1,230sq m
16in/40cm	2,000sq yds/1,670sq m
20in/50cm	2,640sq yds/2,205sq m
24in/60cm	2,930sq yds/2,450sq m

See also: Establishing a lawn Pages 84–85

FOLIAGE PLANTS

Foliage plays a vital role in creating the form of a garden and in giving the planting interest and variety. With some plants, it is the small or large size of the leaves that is distinctive. With others, it may be colour of the foliage—variegated, yellow, red, grey or purple—or its texture that makes it valuable.

In many instances the value lies in shape: the stiff, swordlike foliage of crocosmia or iris and the bold, smooth or puckered leaves of hosta all act as a foil for the softer, less distinctively shaped foliage of other plants in the border.

The contribution of trees, with their wide variety of leaf colour and shape, should not be overlooked. The grey-green young foliage of *Eucalyptus gunnii* offers attractive colour and shape as well as a pleasing sharp scent when the leaves are crushed.

The strong, uncompromising lines of many conifers, clothed in foliage year-round, give solidity and permanence to garden design. And their colour—ranging from gold and bright green to blue-green and almost black—is invaluable, enlivening the garden in winter and providing a backdrop for summer-flowering plants.

The list of trees and shrubs whose foliage gives brilliant autumn colour is almost endless. Among the most splendid trees are *Acer* spp., *Liquidambar styraciflua* (Sweet gum), a native of North America, and *Ginkgo biloba* (Maidenhair tree). Among the shrubs, the foliage of *Enkianthus* spp. turns bright red, that of *Hamamelis mollis* (Witch hazel) golden yellow.

The popular camellia can be enjoyed not only for its showy flowers but for the pleasure of its glossy green leaves in winter. *Olearia* 'Waikariensis', with its metallic-hued leaves also brightens up a winter garden, as do the gold-variegated leaves of *Eleagnus pungens* 'Maculata'.

A well-planned design uses foliage plants to give depth and perspective—an important consideration in a small garden.

PLANTS WITH AROMATIC LEAVES

Aloysia triphylla (Lemon verbena)
Choisya ternata (Mexican orange blossom)
Laurus nobilis (Sweet Bay)
Mentha spp. (Mint)
Monarda spp. (Bergamot)
Myrtus communis (Common myrtle)
Nepeta musinii (Catmint)
Rosmarinus officinalis (Rosemary)
Thymus spp. (Thyme)

A corner can be given dramatic emphasis with *Fatsia japonica*, a hardy shrub that has wonderfully tropical-looking large-lobed leaves. The shiny evergreen foliage of *Choisya ternata*, which both catches and reflects light, will enliven a dull wall or wooden fence.

The highly ornamental yucca, with its sea-green, sword-shaped leaves and tall stalk of white flowers, will create a strong vertical line in a border of summer flowers. Even at ground level, additional interest can be created by creeping plants, such as the aromatic, hairy, grey-leaved *Thymus pseudolanuginosus*.

Foliage also adds texture to a garden. A grouping of plants such as *Artemisia pedemontana*, with fine, silvery grey leaves, and *Stachys byzantina* (Lamb's ear) will soften the hard edge of a stone path. And the graceful silvery leaves of the shrubby *Artemisia arborescens* 'Lambrook Silver' or 'Powis Castle' form a pleasing contrast when planted in front of a shrub with dark green or purple foliage such as yew or *Berberis* 'Helmond Pillar'.

The dense, twiggy growth of heathers introduces a rougher, sharper texture that is a welcome foil to the voluptuous colours and shapes of the leaves of many annuals and perennials.

Such contrast is the essential delight of foliage—sometimes bold, sometimes subtle in its visual appeal. The grand display of *Gunnera manicata*, for example, with its enormous leaves, which are larger than umbrellas, is impressively eye-catching in a large garden. While at the other end of the scale, the low-growing *Alchemilla mollis* demands close inspection to appreciate fully its charming fluted leaves that hold drops of water in the centre, like diamonds.

The value of foliage plants in the garden is often neglected in the quest for flowers and colour when planting is planned, but it should not be, for their variety is always rewarding, and often surprising.

The part played by foliage plants in creating the framework of the garden is often overlooked when planting schemes are planned. But it is the pleasing juxtaposition of these plants, with their differently shaped leaves of varied texture and colour, that gives permanence to the garden design.

See also: Evergreen shrubs Pages 114–121
Deciduous shrubs Pages 122–133

HOBBY PLANTS

$\mathcal{S}$ ome popular types of plants are available in so many different forms or varieties that many amateur gardeners and nurseries enjoy specializing in them. Begonias, fuchsias, border carnations and pinks and pelargoniums are examples of such "hobby" plants.

Border carnations and pinks

Long familiar as cut flowers and as rockery or front-of-border edging plants, these well-known hybrid forms of *Dianthus* are easily grown in an open, sunny position and in light, free-draining, alkaline soil that is not over-rich. Pinch out the main shoots of new plants in spring to encourage bushy growth. It is best to raise new plants every 2–3 years from cuttings of strong side-shoots taken in June–August.

Old-fashioned pinks, such as 'Inchmery' and 'Prudence', form low, evergreen clumps with scented, single or double flowers produced in midsummer and are available in laced and fringed forms.

Modern pinks and border carnations are taller and less spreading, with two or three main flushes of carnation-like flowers in the summer. *Good varieties—modern pinks:* 'Alice', 'Doris', 'Joy'; *border carnations:* 'Happiness', 'Santa Claus', 'Imperial Clove'.

Fuchsias

These are mainly frost-tender shrubs, popular for their graceful, pendulous flowers freely borne from midsummer to autumn. Several forms also have colourful foliage. They need a moisture-retentive soil rich in nitrogen and potash.

Hardier varieties, such as *F. magellanica* and *F.* 'Riccartonii', can make attractive hedges for milder areas if planted 30–36in (75–90cm) apart and trimmed in early spring. If grown as decorative shrubs in a border, they are best cut back to 12in (30cm) above ground level in late winter.

The single or semi-double half hardy hybrids make excellent outdoor container or bedding plants, and can be trained as

Overwinter a zonal pelargonium by lifting the plant in the autumn, trimming the roots and top growth and potting it up in a free-draining compost.

To keep mature indoor container plants healthy, regularly remove dead flower heads and yellowing leaves and cut back stems by approximately one-third in early spring.

▼ See also: Cuttings Pages 24–25
Lifting and overwintering Pages 172–173

Fuchsias can make elegant pot plants. Pinch out the growing tips initially to encourage bushy growth. Keep plants well watered and fed with a liquid fertilizer.

standards or grown as shrubs. The showy double forms need cool greenhouse conditions with some shade from hot sun. Trailing or spreading varieties are ideal for window boxes or hanging baskets. Pot plants, or 2–3in (5–7cm) tip cuttings taken in spring, should be overwintered under glass and potted on the following year.

Pelargoniums

Like most fuchsias, these plants are frost-tender, but they are better for sunny or drier conditions. There are four main types: **Regals**, with frilled, green leaves and showy flowers in large, loose clusters; **Zonals**, the common "pot geraniums" with patterned or variegated circular leaves and rounded heads of flowers; **Ivy-leaf** or **trailing geraniums** used for window

boxes or hanging baskets, and **Scented-leaf geraniums,** grown largely for their aromatic foliage. Regals are best as conservatory or houseplants; the other types are all good bedding or container plants.

Begonias

Frost-tender plants, preferring rich, moist but well-drained soil and warm, sheltered conditions with protection from too hot sun. **Fibrous-rooted begonias** include the bedding begonia, *B. semperflorens, B. coccinea,* and *B. haageana;* **Rhizomatous begonias** include the showy leafed *B. rex* hybrids needing warm greenhouse conditions. **Tuberous begonias** produce the well-known pot begonia, *B. tuberhybrida*, with large or smaller double flowers, which can also be used as sheltered bedding plants.

SEASONAL TASKS

WINTER

This is the main season for pruning, tidying the garden and overhauling garden tools. It is also the time to plan any changes you may want to make.

• Remove leaves or debris from beds, borders and rockeries.

• Prune fruit and ornamental trees (if necessary) in early winter, and roses and woody climbers such as jasmine and wisteria in late winter. Tie in spreading growth of climbers and wall shrubs. Cut back late-flowering clematis to 8–12in/ 20–30cm from the ground.

• Plant hardy deciduous shrubs and trees when conditions allow.

• Order seeds of summer plants and summer-flowering bulbs, such as lilies, from catalogues.

• Sow seeds of early bedding plants under glass in late winter.

• Pot up or pot on tender, indoor bulbs such as *Hippeastrum, Nerine* and *Vallota*.

• Feed spring bulbs and flowering plants with a slow-release fertilizer like bonemeal or blood, fish and bonemeal.

• Ensure that all tools and machines are cleaned, sharpened and overhauled.

• Browse through recent gardening books, and plan visits to interesting gardens.

▼ See also: Propagation by seed Pages 14–15
Fertilizers Pages 28–29

SPRING

Warm weather in early spring will bring on rapid growth and may tempt impatient gardeners into premature tasks, but do not expose non-hardy plants to late frosts by setting them out in flower beds too early.

• Cut back soft wood, summer-flowering shrubs such as *Buddleia*, and shrubs grown for winter stems such as *Cornus* or *Rubus*. Finish pruning roses and lightly trim early-flowering clematis.

• Plan summer bedding. Order plants or sow seeds in the greenhouse or under glass.

• Plant shrubs, perennials and summer bulbs such as lilies. Pot on half hardy container and greenhouse plants. Plant out summer bedding; if it is cold, use cloches

• Feed bulbs and garden plants with a general fertilizer.

• Spray aphids with a contact insecticide and, if necessary, use a systemic fungicide against blackspot and mildew.

• Lay turf or sow seed for new lawns. Apply moss-killer or weed and feed on established lawns before mowing.

• Clean out and refill ponds. Divide and replant established clumps of water-lilies and other aquatic plants.

• Take cuttings from new shoots of tender perennials or tuberous plants.

Basic pruning Pages 52–53
Essential tools Pages 62–63

SEASONAL TASKS

SUMMER

This is the peak time for all the basic tasks of the growing season:

- Plant out greenhouse-reared cuttings and annuals early in the season.
- Weed, using hoe or handfork, or apply a systemic weedkiller to pervasive weeds.
- Keep all late-flowering spring bulbs, new plants, bedding and container plants and new lawns well watered. Liquid feed every two weeks. Mulch containers and beds to conserve moisture. Mow lawns.
- Tie or stake taller plants needing support.

- Dead-head or trim spent flowering shoots of summer-flowering annuals, perennials, flowering shrubs and roses.
- Divide and replant Bearded Iris after flowering, removing top leaf growth.
- Spray roses and other disease-prone plants fortnightly with a systemic fungicide. Deal with slugs and snails.
- Prune out one-third of old growth of spring- and early summer-flowering shrubs.
- Plant autumn-flowering bulbs.
- Take and pot up cuttings of fuchsias and other half hardy plants.
- Skim surface weed off ponds.
- Trim evergreen hedges in June–July.

    And, not least, spend some time simply relaxing in your garden and enjoying it.

See also: Identification of weeds Pages 36–37
Eradication of weeds Pages 38–39

AUTUMN

Most of the summer jobs will continue, with cutting back of spent top growth of perennials and harvesting of seeds as priority tasks. Save attractive seed heads for dried flower arrangements.

• Lay new lawn turf or sow seed. Rake out thatch from established lawns and give an autumn feed if necessary.

• Weed and rake beds and borders as annuals are removed and leaves fall.

• Lift, divide and replant overcrowded clumps of hardy perennials. Lift and store tender bulbs and tubers; pot up small, half hardy plants for overwintering under cover.

• Dig over empty ground prior to planting and apply bonemeal and/or compost.

• Plant roses, hardy shrubs, perennials and spring bulbs. Pot winter bulbs for forcing.

• Tidy and clean the greenhouse; insulate it if unheated. Set up seed trays and half hardy plants and cuttings for overwintering.

• Protect containers and tender plants against frost with netting, straw or plastic.

• Take semi-ripe wood cuttings of hardy evergreen and deciduous shrubs.

• Trim evergreen shrubs if necessary, especially Mediterranean types such as *Cistus*, lavender and rosemary.

• Cover ponds with mesh to prevent clogging with fallen leaves, remove pumps.

Lifting and overwintering Pages 172–173
Late-flowering bulbs Pages 184–185

THE
PLANTS

The art of cultivation encompasses a huge range of plants.
These may be species, originally or currently existing in the
wild, or garden hybrids, the products of highly specialized
breeding techniques by modern horticulturists. This chapter
deals with those plants commonly grown to enhance the
garden with their shapes and colours or to provide a useful
function, such as shading a terrace. Many will thrive in most
garden soils, but some are included which have a special
requirement, such as moist or acid soil or protection from
severe cold. A thoughtfully planned garden, developed
with judgement and discrimination, will include a range
of plants—trees, shrubs, perennials, annuals and bulbs—
which, working harmoniously together, will provide
year-round colour and interest.

Since plants require an appropriate setting, the best ways of
siting, cultivating and training them are explained.

The mature size of a plant (in, say, 10 to 15 years' time) is an
important consideration in planning a garden. Trees and
shrubs in particular need to be correctly postioned for size.

Once the garden has been established, a patient, efficient
routine will replace the initial hard work, and the
gardener, gratified by a sense of achievement, will find
time to enjoy its beauty.

DECIDUOUS TREES/1

These trees are of great ornamental value in the garden. Despite being deciduous, with the implication of stark bareness in winter, many of them offer interest all year round. Bark and shape compensate when the foliage is lost, and some offer berries and unusual leaf colour. The varieties shown here are well suited to smaller town gardens.

1 *Parrotia persica*
(Persian ironwood)
A small tree. Bark of older stems is flaky and grey; leaves turn gold and red in autumn. Inconspicuous flowers without petals but crimson stamens in March. Hardy, thriving on both acid and chalky soils. Height 10–18ft/3–5.5m

2 *Magnolia soulangiana* 'Alexandrina'
A small tree valued for its flowers; the seeds are also interesting. Needs rich soil, much moisture but good drainage. Height 10–15ft/3–4.5m.

5 *Acer platanoides* 'Crimson King'
(Norway maple)
Large, fast-growing tree with red leaves all season. Often used as an ornamental street tree. Most garden soils and situations; thrives in sun. Height 30–35ft/9–10.5m.

4 *Catalpa bignonioides*
(Indian bean tree)
With its bold leaves, this wide-spreading tree is a splendid feature on an expansive lawn. Late summer blooms, white with yellow and purple markings. Hardy, preferring sun and a well-drained soil. Height 15–20ft/4.5–6m.

3 *Amelanchier lamarckii*
(June berry, snowy mespil)
A small tree with twiggy, spreading habit. Leaves rich copper in autumn; in spring, prolific white flowers. Tolerates most soils and climates. Height 10ft/3m.

6 *Cratageus oxycantha (laevigata)*
(Hawthorn)
A small tree, densely round, often with branches touching the ground. Deep pink or white flowers in spring, with conspicuously red foliage in autumn. Thrives in most soils and climates, including wind. Height 15–20ft/4.5–6m.

9 *Rhus typhinia* **'Laciniata'**
(Stag's horn sumach)
Widespreading, sparse branches
with finely toothed foliage turning
orange-scarlet in autumn. Flowers
insignificant, but fruit attractive.
Thrives in fertile soil. If pruned
regularly, produces larger
than normal foliage.
Height 10–15ft/3–4.5m.

8 *Laburnum* x *watereri* **'Vossii'**
(Golden rain tree)
Small ornamental tree with yellow
pea-like flowers in long racemes.
Poisonous, especially the seeds, but
attractive. All types of soil.
Height 30ft/9m.

7 *Prunus serrula* **'Amanogawa'**
Small to medium-sized tree notable
for its beautiful, shiny coppery bark
and clusters of white blossom in late
spring. Prefers a sunny position and
good soil. Height 30ft/9m.

DECIDUOUS TREES

Trees are always popular, even with confirmed city dwellers, and certainly most gardeners wish to grow at least one. The successful cultivation of trees is not, however, an entirely "natural" process; it is an exercise that needs careful attention.

Do not buy on impulse. Few people have the space for more than a single tree in their gardens, so the height, habit and foliage must be carefully chosen to suit the surroundings.

Planting used to be confined to the dormant season, when deciduous trees carry no leaves, since much moisture is lost through the leaves, and growing trees were simply lifted from the earth to be replanted as quickly as possible. Planting had to be done in autumn, before the cold winter weather set in, to lessen the likelihood of damage to the roots, or in spring, when the threat from frost had passed.

The modern practice of growing trees in containers has largely altered this old routine. Now, with their roots safely protected by the container, trees can be planted at almost any time. Nevertheless, certain essential steps should still be followed.

• Dig a hole approximately twice the size of the rootball of the tree.
• Mix the soil removed with well-rotted manure or compost and one or two handfuls of bonemeal or blood, fish and bone.
• Fork the soil at the bottom of the hole to break it up.

1 Leyland cypress; **2** Horse chestnut; **3** Weeping willow; **4** Prunus 'Kanzan'; **5** Bay; **6** Holly; **7** Paperbark maple; **8** Snowly mespil; **9** Crab apple

a height after 10 years; *b* height after 20 years; *c* ultimate height

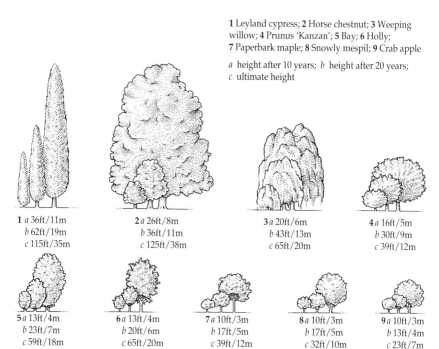

1 *a* 36ft/11m
b 62ft/19m
c 115ft/35m

2 *a* 26ft/8m
b 36ft/11m
c 125ft/38m

3 *a* 20ft/6m
b 43ft/13m
c 65ft/20m

4 *a* 16ft/5m
b 30ft/9m
c 39ft/12m

5 *a* 13ft/4m
b 23ft/7m
c 59ft/18m

6 *a* 13ft/4m
b 20ft/6m
c 65ft/20m

7 *a* 10ft/3m
b 17ft/5m
c 39ft/12m

8 *a* 10ft/3m
b 17ft/5m
c 32ft/10m

9 *a* 10ft/3m
b 13ft/4m
c 23ft/7m

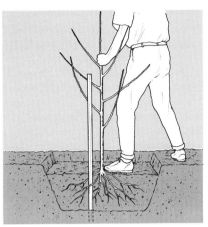

Dig a hole at least 12in/30cm deeper than the level at which the tree will be planted. Drive a stake firmly into the hole. Tease out the tree's roots at the sides and bottom before planting.

Mix the dug out soil with manure or compost and bonemeal, or blood, fish and bone meal. Replace the mixture, firming it in with your foot when the hole is half full and again when it is full.

• Drive a 2-in/5-cm stake into the hole on the windward side of the tree. The stake needs to be roughly equal in height to the tree, plus some 18in/45cm—the amount that is driven into the soil.

• Remove the tree from the container, or, if its roots have been wrapped in sacking or plastic, remove that. Loosen the roots around the sides and bottom.

• Set the tree in the hole so that the old soil line on the trunk is level with the top of the hole.

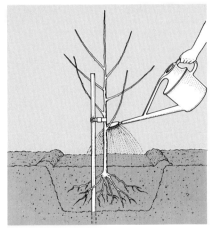

• Fork 6in/15cm of manure or leaf mould into the hole, then refill it with the soil mixture, treading it down gently, until it reaches the level of the surrounding earth.

• Tie the sapling to the stake, using tree ties; attach one close to the ground and again every 5ft/1.5m. Tighten the ties against the stake, not the tree trunk.

• Finally, water the tree thoroughly and mulch around the base.

Attach tree ties, tightening them against the stake. Water the tree copiously, mulch at the base and keep an area some 3ft/90cm in diameter around it free from grass and weeds.

See also: Established trees Pages 104–105

DECIDUOUS TREES/2

The sense of scale in a garden is influenced more by trees—the largest and most permanent plants in it—than by any other plant. Careful juxtaposition of large and small species helps to create a feeling of space and perspective. And with their variety of shapes, growth habit, flower and leaf colour, deciduous trees make a valuable contribution to the overall design and structure of the garden.

1 *Gleditsia triacanthos* **'Sunburst'**
(Honey locust)
Slow-growing tree with graceful, compact habit. Beautiful bright yellow foliage in early summer. Any well-drained soil; tolerates atmospheric pollution. Height 70ft/21m.

2 *Sorbus aria* **'Lutescens'**
(Whitebeam)
Tree of rounded habit grown for its ornamental creamy-green foliage, richly coloured in autumn. Prefers moisture-retentive but well-drained soil. Height 50ft/15m.

3 *Prunus* x *amygdalopersica* **'Pollardii'**
(Flowering almond)
Beautiful small tree with clear pink flowers in early spring. Grows in a sheltered sunny position; tolerates chalk. Height 22ft/6.7m.

4 *Malus* **'Golden Hornet'**
(Flowering crab)
Small tree of bushy habit. Flowers like apple blossom in early summer, followed by bright yellow fruit in autumn. Well-drained, fertile soil. Height 15–18ft/4.5–5.5m.

9 *Salix caprea* 'Pendula'
(Kilmarnock willow)
Umbrella-shaped tree with stiff
pendulous branches. Silvery
catkins in late winter, early
spring. Flourishes in damp
conditions and loamy soil.
Height 30ft/9m.

8 *Pyrus salicifolia* 'Pendula'
(Willow-leaf pear)
Small to medium tree of graceful.
drooping habit. Green to silver-grey
foliage and white flowers in early
summer. Fairly hardy and drought
tolerant. Height 15–25ft/4.5–7.6m.

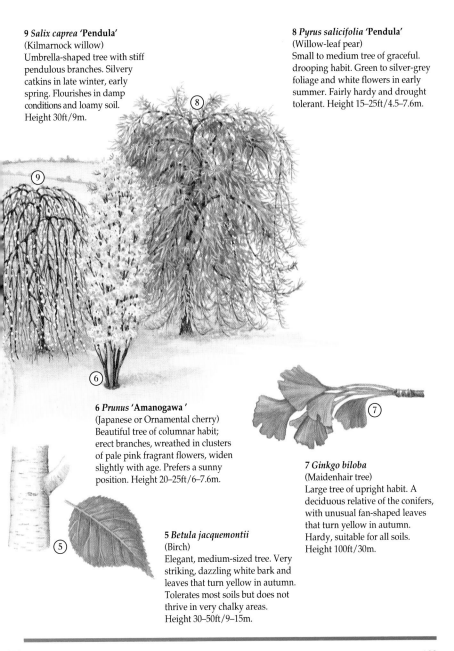

6 *Prunus* 'Amanogawa '
(Japanese or Ornamental cherry)
Beautiful tree of columnar habit;
erect branches, wreathed in clusters
of pale pink fragrant flowers, widen
slightly with age. Prefers a sunny
position. Height 20–25ft/6–7.6m.

7 *Ginkgo biloba*
(Maidenhair tree)
Large tree of upright habit. A
deciduous relative of the conifers,
with unusual fan-shaped leaves
that turn yellow in autumn.
Hardy, suitable for all soils.
Height 100ft/30m.

5 *Betula jacquemontii*
(Birch)
Elegant, medium-sized tree. Very
striking, dazzling white bark and
leaves that turn yellow in autumn.
Tolerates most soils but does not
thrive in very chalky areas.
Height 30–50ft/9–15m.

ESTABLISHED TREES

A fully grown tree is generally capable of looking after itself. It does not need regular pruning, though it deserves some attention such as the removal of dead branches and the eradication of pests and diseases where this is possible.

Young trees should be well tended. Keep an area 36in/90cm in diameter around the base clear of grass and weeds for a few years—the tree should not have to compete with other plants.

It is also important to keep a tree well watered while it is becoming established, that is, throughout the first spring and summer of its life after planting and in dry spells for the next year or two. A general-purpose fertilizer, such as blood, fish and bone meal, should be applied in late spring, followed by a thick organic mulch.

Some trees may suffer from mildew or leaf curl, but these are not usually major problems and can be endured. Coral spot is more serious; prune infected branches back to healthy wood the moment you notice the tell-tale pinkish marks on the bark and burn the diseased wood. Then, if the tree is small enough, you should spray it with thiophanate-methyl, repeating the treatment two weeks later.

The branches of a large tree cast a wide shadow, and the roots, if they are shallow, deplete the soil over a large area. Take these facts into account when planning the garden and plant shade-loving ferns, hellebores and euphorbias, or pave beneath the tree and turn it into a shady sitting-out area, with sweetly scented plants in pots.

TREES TO AVOID
Some trees are unsuitable for most gardens. They may be too large, have invasive roots or anti-social habits—lime drops sticky honeydew, sumach suckers freely—and all parts of yew and the seeds of laburnum are poisonous. Check before planting.

The most serious disease that can affect a tree is honey fungus. This can kill established specimens and is extremely difficult to combat, but if old stumps are removed, it is less likely to strike.

The most easily recognized sign of the fungus is the presence of dark strands, which look like bootlaces, in the soil near an ailing tree. Sometimes toadstools with rough brownish caps up to 6in/15cm across may appear near the tree trunk. If loose bark is peeled back, strands of the fungus may be seen on the trunk.

The only way to deal efficiently with infection by honey fungus is to destroy the diseased tree and to dig out the entire stump and as much of the root system as possible. All diseased wood should then be burned and the soil replaced. Any subsequent planting should be of trees that are in some degree resistant to the fungus, such as beech and hawthorn.

Many types of tree stump will become loose in the ground as their roots decay. It is then possible, with help, to excavate around the roots and lever the tree out with a crowbar. If you do not have the time or patience to wait for this to happen, the best idea is to get in a contractor who will remove the stump.

Do not waste your money on any of the "chemical treatments" that spuriously claim to loosen tree stumps, they are unreliable. And do not attempt to burn a tree stump to get rid of it; once alight, it can smoulder for a long time, with the fire spreading underground into the dead roots. In peaty soil, in hot weather, this could be potentially dangerous.

TREES IN CONTAINERS

Small trees will grow well in large wooden or ceramic containers. Use a soil-based compost (or peat-based compost on a balcony—it does not weigh so much). Among the trees suited to container growing are:

- *Laurus nobilis* (Bay)
- *Magnolia* x *soulangiana*
- *Chamaecyparis lawsoniana* 'Ellwoodii' (Lawson cypress)
- *Trachycarpus fortunei* (Fan palm)
- *Juniperus* x *media* 'Old Gold'
- *Robinia pseudoacacia* 'Frisia' (Black locust)

Established trees may occasionally need lopping: a large branch which has become unreliable or dangerous or is causing trouble must be removed. If the branch is very large and heavy, it may be better to call in a professional tree surgeon, otherwise:

- Make a small cut under the branch a short distance from the trunk, then saw the top diagonally toward the trunk.
- Saw the resulting stub close to the trunk, but do not cut into the swollen collar at the base of the branch.
- Pare away the rough edges, using a pruning knife.
- Paint exposed surfaces with fungicide.

If you merely wish to trim a tree, use the same techniques as for trimming a hedge, cutting off the growing tips of the foliage and taking only a small part of the stem.

It is advisable to study your local authority or municipal regulations regarding tree cultivation and preservation if you want to plant or remove a tree.

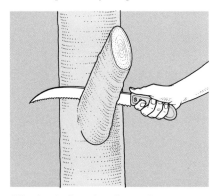

When lopping heavy branches, cut them out in sections, using a special pruning saw. Cut the last section at an angle close to the trunk, leaving the bark ridge and collar on the branch intact.

See also: Pests and diseases Pages 40-47

EVERGREEN TREES

Among evergreen trees, conifers comprise a large group. They have developed narrow, tough leaves, or needles, to cope with sharp variations in temperature and moisture. But there are also several broadleaved evergreen species worth considering as garden plants, for their broader leaves offer an interesting contrast in the winter garden.

1 *Abies koreana*
A slow-growing conifer of neat habit. Favoured for its leaf colour and the upright cylindrical cones borne when tree is quite small. Thrives in containers but roots must be kept damp. Likes a sunny, sheltered spot. Height 20ft/6m.

3 *Taxus baccata* **'Fastigiata Aureomarginata'** (Irish yew) Small, erect tree, making a dense, compact column of tightly packed variegated foliage and branches. Most soils, including chalk; tolerates shade. Height 30–50ft/9–15m.

2 *Ilex aquifolium* **'Golden Queen'** (Common holly)
A small tree or large bush, this is a beautiful, useful evergreen. Slow-growing, but tolerates most soils and many different conditions. If fruit is wanted, a female form must be cultivated. Height 10–18ft/3–5.5m.

4 *Chamaecyparis lawsoniana* **'Ellwoodii'**
Medium to large conifer of columnar habit and fairly slow-growing, taking 10 years to reach 6ft/2m. Popular and appreciated for its feathery blue-green foliage. Prefers good, well-drained soil; does not like windy, exposed sites. Height 18ft/5.5m.

6 *Eucryphia* x *nymansensis* **'Nymansay'**
Magnificent small to medium tree, not always easy to cultivate; takes several years to flower. Needs full sun and deep lime-free loam; does not do well in exposed areas. Height 15ft/4.5m.

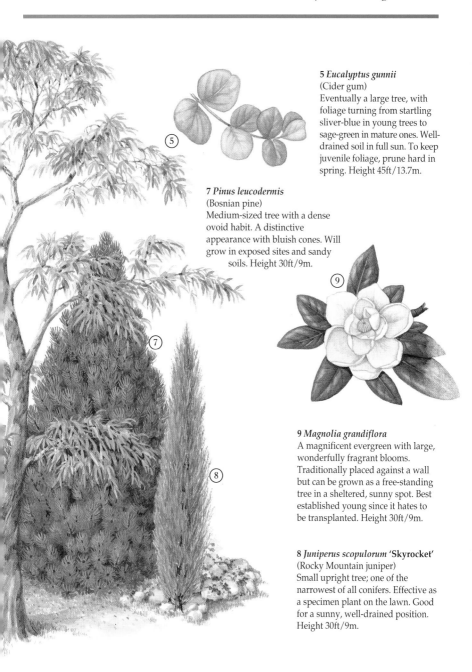

5 *Eucalyptus gunnii*
(Cider gum)
Eventually a large tree, with
foliage turning from startling
sliver-blue in young trees to
sage-green in mature ones. Well-
drained soil in full sun. To keep
juvenile foliage, prune hard in
spring. Height 45ft/13.7m.

7 *Pinus leucodermis*
(Bosnian pine)
Medium-sized tree with a dense
ovoid habit. A distinctive
appearance with bluish cones. Will
grow in exposed sites and sandy
soils. Height 30ft/9m.

9 *Magnolia grandiflora*
A magnificent evergreen with large,
wonderfully fragrant blooms.
Traditionally placed against a wall
but can be grown as a free-standing
tree in a sheltered, sunny spot. Best
established young since it hates to
be transplanted. Height 30ft/9m.

8 *Juniperus scopulorum* 'Skyrocket'
(Rocky Mountain juniper)
Small upright tree; one of the
narrowest of all conifers. Effective as
a specimen plant on the lawn. Good
for a sunny, well-drained position.
Height 30ft/9m.

EVERGREEN TREES

M ost gardeners are keen to grow some evergreens, for they help to give an air of maturity to even the newest garden. This group includes conifers and a few broadleaved trees, such as holly and the evergreen oak, *Quercus ilex*.

Conifers are among the simplest plants to care for since, with careful selection, it is possible to have varieties that do not need staking or pruning and are hardy with a long life expectancy. The main requirements for most types of conifers are simply regular watering in dry spells and an annual feed of conifer fertilizer.

The foliage of conifers ranges in colour from the dark, almost black, green of *Taxus baccata* (Yew) to the frosty blue needles of *Picea pungens* (Colorado spruce) and golden-yellow forms of many easily available trees. There is also a wide variety of shapes, from the narrow column of Lawson's cypress, *Chamaecyparis lawsoniana*, to the bushy plumes of *Cryptomeria japonica*, the vast, wide-spreading branches of *Cedrus libani*, (Cedar of Lebanon), and the prostrate, feathery *Juniperus horizontalis*.

You should have no difficulty in finding a suitable tree for your garden; catering for the diminishing size of gardens and the popularity of conifers, horticulturists have produced trees that reach only 12–36in/ 30–90cm at maturity (see box), but there are others that soar to gigantic heights.

Indeed, if there is one disadvantage to conifers, it is that the information given by nurseries tends to underestimate their ultimate size. So, before buying, check the predicted heights of the plants on offer in a reliable garden encyclopedia to ensure that you get trees that are right for your garden.

The broadleaved evergreens, too, are a valuable element in the garden, for apart from providing foliage in winter many bear attractive flowers or berries. *Magnolia grandiflora*, for instance, as well as its leathery leaves with russet felt underneath, has huge waxy blooms in the summer. It prefers full sun, good drainage and a rich soil. Plant it in a sheltered spot, where it does not get very early morning sun—this tends to shrivel frost-wet buds.

Ilex, or holly, is among the most popular of evergreens. It is hardy, will grow in almost any reasonable garden soil and tolerates shade and sun alike. There are several varieties available with leaves

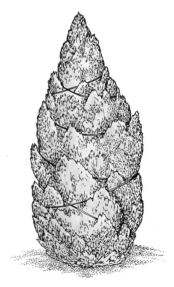

The weight of snow settling on the foliage of conifers can snap the branches, which spoils the shape of columnar trees especially. It is a good idea, therefore, in areas experiencing severe winters, to wire in branches or tie them in with rope before the worst of the weather arrives.

margined or blotched in white or golden-yellow which, together with the scarlet berries, enliven the winter garden.

Eucalyptus gunnii (Cider gum) can be allowed to reach its natural height of 45ft/13.7m or it can be kept constantly trimmed to around 6ft/2m to retain interesting colours and shape in the foliage. The young leaves, often borne on pink stems, are rounded and vary from bright blue-green to silvery-white, while the mature leaves are long and narrow and much darker. This eucalyptus has also smooth, attractively coloured bark.

Other interesting small evergreen trees include *Arbutus* (Strawberry tree), *Phillyrea latifolia* and *Pittosporum tenifolium*, all succeeding best in a warm, sheltered position. The popular bay tree, *Laurus nobilis*, is not only a good evergreen for dry, sunny spots, but also makes an excellent subject for topiary or containers. It has been used as a decorative large tub plant since Roman times.

One of the most beautiful and unusual of broadleaved evergreen trees is *Eucryphia* x *nymansensis*. It grows quickly, forming a column of tough, shiny green leaves, some of which consist of three small leaflets. In autumn, it is covered in large white flowers, rather like single roses in appearance. Although this eucryphia is less fussy than other varieties, it prefers a sheltered spot and moist, loamy soil.

Evergreens should be planted in the same way as deciduous trees. Site them so that they can be seen and enjoyed from the house in winter, and use them to screen unsightly aspects of the garden at this time of the year. Dwarf conifers are excellent in the rock garden or planted in containers.

GENUINELY DWARF CONIFERS

At maturity (after 10–15 years' growth) the height of many of the species listed below will vary from under 12in/30cm to 36in/90cm. Few will exceed 39in/1m in height, though some may do so in spread. All of them make excellent rock garden plants and they are easily grown in good, well-drained soil.

• *Chamaecyparis lawsoniana* 'Gimbornii'—Soft, blue-green foliage, compact, globular shape.
• *Chamaecyparis obtusa* 'Nana'— Black-green foliage in shell-like sprays, upright habit.
• *Juniperus communis* 'Compressa'— Fine grey-green foliage and very neat columnar growth.
• *Juniperus squamata* 'Blue Star'— Silver-blue foliage, spreading but compact growth.
• *Picea glauca* 'Alberta Globe'— Dense green spruce, forming a low, neat mound.
• *Pinus mugo* 'Mops'—Dense dark green pine, with very low bun-shaped growth.
• *Taxus baccata* 'Repandens'— Green-foliaged yew, with a prostrate, spreading form.
• *Thuja orientalis* 'Aurea Nana'— Dense, upright, fan-shaped foliage, which is bright yellow in a sunny position.

HEDGES

Hedges can provide protection from wind and privacy; as a backdrop to other plants; to give form to the garden; and, with ornamentals, to give colour, flowers and scent. As the height of hedges is decided by the gardener, heights are given only where plants are not usually clipped back.

6 *Fagus sylvatica*
(Beech)
An excellent hedge; green foliage changes to yellow in summer and brown in autumn. Clip in mid-summer and late spring. Tolerant of most soil types; deep, well-drained soil is best.

1 *Escallonia* **'Apple Blossom'**
Evergreen, makes a perfect hedge and windbreak; particularly popular in coastal areas. Pink and white flowers in midsummer. Can be damaged by wind or excessive cold but regenerates itself. Reasonable garden soil in sun or part shade. Trim after flowering.
Height 10ft/3m.

2 *Buxus sempervirens* **'Marginata'**
(Box)
Slow-growing evergreen of dense habit; ideal for edging large beds or creating formal structures. The upper leaves of terminal shoots are often tipped with yellow. Grows in most soils in sun or shade; tolerates an exposed site.
Clip in summer.

4 *Rosmarinus officinalis*
(Rosemary)
An aromatic evergreen that makes an initially dense hedge. All varieties have blue flowers. Clip lightly when flowering is over. Well-drained soil in full sun. Height 3½ft/1.1m.

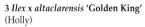

3 *Ilex* x *altaclarensis* **'Golden King'**
(Holly)
A valuable evergreen forming a large hedge that withstands pollution and maritime exposure. This variegated form is best in sun and tolerates most soils. Trim in late summer.

5 *Cratageus monogyna*
(Hawthorn)
A good thorny windbreak with a beautiful display of blossom in spring. Suited to a large boundary. Slow to establish, followed by vigorous growth. Any soil, in sun or shade. Trim in summer.

8 *Rosa rugosa*
(Japanese rose)
Species rose with mound-like form and a strong suckering habit. Blooms all through summer; attractive hips in autumn; the dense, coarse foliage turns gold in autumn. Well suited to seaside gardens. If necessary, prune lightly in winter. Height 7ft/2.1m.

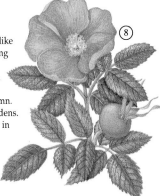

7 *Taxus baccata*
(Yew)
Dark evergreen with a dense, compact habit. Regenerates well from old wood, a worthy quality in a hedge, offsetting early slow growth. Tolerates most situations and soils, even chalk. Trim in early spring and late summer.

9 *Lavandula spica*
(Lavender)
Aromatic, with semi-evergreen greyish leaves. Larger or more compact forms are available, with flowers varying from white to pink to dark purple. Needs well-drained soil in full sun. To keep bushy, clip just after flowering. Height 3–4ft/1–1.2m.

11 *Chamaecyparis lawsoniana* 'Allumii'
A popular evergreen, it eventually creates a dense screen. Favours a moist, well-drained soil; dislikes windy or exposed sites. Trim lightly but regularly to keep thick and compact.

10 *Berberis thunbergii atropurpurea*
A deciduous species suitable for smaller gardens. Coppery-purple leaves turn red in autumn and berries are an added attraction. Reasonably fast-growing, it needs light pruning after flowering. Height 4–5ft/1.2–1.5m.

12 *Forsythia* x *intermedia* 'Lynwood'
A deciduous species. Yellow flowers wreathing bare branches make a showy display in early spring. Any reasonable soil, preferably in sun. Prune carefully, cutting back only long shoots that have flowered heavily. Height 8ft/2.4m.

HEDGES, WINDBREAKS AND DIVIDERS

The boundaries of many gardens require some demarcation. You may want to screen off part of the garden—and most sites need a windbreak of some sort. Faced with such situations, the gardener must decide whether to put up a fence, build a wall or grow a hedge.

Fences

These are relatively inexpensive, quick and easy to erect, take up little space, and provide good support for climbing plants. But wire fences are ugly, and wooden fences can be boring in appearance.

Walls

Initially expensive, whether of stone, brick or even concrete blocks, walls are nevertheless attractive, robust and long lasting. Maintenance costs are low, and they provide excellent support for plants.

Hedges

All hedges take time to establish and use a lot of space. Although quite expensive to plant, they then need care and cultivation rather than further expenditure.

It can be tempting when you take on a garden quickly to erect a wooden fence, but think carefully before doing so. Your garden may be spoiled by the monotony of woodlap, even if you hide it with plants, and it may rot and have to be replaced.

Hedges are slow growing, but they are attractive, especially informal hedges, which are usually composed of flowering plants, and they afford cover for wildlife. They also provide an excellent windbreak, dissipating the flow of the wind without creating eddies on the leeward side as a wall will do.

There are several hedging plants that make a good windbreak. Try beech, *Fagus sylvatica*, for a dense, tall hedge which

AVERAGE GROWTH RATES

Before planting a hedge, work out how many plants you will need (so you can compute the cost) and how long it will be before it will perform the function you require of it.

Planting distance (PD) and height (H) after 5 years are given. Average height at planting: 12–18in/30–45cm; box (5–8in/13–20cm).

Berberis thunbergii—deciduous hardy shrub; dense, with bright red autumn fruits and leaves. PD 18in/45cm; H 5ft/1.5m.

Buxus sempervirens (Box)—Hardy evergreen shrub with dark green glossy leaves; a good formal hedge. PD 12in/30cm; H 2–3ft/60–90cm.

Fagus sylvatica (Beech) Hardy, deciduous; leaves colour and remain on branches all winter. PD 12in/30cm; H 5ft/1.5m.

Forsythia x intermedia 'Lynwood'— Hardy deciduous shrub; yellow flowers on bare stems in spring. PD 12in/30cm; H 6ft/2m.

Ilex 'Golden King' (Holly)—Hardy, evergreen small tree; dark green leaves with yellow margin and grey-green blotches. PD 18in/45cm; H 4ft/1.2m.

Rosa rugosa—Dense-growing rose; prickly stems, wrinkled foliage, large pink, scented flowers and round red hips. PD 18in/45cm; H 5ft/1.5m.

Taxus baccata (Yew) Evergreen conifer, suitable for formal hedges and topiary work; female has red berries. PD 15in/38cm; H 4ft/1.2m.

Layering a hedge helps to thicken it and prevent legginess. Cut thick branches partially through at the base, bend them almost horizontal and secure them to stakes driven into the ground at intervals. Cut back side branches and trim the tops to a uniform height.

keeps its dead, russet-coloured leaves all through winter, or hawthorn, *Crataegus monogyna*, with masses of white flowers in spring. Some gardeners consider *Escallonia* 'Apple Blossom' the perfect hedge for mild areas. It forms a decorative and sturdy barrier against the wind and is excellent in a seaside garden.

If a formal hedge is required, turn to the traditional hedging plants. Beech, again, can be clipped into a smooth, regular shape, as can yew, *Taxus baccata*, and box, *Buxus sempervirens*; choose 'Gold Tip 'if you want a colourful low hedge. Most *Pyracantha* (Firethorn) species can be trained into formal regularity, but they will not bear many berries if they are clipped back too hard.

Lavender, *Lavandula angustifolia* 'Hidcote' and rosemary, *Rosmarinus officinalis*, with aromatic foliage and pleasing flowers, can make good low, informal hedges, useful for providing a visual separation of one part of the garden from another.

Pruning hedges

Most formal hedges need clipping in spring and in autumn. Shape the hedge so that the base is wider than the top; this allows the lower stems to get air and light, and snow will slide off it. If the hedge grows long, leafless stems at the base— becomes "leggy"—prune it back hard. Remember, however, that except for yew, most conifer species will not sprout from old wood and must have the green growth trimmed regularly if they are to stay dense and bushy. Trim informal hedges after they have flowered.

Choose your tools with care. You will need secateurs, which come in a range of models for cutting soft stems and hard, woody branches. If you can afford it, the power hedge trimmer is a great labour-saving device.

See also: When to prune Pages 52–53
Pruning shrubs Pages128–129

EVERGREEN SHRUBS

Many evergreen shrubs produce flowers and berries; conifers are an exception. However, all come into their own in winter, when their foliage provides a pleasing contrast to the bare branches and stems of other plants.

1 *Pyracantha* **'Orange Glow'**
(Firethorn)
Vigorous, of dense habit, bearing masses of hawthorn-like flowers in early summer, then orange fruit through autumn and winter. Needs ordinary soil; tolerant of exposure, pollution and some shade.
Height 10–12ft/3–3.6m.

2 *Aucuba japonica*
'Crotonifolia'
This dense, rounded bush has large, brightly variegated leaves, small flowers in panicles in spring, and red berries in winter. Thrives in sunless sites and most soils.
Height 8ft/2.4m.

3 *Daphne retusa*
Clusters of purplish scented flowers appear in spring on this small shrub. It is hardy but needs humus-rich soil and shelter. No pruning, but appreciates early season mulching.
Height 3ft/1m.

4 *Viburnum davidii*
A splendid evergreen forming an attractive mound and making good ground cover. Favoured for glossy leaves and turquoise berries in winter. Plant male and female clones. Needs little attention once established. Height 24–36in/60–90cm.

11 *Choisya ternata* (Mexican orange blossom) Rounded habit; sweet-scented flowers in spring and early summer; leaves aromatic when crushed. Tolerates sun but prefers a sheltered position. Height 6ft/2m.

10 *Cotoneaster salicifolius floccosus* Arching branches covered in summer with white or pink flowers favoured by bees, then masses of small red fruit. Tolerates most soils and conditions. Height 12–15ft/3.6–4.5m.

9 *Mahonia* x **'Charity'** Upright habit. Large clusters of scented flower spikes in late winter, then blue-black berries. Any well-drained soil in full sun. Prune only old, leggy shoots. This variety is resistant to rust and permitted in U.S. wheat-growing areas. Height 8–10ft/2.4–3m.

8 *Hebe salicifolia* (Veronica) Medium-sized shrub with white or lilac flowers on long racemes in summer. Succeeds in any well-drained soil, but vulnerable to extreme cold. Trim lightly in spring. Height 5–10ft/1.5–3m.

7 *Elaeagnus pungens* **'Maculata'** Fast-growing, medium-sized shrub with bold, variegated foliage, most intense in winter. Excellent wind resister. Thrives in fertile soil; prefers clay to chalk. Cut out green-leaved shoots. Height 8–12ft/2.4–3.6m.

6 *Skimmia japonica* A small shrub appreciated for its flowers, red or white berries , bright foliage and aroma. Male and female forms needed to ensure fruiting. Likes partial shade and acid soil. No pruning. Height 3–4ft/1–1.2m

5 *Berberis darwinii* A large shrub with clusters of orange flowers in spring and pleasing blue-black berries. Hardy and tolerant of most soils. Pruning generally unnecessary. Height 8–10ft/2.4–3m.

EVERGREEN SHRUBS

Every garden is enhanced by broad-leaved evergreen shrubs, for many are of considerable ornamental interest and provide structure for the garden and solace to the eye amid bare winter stalks

Apart from box and conifers, which can be used for hedges as well as ornamentally, there are many evergreens that will provide special interest at different seasons. Cotoneasters are indispensable. Try growing the large *Cotoneaster salicifolius*, which reaches 15ft/4.5m in both height and spread. It has large, glossy green leaves, flattened heads of white flowers and, later, bright red berries. *C. conspicuus* is a smaller low-growing type with arching branches.

Another rewarding group is the genus *Daphne. D. collina, D. odora, D. tangutica* and *D. retusa* all grow slowly to 36in/90cm and have beautiful, fragrant pink or white flowers from late winter to spring.

Apart from the aesthetic value of evergreen shrubs, they are generally easy to maintain. They benefit from a mulch in the spring and a top dressing of a balanced fertilizer such as that used on roses. If you live in an area that has a severe winter, try to brush the snow off their branches, which might otherwise break under the weight. But even without this care, most will survive and remain healthy.

Few evergreen shrubs need pruning, although trimming to retain the shape and to keep plants free of old, dead wood is required periodically. Apart from the occasional incidence of honey fungus and coral spot disease, most are relatively pest- and disease-free.

Most can be propagated from seed or from semi-ripe cuttings, and some can also be propagated by layering.

EVERGREEN SHRUBS WITH COLOURED OR VARIEGATED LEAVES

- *Aucuba japonica* 'Crotonifolia': dark green leaves blotched yellow.
- *Euonymus fortunei* 'Silver Queen': dark green with a broad white edge.
- *Ilex aquifolium* 'Argentea Marginata': green leaves with cream margins, pinkish when young.
- *Mahonia aquifolium*: holly-like leaves often turn reddish in winter.

The prostrate conifer, *Juniperus horizontalis* 'Emerald Spreader' (top), and the evergreen creeping sub-shrubs *Pachysandra terminalis* (bottom) and *Vinca major* make excellent ground cover and suppress weeds by shading or smothering them. Both are available in attractive variegated forms.

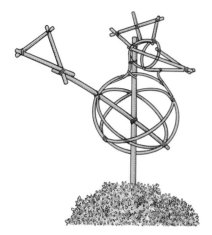

Fashion the desired shape from wire and metal rods, or use wire netting. Stake it firmly into the evergreen shrub you wish to train.

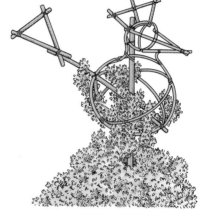

As they grow, tie shoots to the frame with plastic-covered wire. Check periodically that ties are not cutting into the stems.

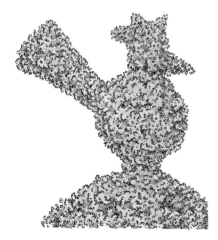

Pinch out shoots to encourage bushing and, once the shape has been covered, clip twice a year to maintain it.

TOPIARY

The best subjects for topiary—the art of training shrubs and trees into decorative shapes—are already established evergreens such as yew, box and holly. An art much practised during the 17th and 18th centuries, it is coming back into fashion in modern gardens.

Sometimes the growth pattern of the plant will suggest a shape that only requires clipping to accentuate it, or a frame can be created from wire or wire netting to represent a shape. It takes time and patience to train a plant in this way, and regular, careful clipping to maintain it.

See also: Layering Pages 26–27
Pests and diseases Pages 40–47

ACID-LOVING SHRUBS

Among the most decorative garden plants are many of the acid-loving shrubs. They are easy to grow in peaty or woodland gardens, but where the soil is neutral or chalky, it is best to plant these shrubs in containers or tubs. They all need acid, moisture-retentive but well-drained soil and little or no pruning.

1 *Camellia* x *williamsii* **'Donation'**
A medium-sized evergreen shrub of erect, vigorous growth. Much loved for its prolific flowers and glossy foliage. Plant in a sunny spot, away from direct morning sun; mulch in spring. A good container plant. Height 6–8ft/2–2.4m.

2 *Kalmia latifolia*
(Calico bush, Mountain laurel)
A charming evergreen shrub, with clusters of unusually shaped clear pink flowers in spring and early summer. Grows in sun or partial shade. Height 6–10ft/2–3m.

3 *Rhododendron yakushimanum*
Compact, dome-shaped small shrub, with beautiful heads of pink-white blooms. Well suited to urban gardens and containers. Height 3ft/1m.

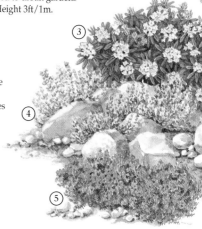

4 *Calluna vulgaris* **'Silver Queen'**
(Heather)
Hardy evergreen, ideal ground cover. Both flowers and foliage have decorative appeal. Easily grown in lime-free soils; loves sun but tolerates light shade. Good for dried flower arrangements. Height 24in/60cm.

5 *Erica cinerea* **'P. S. Patrick'**
(Heather)
Popular, low-spreading shrub with attractive foliage and flowers in midsummer. Loves sun but will grow in partial shade. Well suited to poorer, acid soils. Height 12in/30cm.

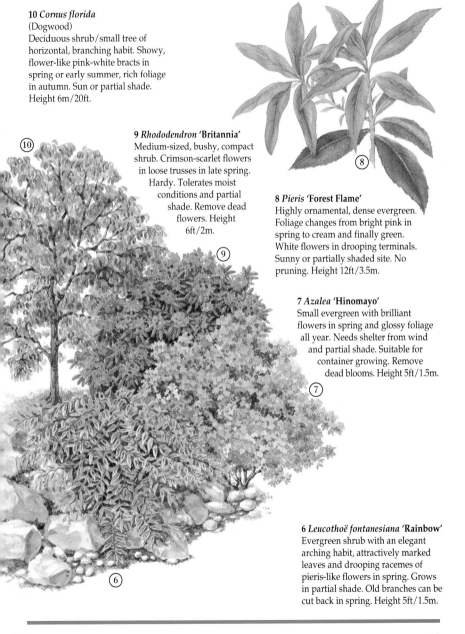

10 *Cornus florida*
(Dogwood)
Deciduous shrub/small tree of horizontal, branching habit. Showy, flower-like pink-white bracts in spring or early summer, rich foliage in autumn. Sun or partial shade. Height 6m/20ft.

9 *Rhododendron* **'Britannia'**
Medium-sized, bushy, compact shrub. Crimson-scarlet flowers in loose trusses in late spring. Hardy. Tolerates moist conditions and partial shade. Remove dead flowers. Height 6ft/2m.

8 *Pieris* **'Forest Flame'**
Highly ornamental, dense evergreen. Foliage changes from bright pink in spring to cream and finally green. White flowers in drooping terminals. Sunny or partially shaded site. No pruning. Height 12ft/3.5m.

7 *Azalea* **'Hinomayo'**
Small evergreen with brilliant flowers in spring and glossy foliage all year. Needs shelter from wind and partial shade. Suitable for container growing. Remove dead blooms. Height 5ft/1.5m.

6 *Leucothoë fontanesiana* **'Rainbow'**
Evergreen shrub with an elegant arching habit, attractively marked leaves and drooping racemes of pieris-like flowers in spring. Grows in partial shade. Old branches can be cut back in spring. Height 5ft/1.5m.

SHRUBS FOR ACID SOIL

Some of the most beautiful ornamental shrubs prefer an acid soil, as do the ever-popular heathers, or *Ericas*. These shrubs are not able to absorb sufficient iron for healthy growth from alkaline soils, so before planting them, determine your soil type with a pH test.

Slightly alkaline soil can be treated with peat or chemical acidifiers, but this is not usually satisfactory. So, in chalk areas or where the pH level is neutral, to avoid possible failure—and certainly expense—it is a good idea to grow such shrubs in pots or specially prepared beds containing an ericaceous or peat-based compost. Luckily, many of them are happy in containers, which means that even on a balcony or patio garden you can enjoy a variety of acid-loving shrubs.

Rhododendrons and azaleas are favourite plants for such treatment. The brilliance and profusion of their blossom in the spring is breathtaking and some of them, such as the azalea *Rhododendron luteum* with deep yellow flowers, are strongly and sweetly scented. One of the best evergreen rhododendrons for containers is the compact *R. yakushimanum*, which has pink buds opening to white.

Plant the superb *Pieris* 'Forest Flame', which has dense evergreen foliage with bright red young leaves in spring. During the winter, the long flower panicles carry red-tinged buds, which open into white blossom resembling lily-of-the-valley in late spring.

Camellias, with their bold, glossy foliage, showy flowers in pink, white or red and neat habit of growth, also do well in big tubs. Another large plant which offers interest all through the year and rich

Shrubs in containers can be used to fill awkward corners or hide ugly features, such as manhole covers. Plant a rhododendron or camellia in a large

foliage colours in autumn is *Cornus florida*, the flowering dogwood.

Heathers, such as *Erica cinerea* with its low, spreading habit, will form an attractive "ground cover" when planted around larger shrubs in a tub. Choose 'Mrs Dill' for a splash of bright pink.

Containers must be chosen with care; if there is not space for a decent amount of compost, there will not be enough room for the roots to spread. Check for an internal diameter of at least 10in/25cm, especially in concrete tubs; for although these may look large and wide, the thick walls reduce the interior space.

One of the joys of container gardening is the freedom it gives you to "redesign" by moving the tubs around, so the weight of the filled container must be considered; 4cu yd/1cu m of potting compost weighs

See also: Feeding plants Pages 28–29
Mulching and watering Pages 34–35

tub, a patio rose or *Erica* in a smaller one, matching the shape to the habit of the plant, whether it be spreading or round and bushy.

terracotta and china containers that they are frost proof (not all are), otherwise they can crack in really severe weather. This will expose the plant's roots, and you may lose both expensive plant and costly container.

Acid-loving shrubs should be watered with rainwater where tap water is hard and full of lime or, if this is not possible, sequestered iron should be added to the water. They should also be given a liquid fertilizer every week or two during the growing season; proprietary brands formulated specially for ericaceous plants are available.

Although plants in containers need frequent watering, pots should not be allowed to sit in trays full of water, especially in cold weather, or the roots will become waterlogged and frosted.

approximately 1 ton/1 tonne. A terracotta tub about 16in/40cm high and 14in/36cm wide, filled with compost, can be carried comfortably by the average man. A similar size in concrete will be much heavier; it follows, therefore, that concrete pots are more suitable to be used in a permanent place at ground level.

Plastic pots are cheap but they are impermeable to air and water, so plants can suffer root damage from waterlogging. Treat wooden tubs with a non-toxic preservative before they are used and bore an adequate number of drainage holes in the bottom.

Terracotta containers are particularly attractive, but they can also be expensive, and since they dry out quickly, specimens planted in them will need to be watered frequently. Make sure when choosing

ALTERNATIVES TO PEAT

Peat is the partly decomposed remains of plants which, added to soil, will increase its moisture-holding capacity and its acidity. Peat is a valuable base for seedling and potting composts, but it has little nutrient value, and fertilizers must be added to feed plants.

Environmentalists fear that the continued extraction of peat will destroy the peat bogs with their unique plant and animal life, and several substitutes for peat are now offered. Composted bark, farmyard waste and coconut fibre all serve quite well added to compost.

Shrubs are the foundation of the modern garden. They can be used to create shape and form, having more permanence than herbaceous perennials. Yet they need not be simply a backdrop to offset the flower garden; thoughtful initial planning will ensure that shrubs provide colour and interest year round. Deciduous shrubs are easy to grow and care for, and most have attractive flowers in addition to pleasing foliage and habit of growth. Those illustrated here flower from late winter to early spring, bringing colour—or fragrance—to the garden at a particularly welcome time.

3 *Corylus avellana* 'Contorta'
(Corkscrew hazel)
Hardy large shrub/small tree with curious twisted branches, covered in late winter with pale yellow catkins. The inconspicuous female flowers later produce nuts. Height 10ft/3m.

1 *Jasminum nudiflorum*
(Winter-flowering jasmine)
This large species is deciduous, but its bright flowers borne on green stems in winter compensate for the lack of leaves. Needs support, but will grow well even on a cold, sunless wall. Height 8ft/2.4m.

2 *Daphne mezereum*
A bushy shrub, happy in alkaline soil. In late winter/early spring, it bears dense clusters of sweet-scented flowers on the previous season's bare stems, followed by poisonous scarlet berries. Height 3ft/1m.

5 *Hamamelis mollis* 'Pallida'
(Chinese witch hazel)
Large shrub of upright growth. Pale
yellow, spidery flowers, flushed red
in the centre, wreathe bare stems
from mid- to late winter. Good
autumn leaf colour. Prefers acid,
humus-rich but well-drained soil.
Height 6–8ft/2–2.4m.

4 *Chimonanthus praecox*
(Winter sweet)
Hardy large shrub with a lax habit;
best trained against a sunny wall.
Small cup-shaped flowers borne on
bare branches in late winter are
highly fragrant. Cut out untidy
branches after flowering. Height
8ft/2.4m.

6 *Salix helvetica*
Spreading dwarf shrub
with twiggy growth, grown
for its attractive foliage and
for its brown winter buds
and woolly grey catkins in
spring. Prefers moist loamy
soil. Height 24in/60cm.

7 *Ribes* (Flowering currant)
Compact, upright deciduous
shrub, available in a number
of species, flowering from
early to late spring. Various
forms of *R. sanguineum* are
popular in Britain but are
banned in some areas of
North America. Grows
easily in any well-drained
soil in sun or partial shade
Height 6ft/2m.

8 *Cornus mas*
(Cornelian cherry)
Hardy shrub or small tree with
open growth. Ornamental interest
all year: masses of small star-
shaped flowers in late winter/
early spring are followed in hot
summers by edible, bright red fruit
and colourful autumn foliage. Best
in full sun in fertile,
well-drained soil.
Height 15ft/4.5m.

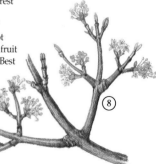

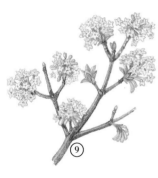

9 *Viburnum* x *bodnantense* 'Dawn'
Hardy large shrub with strong
upright habit. Clusters of sweet-
scented, remarkably frost-resistant
flowers cover the branches from late
autumn to early spring. Fertile soil in
sun or semi-shade. Height 3m/10ft.

THE DECIDUOUS SHRUBBERY

Shrubs make a valuable contribution to the structural aspect of a garden's design, working with trees to provide a permanent background for the perennials and annuals. By the judicious juxtaposition of plants chosen for their growth habit and foliage, flowering times and colours, the deciduous shrubbery can provide interest throughout the year.

Although they are bare of leaves in the winter, many of these shrubs, such as *Cornus alba* 'Elegantissima' (Red-barked dogwood), have attractive stems. Others bloom throughout the coldest months and very early in spring; *Daphne mezereum*, which bears its highly scented mauve-pink flowers in late winter, and *Viburnum x burkwoodii*, with clusters of fragrant pinkish white flowers in early spring, are among the best.

Some shrubs have variegated foliage or splendid autumn leaf colour—*Berberis* 'Rubrostilla' has both reddish leaves and berries, while the clusters of berries on *Callicarpa bodinieri* are an unusual shade of violet and remain on the bush well into the winter.

The shrubs shown in the plan, *opposite*, include those with perfumed flowers, such as the midsummer-flowering *Philadelphus coronarius* 'Aureus' (Mock orange) and *Buddleia alternifolia* (Butterfly bush), and those with an interesting growth habit—for example, the arching stems of *Kerria japonica* 'Pleniflora'.

Throughout the summer, *Potentilla* 'Vilmoriniana' is covered with creamy flowers, while *Weigela florida* 'Variegata', has clusters of pale pink flowers and broad creamy white margins to the leaves. Late-season colour is introduced by the powder-blue flower-heads of *Ceanothus* 'Gloire de Versailles' and the red-centred, bright blue blooms of *Hibiscus syriacus*, a fine upright shrub that needs no pruning.

Most deciduous shrubs will grow in any reasonable garden soil and they are not too fussy about climatic conditions. And few demand hard pruning, needing, in some instances, only cutting back after flowering, or light trimming and shaping and the removal of diseased or dead wood.

They are also, in the main, relatively free from attack by pests and from diseases; coral spot and honey fungus being the most serious that may afflict them.

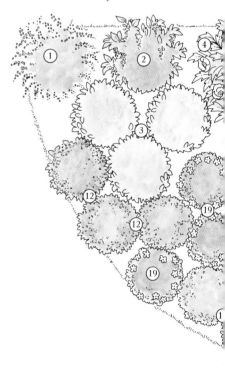

See also: Pests and diseases Pages 40–47
Foliage plants Pages 88–89

KEY TO PLAN
1 *Spiraea arguta*
2 *Leycesteria formosa;* (Himalayan honeysuckle)
3 *Cornus alba* 'Elegantissima' (Red-barked dogwood)
4 *Paeonia lutea ludlowii* (Tree peony)
5 *Buddleia alternifolia* (Butterfly bush)
6 *Philadelphus coronarius* 'Aureus' (Mock orange)
7 *Kolkwitzia amabilis*
8 *Weigela florida* 'Variegata'
9 *Prunus glandulosa* 'Alba Plena' (Bush cherry)
10 *Hydrangea aspera villosa*
11 *Dorycnium hirsutum**
12 *Stephanandra incisa* 'Crispa'
13 *Forsythia* 'Spectabilis'
14 *Indigofera heterantha*
15 *Hibiscus syriacus* 'Bluebird'
16 *Hypericum* x *moserianum* 'Tricolor'*
17 *Hydrangea involucrata* 'Hortensis'
18 *Kerria japonica* 'Pleniflora'
19 *Potentilla davurica* 'Manchu'
* May be semi-evergreen in mild areas

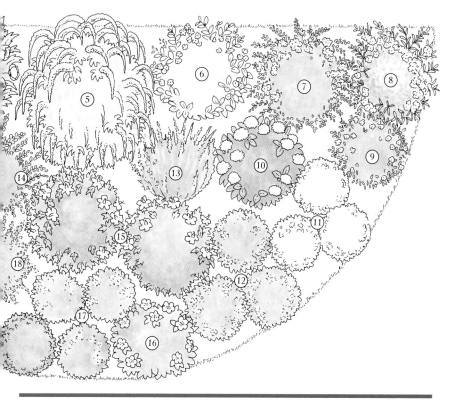

These shrubs, with their mid-season blooms, add to the colourful display of border and bedding plants but, of course, all shrubs can be relied upon to do more than this. In autumn, many offer the delight of berries or brilliant foliage and then present elegant shapes in the lean, stripped winter garden.

1 *Weigela florida* **'Variegata'**
Decorative, hardy, medium-sized shrub. Ideal for urban gardens. Easy to grow, except in very wet soil. Thin out and cut back shoots after flowering. Height 8ft/2.4m.

2 *Cotinus coggygria* (Smoke bush)
A large shrub with feathery heads produced in profusion and good autumn foliage. Young plants need care and water. If space is limited, prune after flowering. Height 15ft/4.5m.

3 *Buddleia alternifolia*
A large shrub that thrives in dry soil and revels in full sun; when placed against a wall will grow tall. Delicately fragrant flowers on drooping branches in early summer; after flowering, thin out "crown". Height 12ft/3.6m.

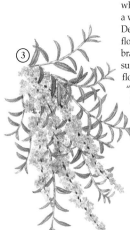

4 *Genista pilosa* (Broom)
A decorative dwarf shrub with characteristic pea-like pods. Needs a sunny spot; useful for poor, dry soil, but does not transplant easily. Requires little attention and no pruning. Height 12in/30cm.

5 *Philadelphus* **'Belle Etoile'** (Mock orange)
Compact shrub of medium size with an arching habit and highly fragrant flowers; gives a good display even on poor soil. Thin out and cut back immediately after flowering. Height 8ft/2.4m.

11 *Kolkwitzia amabilis*
(Beauty bush)
Hardy and adaptable shrub
of medium size. Graceful
arching branches are draped
with sprays of bell-shaped
flowers; cut back branches
with faded blooms after
flowering. Height 10ft/3m.

10 *Hydrangea macrophylla*
Strong growing, medium-
sized shrub in many
varieties. Lace-cap or mop-
head panicles of flowers
range from bright blue in
acid soil to clear pink in
alkaline soil. Prune older
shoots and dead flowerheads
in spring. Height 5ft/1.5m.

6 *Spirea* 'Arguta'
(Bridal wreath, Foam of May)
Dense-growing, free-flowering,
medium-sized hardy shrub, with
slender arching branches. Easily
grown in ordinary soil in sun or
partial shade. Needs no pruning.
Height 8ft/2.4m.

7 *Cytisus scoparius*
(Broom)
Medium shrub, grown for its profuse
flowers; available in various coloured
forms. Does best in neutral soil in
full sun. Prune lightly immediately
after flowering to prevent legginess.
Height 3ft/1m.

**8 *Lavandula angustifolia*
'Hidcote'** (Old English lavender)
Compact form with narrow
leaves and deeply coloured
flowers carried in dense spikes.
Needs good drainage and
plenty of humus; trim when
flowers fade. Height 30in/75cm.

9 *Chaenomeles* x *superba*
(Japonica, Japanese quince)
A beautiful, small to medium
shrub with fruit that is edible
but not very good. Thrives in an
open border or against a sunny
or part-shaded wall. Trim after
flowering. Height 3ft/1m.

PRUNING SHRUBS

Most shrubs do not require heavy pruning, but routine attention to the health of any plant involves cutting out dead or damaged wood, and wayward shoots need to be to trimmed to maintain a plant's shape. Deciduous shrubs need this sort of care in the early stages of their growth, when careful pruning will ensure a graceful habit in the older plant.

Poor growth in young shrubs will not be improved by brutal pruning, and the gardener faced with ailing plants should first look for other remedies. It is worth checking that a plant's needs have been met before resorting to the secateurs. For instance, a sun-loving shrub will not thrive in a gloomy site, and overcrowded plants will languish. Similarly, unhealthy shrubs may be the result of incorrect planting: the soil not properly prepared, the necessary nutrients not provided. This can be corrected by the application of fertilizers, compost, watering and the use of mulch.

When diagnosing the causes of poor growth, the type of soil must also be considered: the shrub may be acid loving, yet has been planted in alkaline soil.

A few shrubs have a naturally untidy habit, never responding even to careful pruning. Usually short-lived species, such as *Cytisus* (Broom), they should be replaced when their growth becomes unsightly. Conversely, some ornamental shrubs need hard pruning to reveal their chief attraction; for instance, *Cornus alba* (Dogwood), grown for the bright red bark in winter of the current season's stems, should be cut back fairly hard in the spring.

If the object of pruning is to help give a good shape to the shrub, cuts must be made judiciously to ensure that new growth will appear where it is wanted. Familiarity with the natural growth pattern of a shrub will help you decide what to prune away, and you will avoid a misguided attempt to alter the plant's natural form too drastically. Any effort to alter the arching pattern of branches in *Acer palmatum* (Japanese maple), for example, would be both absurd and unworkable.

Older shrubs can sometimes be rejuvenated by pruning if they have become leggy and ungainly. Many old deciduous shrubs that have reached this stage will benefit by being cut down to about 12in/30cm above the ground. If this treatment seems too brutal, some of the old wood can be cut out from the base of the plant in winter and, as new shoots appear, further old wood can be removed until the plant is flourishing once again. Some evergreen shrubs, including most conifers, will not make new growth if they are cut hard back. It is best simply to trim these shrubs lightly once a year if necessary.

Shrubs will suffer if pruning is not done with sharp tools and confident cutting. Torn or damaged stems will bring further problems, for wounds can become infected with disease, as can stubs of wood that have not been cut at the right angle or in the right place.

Because poor cutting or incorrect pruning can have long-term adverse effects on the development of a shrub, the gardener who gives patient attention to the growth habit of the plant and to methods of pruning—or who takes time to consider whether the shrub actually needs this treatment—will be rewarded by healthy plants and the elegant appearance that well-kept shrubs impart to a garden.

See also: Compost 30–31
Nutrient deficiencies Pages 32–33

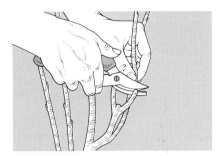

Group One Prune young plants lightly. Only remove unwanted growth that disturbs the shape. This is usually unnecessary on mature shrubs.

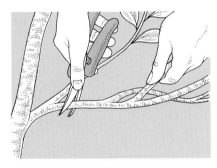

Group Two Cut back old stems after flowering to allow new growth to flourish, so encouraging profuse flowering in the next season.

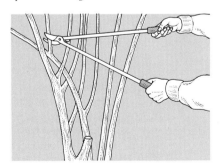

Group Three Prune hard, cutting back stems to near the woody permanent base. Leave a few strong buds, to stimulate vigorous growth.

PRUNING TIMES AND METHODS

Deciduous shrubs can be divided into three groups for the purposes of pruning.

- **Group One**
Shrubs that develop a permanent framework of branches within which future growth is held, neither distorting nor disfiguring the plant's habit; eg *Acer palmatum*, *Viburnum plicatum* and *Magnolia*. The first year after planting, cut out weak shoots or crossed growths; in the second year, remove shoots too low on the trunk and unwanted shoots on main stems. Thereafter cut out only dead or diseased wood.
- **Group Two**
Shrubs that flower early, before the current season's shoots have developed, on wood produced the previous year; eg *Forsythia*, *Deutzia elegantissima* and *Kolkwitzia amabilis*. Prune immediately after flowering and before current wood ripens. Cut flowered stems quite low, so new shoots can grow freely; cut out new shoots that spoil the shape.
- **Group Three**
Shrubs that flower on the current season's growth in mid or late summer; eg *Hypericum calycinum*, *Buddleia davidii* and *Ceratostigma willmottianum*. Prune in spring to prevent new growth forming over and around old, twiggy growth. Cut back all branches to within one or two buds of last year's growth.

DECIDUOUS SHRUBS/LATE SEASON

As summer draws to a close, these shrubs, which have served all season to give depth and foliage interest to the blooms of the annuals and perennials, bring their own blossoms to the garden. Site them so that they may be fully enjoyed as the display of showy colour in the garden begins to fade.

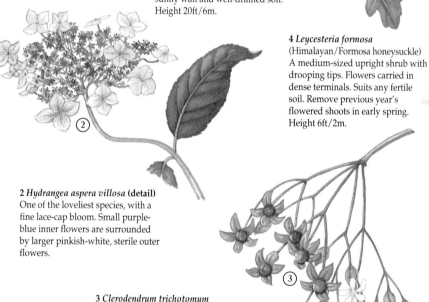

1 *Fremontodendron* **'California Glory'**
(Flannel bush, USA)
A large shrub, semi-evergreen in temperate zones. Flower has no petal but a large yellow calyx. Needs a sunny wall and well-drained soil. Height 20ft/6m.

4 *Leycesteria formosa*
(Himalayan/Formosa honeysuckle)
A medium-sized upright shrub with drooping tips. Flowers carried in dense terminals. Suits any fertile soil. Remove previous year's flowered shoots in early spring. Height 6ft/2m.

2 *Hydrangea aspera villosa* **(detail)**
One of the loveliest species, with a fine lace-cap bloom. Small purple-blue inner flowers are surrounded by larger pinkish-white, sterile outer flowers.

3 *Clerodendrum trichotomum*
Strong-growing, large shrub with fragrant flowers in colourful calyces that later hold blue berries. Pleasing autumn foliage. Sunny, sheltered site in well-drained soil. Pruning unnecessary. Height 10ft/3m.

5 *Buddleia davidii* **'Black Knight'**
Large shrub, with fragrant flowers
that attract butterflies. Adaptable in
any well-drained soil, but loves full
sun and a position against a wall.
Prune back hard in late winter.
Height 15ft/4.5m.

6 *Hibiscus syriacus* **'Blue Bird'**
Medium-sized shrub producing an
effective display of blossoms.
Hardy but needs full sun, well-
drained soil and shelter from wind.
Prone to frost damage. Remove
dead flowerheads. Height 10ft/3m.

7 *Potentilla fruticosa* **'Goldfinger'**
A small, hardy shrub of dense habit.
Flowers summer to late autumn.
Thrives in light soil and prefers full
sun. Pruning not usually required.
Height 3ft/1m.

8 *Hydrangea aspera villosa*
Medium-sized shrub, needs shelter
from the wind and prefers partial
shade with moist roots. Mound
compost around the crown for
protection in winter; prune lightly in
spring. Height 8ft/2.4m.

9 *Ceratostigma willmottianum*
(Hardy plumbago)
Small ornamental shrub with red-
tinted foliage in autumn. Makes
excellent ground cover. Suits dry,
well-drained soil in full sun. Cut
back old flowering shoots in spring.
Height 3ft/1m.

SHRUBS FOR SPECIAL PURPOSES

Deciduous shrubs, rightly regarded as sturdy and functional plants essential to the structure of the garden, are more than simply practical and easy to grow. They have many qualities which can enhance a garden: perfume, texture, form and hardiness as well as attractive flowers and foliage. All these features should be taken into account when determining a planting scheme.

Shrubs which have scented flowers or fragrant leaves should be sited where people sit, or near windows, so the scent can be enjoyed indoors. Among the old favourites that have both perfume and lovely flowers for picking are *Philadelphus* (Mock orange) and *Syringa* (Lilac). Plant the smaller *P.* 'Sybille' and the unusual *S. chinensis*, which has more compact leaves and flowers than the popular hybrids.

Berberis thunbergii atropurpureum, with red foliage and berries that bring autumn colour to the garden, and the silvery-leaved *Eleagnus commutata* may be selected for their foliage. The latter has scented flowers, and both plants like a sunny position, so all these factors should be considered when choosing where to plant them.

The leaves and mauve flowers of *Perovskia atriplicifolia* (Russian sage) are aromatic, especially when crushed, so put it where passers-by may brush against it. *Chimonanthus fragrans* (Winter sweet), with a strong spicy aroma, and sweet-scented *Viburnum farreri* and *Lonicera standishii* are winter-flowering shrubs—plant them in a sunny spot close to the house so their perfume can be enjoyed on dreary days.

Certain shrubs are particularly attractive to birds, bees and butterflies, so gardeners will want to include them in the garden

SHRUBS FOR THE SEASIDE

A garden by the sea needs special care. Since the usually sandy soil does not retain water, moisture-retentive organic material—peat, compost, decayed manure or leaf mould, even some clay—should be dug in. Protection from wind and sea spray is essential: a wooden board fence forms a good shelter while shrubs become established. Deciduous shrubs that will thrive in maritime conditions include:

- *Colutea* spp. (Bladder senna)—attractive seed pods.
- *Cotoneaster horizontalis; C. adpressus*—bright red berries in autumn.
- *Cytisus scoparius* (Common broom); *Genista* spp. (Broom); and *Spartium junceum* (Spanish broom)—all hardy, with mainly yellow flowers.
- *Escallonia virgata*—sprays of white flowers in summer.
- *Euonymus europaeus; E. alatus*—(Spindle tree) **1** rose-red seed pods with orange seeds; **2** purple fruit with bright red seeds.
- *Fuchsia magellanica*—hardy, with profuse small flowers.
- *Hippophae rhamnoides* (Sea buckthorn)—grow male and female for bright orange berries.
- *Hydrangea macrophylla* (Common hydrangea)—hardy; pink, blue and white blooms in summer.
- *Tamarix gallica* (Tamarisk)—feathery foliage and sprays of frothy pinkish flowers in summer.

plan. *Ceanothus* x 'Topaz', *Weigela*, *Fuchsia* and the early-flowering *Daphne mezereum* attract bees, while in autumn birds will enjoy the red berries of the versatile *Cotoneaster* family. Butterflies are particularly drawn to lavender and to *Buddleia davidii*, hence the name Butterfly bush.

The town gardener must also consider the local "unnatural" environment when planting and should look for shrubs that will withstand urban and industrial pollution. There are many varieties to choose from, for shrubs will often thrive in apparently adverse conditions: *Buddleia davidii*, *Ribes sanguineum* (Flowering currant), *Forsythia*, *Hypericum*, *Spartium* (Spanish broom) and *Weigela* spp. are but a few.

Use large-leafed shrubs or those with an an unusual habit to add a sculptural element to the garden. *Acer palmatum* 'Dissectum Atropurpureum', a Japanese maple with lacy bronze-red leaves, reaches only 36in/90cm after 8–10 years, but its layered horizontal branches make a distinctive statement. Another graceful shrub, with sharply toothed foliage, masses of small, pale pink flowers in spring and beautiful peeling bark, is *Neillia sinensis*.

Some deciduous shrubs generally regarded as climbers or wall shrubs can be grown as specimen plants. The flowering quince, *Chaenomeles* x *superba*, for example, is a pleasing addition to the border, while wisteria, a rampant climber, can with the correct pruning and training be transformed into a beautiful shrub.

With imaginative choice and careful siting, planting and feeding, deciduous shrubs can make a major contribution to the impact of a garden and the pleasure to be gained from it.

SOME UNUSUAL SHRUBS

• *Aralia elata* 'Variegata' (Angelica tree)—A showy plant, with large elegant leaves. It prefers shelter and moist, well-drained soil. Height and spread 18ft/5.5m.

• *Hydrangea villosa*—Beautiful mauve- and pink-flowered species for a sheltered woodland site. Height 8ft/2.4m.

• *Stephanandra incisa*—Graceful spreading habit; bright green leaves turning yellow in autumn. Moisture-retentive soil in sun or partial shade. Height 3–5ft/1–1.5m.

• *Daphne genkwa*—Choice lavender-blue flowers on bare branches. Needs rich soil and a sheltered sunny site. Height 4½ft/1.5m.

The tree peony, *Paeonia lutea*, deserves to be more commonly grown. It is a spectacular shrub, reaching a height of 5ft/1.5m with striking, deeply cut leaves and cup-shaped, usually yellow, flowers in summer.

See also: Foliage plants Pages 88–89
Plant lists Pages 210–219

M odern Shrub Roses share many of the characteristics of Old Garden Roses. They flower all summer in a single or repeated flush, bearing single flowers or sprays in a good range of colours. Larger than Bush Roses and very robust, they require only feeding in spring and mid-summer to ensure flourishing growth and prolific blooming. Little pruning is needed.

1 *Rosa rugosa* 'Frau Dagmar Hastrup' (Species Rose)
One of the best of the single-flowered Rugosa Roses, with strong perfume, continuous flowering and attractive red hips. Not as tall as others in this group, it reaches a height of about 4ft/1.2m. Makes a fine hedge.

2 *Rosa* 'Buff Beauty'
Sweet-scented, pale apricot-yellow flowers are borne in large clusters on arching stems with pleasing dark foliage. This Modern Shrub Rose is repeat flowering and medium sized.

3 *Rosa* 'Mme Hardy'
Not a very hardy variety, but a beautiful medium-sized Old Garden (Damask) Rose; the fully double, fragrant white flowers with a green "eye" are borne in mid-season.

4 *Rosa moyesii* 'Geranium'
(Species Rose)
Brilliantly coloured blooms, appearing in mid-season, are followed by lovely flagon-shaped hips. Vigorous, arching growth with small leaves.

5 *Rosa* 'Perle d'Or'
Smooth, pointed buds open to pretty, small blooms that turn from apricot to cream. This repeat-flowering Old Garden (China) Rose is of small to medium size, with an open habit, but not vigorous in growth.

10 *Rosa* 'William Lobb'
The large blooms of this Old Garden (Moss) Rose, borne in mid-season, turn from fuchsia red to pale lavender. A tall, lanky bush of open habit, it makes a good pillar rose if supported.

9 *Rosa* 'Nevada'
At the height of summer the large, slightly fragrant, creamy flowers are so profuse that foliage and stems are hidden; produces some flowers late in the season. This medium-sized Shrub Rose has a wide arching habit and needs space to display itself fully.

8 *Rosa* 'Ballerina'
Clusters of subtly fragrant small, single flowers are borne on large heads all summer. This small Shrub Rose has tiny, glossy, light green leaves and a bushy, thick habit and can be used as a hedge or in the border.

6 *Rosa* 'Canary Bird'
Produces a profusion of flowers early in the season on graceful arching stems; the fresh green foliage has a fern-like appearance. A species hybrid rose of medium size, it can be used as a hedge or, when grafted, a standard, but needs protection in hard winters.

7 *Rosa* 'Frühlingsgold'
Wonderful large semi-double blooms appear early in the season. Allow this medium to large Modern Shrub space for its arching stems, and plant where the fragrance can be enjoyed. Light green foliage.

SHRUB ROSES

Think of these plants simply as shrubs rather than as a special type of rose and they will lose some of their rather intimidating mystique. They should be cultivated in the same way as other shrubs, with careful digging and preparation of beds and proper routines for watering and feeding.

The difference is largely that Shrub Roses produce some of the most glorious blooms seen in the garden. They tend to flower at the height of summer and, although most have a clearly defined, often rather short, flowering period, their strong scents and beguiling colours, and lovely flower shapes add to the delights of the season.

Shrub Roses require a minimum of pruning, even managing to survive quite well for a few years without much attention from the secateurs. However this is no reason to neglect your plants, and they will benefit if you cut out the oldest third of the stems every spring and remove dead or diseased wood.

Although there are some lovely 20th-century examples, Shrub Roses are often referred to as "old-fashioned", for many of them have been known for centuries.

Shrub Roses come in great variety. *Rosa* 'Mme Hardy', a much-loved old damask rose, is considered one of the most beautiful of the white shrubs. It is quite different in appearance from the popular Modern Shrub 'Ballerina', which carries large clusters of small pink blooms. *Rosa rugosa* 'Frau Dagmar Hastrup' makes an excellent low-growing hedge, while the arching beauty 'Frühlingsgold' deserves to be grown as a specimen plant so that its prolific creamy-yellow blooms can be fully appreciated.

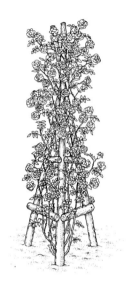

Roses are not self-supporting; they must be trained on a support such as this tripod. Gently tie in the stems with plastic-covered wire.

The fleshy fruit case left after flowering, the rose hip, can be attractive; this one is from *Rosa rugosa*.

ROSE TERMINOLOGY

The classification of roses is a continuing source of argument among the experts, but it is generally agreed that roses can be divided into five main categories:

1 Shrub Roses can be of almost any size, but the name is generally used to describe a plant that retains its habit and size without extensive pruning.

2 Bush Roses when in flower are difficult to distinguish from Shrubs, but they lose shape and flowering efficiency if not pruned annually.

3 Standard Roses are budded on the top of a bare stem varying in height from 30in/75cm to 5ft/1.5m, so the flowering head is raised.

4 Miniature Roses could be called either very small shrubs or very small bushes. A Miniature is both a form and a category, for only certain varieties may be grown in this way.

5 Climbers and Ramblers produce long, pliable shoots requiring support.

There are also different types of rose:

Alba Roses—very old, hardy, scented and early flowering.

Bourbon Roses—19th-century repeat-flowering; shrubs and a few climbers.

Centifolia (Provence) Roses—very old, extremely prickly, loose-growing shrubs.

China Roses—mid-19th century, long-flowering small shrubs; some climbers.

Damask Roses—16th-century, mostly once-flowering, scented shrubs.

Floribunda Roses (Cluster-flowered Roses)—resulted from crossing Hybrid Teas with Hybrid Polyanthas. Cluster-flowered, with a long flowering season and many flowers open at the same time. Need annual pruning.

Gallica Roses—thought to be the oldest rose, scented, often thornless.

Hybrid Musk Roses—early 20th-century, disease-free shrub; free flowering, with flowers in clusters.

Hybrid Perpetual Roses—Victorian shrub, repeat-flowering, scented.

Hybrid Tea Roses (Large-flowered Roses)—originated late in the 19th century by crossing Hybrid Perpetuals with Tea Roses. Usually fairly small bushes requiring annual pruning.

Moss Roses—a sub-group of Centifolia Roses; stems and buds have an unusual mossy appearance.

Noisette Roses—vigorous climbers, but not fully hardy.

Polyantha Pompons—mass of pompon flowers in clusters on dwarf type of recurrent-flowering Shrub Rose.

Portland Roses—upright, cluster-flowered bushes.

Rugosa Roses—very thorny, disease-resistant shrubs with large, highly scented flowers, large hips and good autumn leaf colour.

Spinosissima (Scotch) Roses—very thorny, ferny foliage and summer flowering.

Sweet Briar Roses—vigorous shrubs with scented foliage.

Tea Roses—similar to China Roses, but slightly tender.

Wichuriana Roses—typical Ramblers, flowering once in early summer, need much pruning.

See also: Feeding and fertilizing Pages 28–33
Pruning shrubs Pages 52–53

HYBRID TEA AND FLORIBUNDA ROSES

The Hybrid Tea and Floribunda Roses, now often called Large-flowered and Cluster-flowered Roses, are those most commonly grown by gardeners. Both types form bushes, but the floribundas are often more branched and bushy. Both bloom more than once—in summer and autumn. The flowers of Hybrid Tea Roses are, however, usually double and more sweetly scented and they are excellent cut flowers.

2 *Rosa* 'Queen Elizabeth'
One of the most popular floribundas; forms a large vigorous bush of upright habit suitable for hedging. The large double flowers are long stemmed and slightly fragrant.

1 *Rosa* 'Madame Butterfly'
An early Hybrid Tea Rose, a sport of the famous 'Ophelia'. Creamy coloured flowers, tinged faintly pink, with a good perfume. Upright growth to 4½ft/1.3m.

5 *Rosa* 'Korresia'
(syn. *R.* 'Friesia')
Bushy, upright floribunda, of medium size. The large, urn-shaped double flowers, borne in sprays throughout the season, are brightly coloured and strongly scented.

3 *Rosa* 'Grandpa Dickson'
Tall, upright Hybrid Tea Rose. The well-formed, faintly fragrant flowers have long, slightly pointed creamy yellow petals that turn pink around the edges as the rose ages.

4 *Rosa* 'Allgold'
Vigorous and disease-resistant Floribunda Rose that forms a small bush of branching habit. The flowers, which withstand rain and do not fade in bright sun, are borne over a long period.

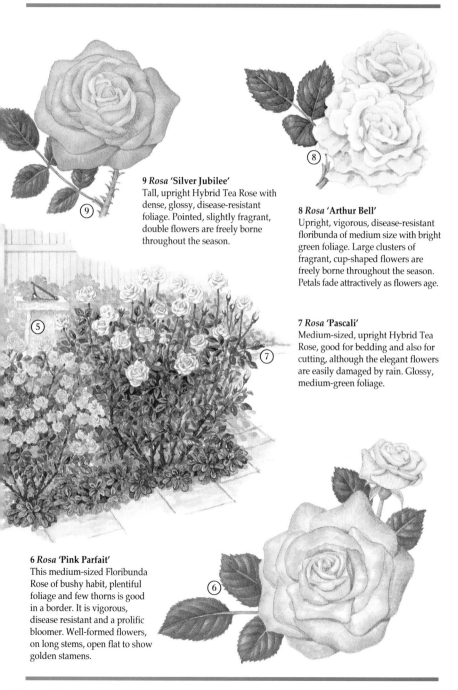

9 *Rosa* **'Silver Jubilee'**
Tall, upright Hybrid Tea Rose with dense, glossy, disease-resistant foliage. Pointed, slightly fragrant, double flowers are freely borne throughout the season.

8 *Rosa* **'Arthur Bell'**
Upright, vigorous, disease-resistant floribunda of medium size with bright green foliage. Large clusters of fragrant, cup-shaped flowers are freely borne throughout the season. Petals fade attractively as flowers age.

7 *Rosa* **'Pascali'**
Medium-sized, upright Hybrid Tea Rose, good for bedding and also for cutting, although the elegant flowers are easily damaged by rain. Glossy, medium-green foliage.

6 *Rosa* **'Pink Parfait'**
This medium-sized Floribunda Rose of bushy habit, plentiful foliage and few thorns is good in a border. It is vigorous, disease resistant and a prolific bloomer. Well-formed flowers, on long stems, open flat to show golden stamens.

HYBRID TEA AND FLORIBUNDA ROSES

Modern Bush Roses are divided into two main categories, both derived from crosses. The first type, Hybrid Tea Roses, now called Large-flowered Roses, resulted from crossing Hybrid Perpetuals with Tea Roses. The second type, the Floribundas, now known as Cluster-flowered Roses, were created by crossing Hybrid Teas with Hybrid Polyanthas.

• Hybrid Tea Roses generally have large fully double or semi-double flowers held singly or not more than two or three per stem. Many are sweetly scented.

• Floribunda Roses carry clusters of flowers. These are usually smaller than those of Hybrid Tea Roses and often with only little scent.

The modern varieties of both types are characteristically repeat flowering, with the main flush in May/June and a second one in September.

The flowers of the two groups share a wide variety of colour from white through yellow and apricot to deep red. Some types can reach more than 6ft/2m in height, but most are smaller.

The most widely grown of all roses, Bush Roses are often planted in large beds to give maximum impact from colour and perfume. This is not usually possible in a small garden, where they can, instead, be planted in small groups of two or three as part of a mixed border. It is best to use the same varieties in a group so that colours harmonize and plants are roughly the same height.

The cultivation of roses follows much the same pattern as that of other flowering shrubs. They should be planted in a hole big enough to give the roots room to spread, in good rich soil. Thereafter, they need a top dressing of fertilizer, preferably a special rose fertilizer, twice a year, in spring and again in midsummer. This feed should be given, after the initial flush of blooms has faded and dead-heading has been completed, to encourage a second flowering.

Pruning need not be a complex and alarming project, for there are a few simple rules which, if carefully followed, will ensure that the shape of the bush is maintained and its flowering potential maximized. The method of pruning Hybrid Tea Roses, which should be encouraged to make substantial new growth in a season, differs slightly from that used for Floribundas, which tend to produce less new growth in a year. The two methods are explained opposite.

BUYING ROSES

Roses can be bought as:

• Bare-rooted plants—dug up and packed in waxed paper, hessian or plastic for posting or, at a garden centre, with roots wrapped in peat.

• Pre-packaged plants—usually in a plastic bag, roots wrapped in peat.

• Container-grown plants from nurseries or garden centres.

Bush Roses should have well-ripened wood that feels firm when squeezed and a strong, fibrous root system. There must be two shoots, preferably more, thicker than a pencil, and no white shoots or open buds.

Climbing Roses should be checked as for Bush Roses, but ideally stems should be at least 30in/75cm long.

PRUNING HYBRID TEA ROSES

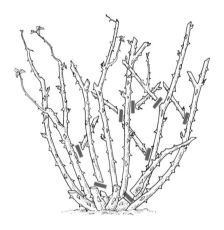

Prune in late winter. Remove any dead or diseased wood and branches that cross over each other. Take them off close to the main stem. Cut back remaining shoots by about half; on a weak plant, remove a little more.

PRUNING FLORIBUNDA ROSES

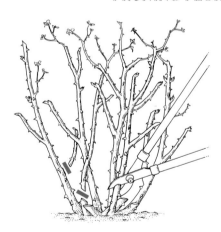
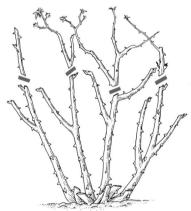

In early spring, cut back one-third of the old wood, removing it from the base of the plant. Then cut back the shoots that remain, shortening them by about one-third of their length. These simple procedures should guarantee the healthy growth of these roses.

BUSH AND MINIATURE ROSES

The Miniature Rose has added another dimension to rose growing. Mostly bred from the dwarf China Rose *Rosa chinensis* 'Roulettii', these little bushes can be raised indoors, yet still produce a dense growth bearing flowers of varied and unusual colours over a long season. Both the bush and miniature varieties, as well as the recently introduced small Patio Roses are easily grown in containers, and they will make a delightful display in a small town garden, on a terrace or even a balcony.

1 *Rosa* 'Cricri'
Small, double, salmon and coral pink rosette-shaped flowers on a rather tall plant, with upright habit and somewhat tough, disease-resistant foliage.

2 *Rosa* 'Fragrant Cloud'
Small, upright Large-flowered Rose. of upright habit and vigorous growth. The foliage is dark, glossy green and flowers clear, pure-coloured with frilled petals and excellent fragrance.

3 *Rosa* 'Whisky Mac'
Small and bushy Large-flowered Rose with fragrant double blooms of unusual amber colour and glossy bronze foliage. Prone to disease.

9 *Rosa* 'Sutter's Gold'
Tall Large-flowered Rose of upright habit; growth is slow and can be straggly. Clear green foliage and sweetly scented flowers on long stems. Very good cut flowers.

8 *Rosa* 'Alec's Red'
Medium-sized, vigorous grower of upright habit. Large, rich-coloured, very fragrant blooms are rain resistant but do not like the heat. Good cut flower.

7 *Rosa* 'Matangi'
Small, vigorous, Cluster-flowered Rose of upright habit. Glossy green foliage. Slightly scented flowers described as "hand-painted", on account of the silvery central eye. Not a good cut flower.

4 *Rosa* 'Magic Carousel'
A bushy Miniature Rose, slightly taller than average at 18in/45cm. Faintly scented, rosette-shaped double flowers in summer and autumn.

5 *Rosa* 'Easter Morning'
Miniature Rose of upright habit. Dark green glossy foliage. Slightly fragrant, cup-shaped flowers are borne during summer and autumn.

6 *Rosa* 'Orange Sensation'
Small, Cluster-flowered Rose of spreading habit. Dark green glossy foliage, and fragrant double blooms in mid-summer and early autumn. Prone to disease but rain resistant.

STANDARD AND MINIATURE ROSES

These forms of roses can be used in a variety of ways. Most Standard Roses are tall enough to stand on their own as specimen plants and can be used to create a formal feature or give height in the border. Miniature Roses are well suited to beds, rockeries or containers, in which they can be grown indoors or on a terrace or patio.

Standard Roses

Because of their height, these can be prone to wind damage, and it is wiser to avoid planting them in an exposed position. Roses may succumb easily to the force of the wind because they are not deeply enough rooted or because superfluous top growth has not been removed before the onset of windy weather. An inadequate root system can be attributed to poor watering and cultivation, or to improper planting.

Most modern Bush Roses, including Standard Roses, are grown as grafted stock. This means the plant has been grafted on to another species which is used as the root stock. The graft shows as a swelling at the base of the stem. When planting Shrub and Bush Roses, this swelling should be buried 1in/2.5cm below the surface of the soil. The grafting point on a Standard Rose is at the top of the stem, and the uppermost roots of these roses, which are on the parent stock, should be 4in/10cm below the surface.

Suckers frequently appear on grafted rose plants and must be removed. These shoots grow from the original rootstock, below the grafting point; they sometimes form on the stems of Standard Roses and should be cut off close to the stem.

Standard Roses need reinforcement against the wind and must be staked.

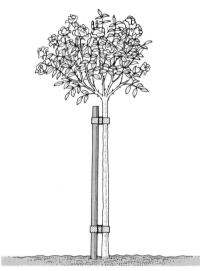

Standard Roses need staking, but make certain that the stake is on the windward side of the rose and that the roots are deeply planted. Fasten the stem loosely to the stake with ties; allow the plant to settle, then tighten the ties against the stake.

• Treat the lower 18in/45cm of a stake some 4ft/1.2m tall and 2in/5cm in diameter with wood preservative.
• Drive the stake into the planting hole on the windward side with the top of the treated area level with the final soil level.
• Trim any of the top roots that are growing upward.
• Put two or three spadefuls of compost into the planting hole.
• Plant the rose so that the stem is close to the stake.
• Use the old soil mark on the stem as a guide to the new planting level.
• Fasten the rose to the stake with ties, or wrap sacking around the stem at intervals, then tie tarred twine around the sacking and on to the stake.

Roses are fairly undemanding about their environment but will not thrive in deep, continuous shade or under trees. They will tolerate some shade, but prefer full sun and a sheltered wind-free spot. Most Bush Roses like a neutral, moisture-retentive soil with plenty of nutrients and humus. Clay soil suits most modern roses.

Miniature Roses

If these are going to be kept as indoor plants, they need warmth, light and humidity. If these are provided, Miniatures will produce successive flushes of blooms continuously from spring to autumn.

• Half-fill a 2-in/5-cm deep waterproof tray with gravel.

• Keep this 1in/2.5cm of gravel moist, but water must not cover the gravel.

• Place the tray near a sunny window, but at the height of summer the plants will need to be shaded from the midday sun.

• Water the pots of Miniature Roses thoroughly, and stand them on the gravel.

• Water each time the soil in the pots

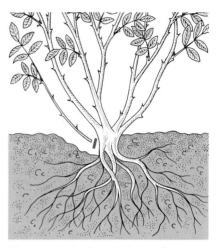

To remove a sucker from a Bush Rose, dig away the soil to find its junction with the root stock. Cut the sucker off cleanly with secateurs, or pull it off. Selective weedkillers are not suitable as they can damage the whole plant

shows signs of slight drying and give a liquid feed at the same time.

• Mist the leaves frequently.

Dead-heading

Apart from the aesthetic effect of removing dead flowers from plants, this is a form of garden hygiene. Dead tissue rots and permits the growth of fungi, so the removal of dead flowers will help to keep the plant healthy. It also stimulates new bud and leaf growth.

There is, however, no point in dead-heading some of the Old Rose varieties, since they have only one period of flowering and dead-heading will not encourage more flowers to form. Additionally, many of these roses produce attractive hips in the autumn and removing the dead blooms naturally removes the hips as well.

Dead-head roses by cutting back to the first outward-facing leaf with five leaflets. In this way you ensure that you cut into strong wood with a strong bud, encouraging new leaves and flowering shoots to form lower down on the stems.

See also: Shrub Roses Pages 136–137

CLIMBING AND RAMBLING ROSES

The rose's variety of form and colour, fragrance and long flowering season make it a plant of exceptional merit. Where long-lasting colour or vertical interest is required, Climbing and Rambling Roses are ideal, for they combine the rose's beauty with the adaptability of a climber.

1 *Rosa* 'American Pillar'
Single blooms without fragrance. Flowers once in midsummer. Typical climber. Vulnerable to mildew; prune out flowering stems as blooms die.

2 *Rosa* 'Handel'
Double, bicoloured blooms borne over a long period. Abundant glossy foliage. Withstands rain. Light pruning, cut away dead wood.

3 *Rosa* 'Parkdirektor Riggers'
Hardy, flowering throughout summer. Dark green foliage. Prone to mildew and black spot. Light pruning to cut out tired wood.

4 *Rosa* 'Iceberg'
Large trusses of pure white flowers in almost continuous bloom all summer. Slight fragrance. Medium green, glossy foliage. Vigorous branching habit. Light pruning only.

6 *Rosa* 'Aloha'
Slow and limited growth, so suits a restricted site. Full deep pink blooms with fragrance. Repeat flowering throughout season. Resistant to heavy rain. Prune lightly. A superb rose.

5 *Rosa* 'Schoolgirl'
Tall, upright climber, flowering through summer to autumn, but not profusely. Glossy foliage. Light pruning only.

7 *Rosa* 'Danse du Feu'
Very popular climber. Medium-sized semi-double blooms of vivid scarlet that fade to delicate purple in old age. Repeat flowering. No fragrance. Bronze-tinted foliage. Prune lightly.

8 *Rosa* 'Gloire de Dijon'
Old Victorian climber. Large flowers with sweet scent all summer. Train against a wall in a warm, sheltered spot. Spray against mildew and blackspot. Little pruning needed.

14 *Rosa* **'Golden Showers'**
Bright blooms that fade attractively. Prolonged flowering season. Excellent for small gardens. Resistant to rain. Growth initially bushy, then climbing. One of the most popular Climbing Roses.

13 *Rosa* **'Maigold'**
Semi-double flowers with strong scent in early summer. Attractive, medium green foliage, but very thorny growth. Popular climber.

12 *Rosa* **'Albertine'**
Wonderful Rambling Rose; vigorous branching habit. Fragrant double blooms in early summer; mid-green foliage. Dislikes heavy rain and is prone to mildew. Prune old flowering shoots in autumn.

11 *Rosa* **'Zéphirine Drouhin'**
(Thornless rose)
Semi-double, very fragrant climber. Repeat flowering but needs dead-heading to produce new blooms. Light green foliage. Prune lightly. A martyr to mildew.

9 *Rosa* **'Madame Alfred Carrière'**
Large, fragrant blooms in summer and autumn. Quick grower in a shady site. Light green foliage. Lightly prune any old shoots.

10 *Rosa* **'Josephine Bruce'**
Repeat flowering, with magnificent dark red blooms, but best display in early summer. Matt, medium green foliage. Spreading habit. Prone to mildew. Light pruning only.

CLIMBING AND RAMBLING ROSES

It may be difficult for the novice to distinguish between these two categories of rose, some of which are descended from true climbing species, while others are mutants or "sports" of Bush Roses.

Rambling Roses produce copious trusses of scented flowers in one mid-summer flowering. They have a vigorous, sprawling habit, producing long new shoots after the main crop of flowers, which bloom on the previous year's growth; 'Dorothy Perkins' fits this description and is a true Rambler. The so-called Pseudo-Rambler produces few new basal shoots, so most blooms appear high up on the old wood; 'Albertine' and 'Albéric Barbier' are typical. Some newer hybrid forms, such as 'The New Dawn', have good repeat flowering and less rampant, more easily managed growth.

Climbing Roses, particularly modern varieties such as 'Compassion', have a stiffer, more upright habit of growth, which makes them suitable for training against a pillar or wall. They are more popular than Ramblers on account of their repeat flowering and larger flowers, usually produced in more than one flush. A different type again is the thornless Bourbon climber 'Zéphirine Drouhin'.

Climbing and Rambling Roses need correct feeding and pruning to perform really well and most take a year or two to flower prolifically. Since they have only long, snaking growth and backward-facing thorns to support themselves, they also need careful training.

• Do not encourage purely vertical growth, for the plant will carry its flowers only at the top of its stems.

• If the rose is growing against a wall, fix wires or a trellis to it. Gently bend the stems horizontal, tying them to the support; this interrupts the upward flow of the sap causing lateral stems to appear, and producing a dense, spreading habit.

• If the rose is to climb a vertical support, train stems around it, so they spiral upward.

• Tie stems quite loosely; tight bindings will cut into them as they thicken.

PESTS AND DISEASES OF ROSES

In order of frequency/severity

Aphids (Greenfly)—can severely damage young shoots. Spray as soon as seen with contact insecticide.

Black spot—dark spots on leaves cause them to yellow and fall. Spray every two weeks with a systemic fungicide.

Caterpillars, leaf-cutter bees, sawflies—pieces eaten from leaves usually more unsightly than serious. Spray with systemic insecticide.

Powdery mildew—white powdery coating, which distorts leaves in dry weather. Treat as for black spot.

Die-back—frost damage or fungal diseases may cause shoots and branches to die off. Cut back healthy wood; paint exposed ends with fungicide. Spray as for black spot.

Grey mould—grey powdery mildew on buds, shoots and spent flowers. Treatment as for die-back.

Rust—minute rust-coloured spots on leaves or stems. Treat as for die-back.

▼ See also: Pests and diseases Pages 40–47
Supporting climbers Pages 48–49

PRUNING CLIMBERS AND RAMBLERS

Climbers Between late autumn and spring, prune the lateral branches that have flowered to within 6in/15cm of main stems. Cut out any weak wood, then tie the leading shoots to the support, using plastic-covered wire.

True Ramblers Prune in midsummer, after flowering. Cut away the flowered lateral shoots and thin out the main stems so that only a base of main stems is left. One or two laterals may be spared, but cut their shoots down to 6in/15cm. Tie in the remaining laterals.

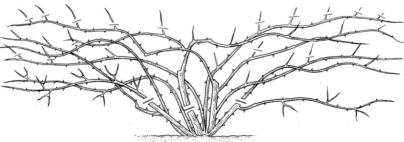

Pseudo-Ramblers In midsummer cut back old main stems just above the union with replacement laterals. Cut back flowered laterals to within 6in/15cm of replacement laterals, which should be tied in to stimulate horizontal growth.

CLIMBERS/1

Climbing plants are an asset in any garden. They can cover ugly walls, ornament old tree-stumps and give shade over a pergola. In a small garden, they bring foliage where there is no space to grow trees, and many have beautiful and fragrant flowers. If they seem too tall, remember, climbers can also be trained sideways to cover large walls.

1 *Passiflora caerulea*
(Passion flower)
Climbs by tendrils; train against a sunny wall. Showy flowers in mid-season. Needs free-draining soil and protection against frost; in spring, prune damaged and unwanted shoots. Height 8–10ft/2.4–3m.

2 *Solanum crispum*
(Chilean potato vine)
A showy, quick-growing, semi-evergreen climber for sheltered gardens. Give it full sun in any reasonable garden soil; in spring cut back damaged or unwanted shoots. Height 15–18ft/4.5–5.4m.

3 *Cobaea scandens*
(Cup-and-saucer vine)
A quick-growing, leafy tendril climber, usually treated as a half hardy annual in frost-prone areas. Cup-shaped flowers from summer to autumn. Can be trained up trellis or netting. Height 10ft/3m.

4 *Humulus lupulus* 'Aureus'
Vigorous herbaceous climber with twining growth. Insignificant flowers but attractive yellow foliage and hop fruits in late summer. Reasonable garden soil in sun or part shade. Height 10ft/3m.

5 *Lonicera periclymenum* 'Belgica'
(Early Dutch honeysuckle)
Colourful, fragrant form, flowering in late spring. Bushy scrambling habit of growth well suited to fences and arches. Grows best in sun, with roots in well-watered, shaded soil. Prune lightly after flowering. Height 15–20ft/4.5–6m.

9 *Wisteria floribunda* 'Macrobotrys'
Deciduous, twining climber,
eventually very large; best trained
against a high wall or over a large
pergola in full sun. Sweet-scented
flowers in long, graceful racemes.
On established plants, cut back
new long shoots in late winter
and midsummer if necessary.
Height 30ft/9m.

8 *Hydrangea petiolaris*
(Climbing hydrangea)
A self-clinging, woody, branched
deciduous climber with lacy white
flowerheads in summer; attractive
foliage turns yellow in autumn. A
slow starter, but will eventually
cover a large wall. Good for shade in
ordinary garden soil. Trim any large
or untidy growth after flowering.
Height 40ft/12m.

6 *Campsis radicans*
(Trumpet vine)
Deciduous climber with ivy-like,
self-clinging aerial roots and
vigorous growth. Showy clusters of
flowers in late summer and autumn,
but needs plenty of hot sun to
perform really well. Fertile soil in a
sheltered spot. Height 30ft/9m.

7 *Vitis coignetiae*
(Japanese crimson glory vine)
Vigorous deciduous climber with
bold foliage and superb autumn
colours. Will festoon large walls and
tall trees. Hardy, but best in a
sheltered position. If necessary, cut
back in winter. Height 70ft/21.3m.

CLIMBING PLANTS

For the gardener with limited space, climbing plants are a boon. They take up only a small amount of ground space and, if the garden is not large enough for growing trees, their height provides perpendicular interest.

Climbers can serve many practical purposes in the garden; they can be used to obscure awkward corners, cover stark or ugly buildings, decorate leafless tree stumps or grace the fences, pergolas and arches that mark the garden landscape.

A "climber" is a plant that has a sprawling or climbing habit. Many have developed mechanisms such as tendrils or aerial roots that enable them to attach themselves to a support, whether it be a wall, pole, tree or trellis. Others, such as Climbing and Rambling Roses which have developed no special aids for climbing, can be trained to grow up these supports, but will need to be loosely tied in—at least in the initial stages.

Self-clinging climbers

These plants have suckers which attach themselves to the surface of the support. Some, such as *Hedera* spp. (Ivy) and *Campsis radicans* (Trumpet vine), have their suckers on modified aerial roots, while most species of *Parthenocissus*, *P. tricuspidata* (Boston ivy) for example, carry them on modified leaves.

Twining climbers

Plants such as *Wisteria floribunda* and *Humulus lupulus* (Hop), have long, winding stems; others, including *Passiflora caerulea* (Passion flower), have clinging tendrils that twine around the support. The leaf stalks of *Clematis* spp. perform this function.

There are advantages in growing climbers on a wall or wooden fence, for these afford protection against wind and a wall will also retain daytime warmth, which will combat the chilling effects of frost. Paradoxically, a wall that gets no early morning sun in winter is often the best place for a tender plant, since it is not low temperatures that cause damage, but rapid thawing of frozen plant tissues.

The soil at the base of a wall is, however, often poor and it must be well prepared before the climbers are planted.

Planting climbers

- Dig the planting hole at least 12in/30cm away from the wall if possible, and clear away any builder's rubble.

- Because the soil is usually poor, mix it with compost or well-rotted manure and even some moisture-retentive leaf mould before replacing it.

- Set the climber's roots at an angle to the support and give them shade initially to

Virginia creeper (*Parthenocissus*) is a self-clinging tendril climber. The broad tips of the tendrils have little suction pads on them that adhere tightly to the support, be it wood or brick.

help retain moisture. This can be provided temporarily by placing a large stone or slab on the soil covering the roots.

• The new climber may not be sufficiently tall to reach the permanent support right away; if so, it will need a cane set at an angle to support it while it grows.

• Water the climber regularly and thoroughly, particularly if it is planted against the house or other building; the roof overhang may prevent rain from reaching it.

• Apply mulch and fertilizer to the plant in spring.

The warmth and shelter provided by walls and fences suits climbers, but it also appeals to pests and encourages a few diseases. Inspect plants regularly, since mildew often occurs in these conditions; the pests that tend to lurk here are red spider mites and aphids.

Wisteria clings by means of long, pliant, twining stems; since these become very thick with age, the support must be long lasting and sturdy enough to bear the plant's considerable weight.

CLIMBERS FOR SUN

• *Actinidia kolomikta*—moderately hardy, deciduous, woody-stemmed, twining; large leaves, tipped pink and white. Height 12ft/3.6m.

• *Campsis radicans* (Trumpet vine)— half hardy, fast-growing woody-stemmed, self-clinging; red, orange or yellow flowers in late summer/ autumn. Height 40ft/12m.

• *Solanum crispum* (Chilean potato vine)—moderately hardy, evergreen or semi-evergreen, needs support. Mauve/purple flowers in summer. Height 20ft/6m.

• *Trachelospermum jasminoides* (Star jasmine)—half hardy evergreen, twining and self-clinging. Fragrant white flowers followed by long seedpods in pairs. Height 28ft/9m.

CLIMBERS FOR SHADE

• *Hedera helix* 'Goldheart' (Ivy)— evergreen, self-clinging ; leaves dark green with yellow centre. Slow to establish. Height 20ft/6m.

• *Humulus lupulus* 'Aureus' (Hop)— twining; female plants bear greenish flowers, which in autumn become hops. Height 20ft/6m.

• *Parthenocissus henryana* (Chinese virginia creeper)—deciduous tendril climber; autumn leaf colour best in cool, shady site, Height 30ft/9m.

• *Tropaeolum speciosum* (Climbing nasturtium)—twining perennial, dies down in winter; tuberous roots need moisture and shade. Scarlet flowers, then blue berries. Height 10ft/3m.

If care is taken with siting and planting, most climbers do not demand too much time. To achieve a controlled, formal look, you will need to prune and train a climber into the required shape, but many climbers survive perfectly well with a light trimming.

However, all climbers which do not cling to flat surfaces by means of aerial roots will require some form of support, so think carefully about where to put the necessary arches, trellises or pergolas, matching the site to the plants' needs.

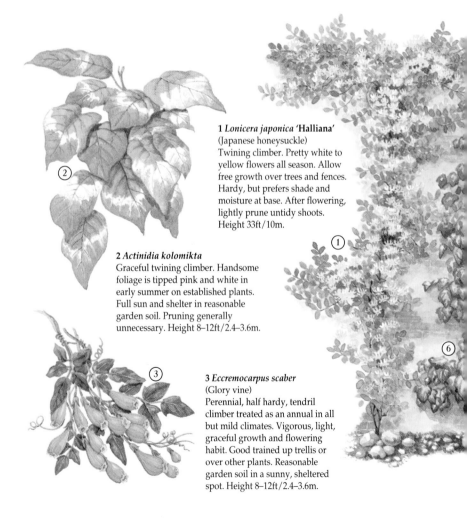

1 *Lonicera japonica* 'Halliana' (Japanese honeysuckle) Twining climber. Pretty white to yellow flowers all season. Allow free growth over trees and fences. Hardy, but prefers shade and moisture at base. After flowering, lightly prune untidy shoots. Height 33ft/10m.

2 *Actinidia kolomikta* Graceful twining climber. Handsome foliage is tipped pink and white in early summer on established plants. Full sun and shelter in reasonable garden soil. Pruning generally unnecessary. Height 8–12ft/2.4–3.6m.

3 *Eccremocarpus scaber* (Glory vine) Perennial, half hardy, tendril climber treated as an annual in all but mild climates. Vigorous, light, graceful growth and flowering habit. Good trained up trellis or over other plants. Reasonable garden soil in a sunny, sheltered spot. Height 8–12ft/2.4–3.6m.

4 *Parthenocissus tricuspidata*
(Boston ivy)
Tall, spreading self-clinging vine
with spectacular autumn foliage
colour. Fertile, free-draining soil
in sun or part shade. Remove
unwanted growth in spring.
Height 40–60ft/12–18m.

5 *Trachelospermum jasminoides*
(Star jasmine)
Twining evergreen climber with
clusters of highly scented flowers in
summer. Prefers a warm, sheltered
wall in mild areas. Pruning
generally not necessary but can be
trimmed lightly after flowering.
Height 12–15ft/3.6–4.5m.

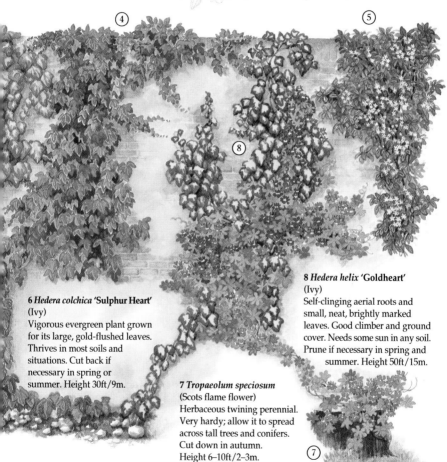

6 *Hedera colchica* **'Sulphur Heart'**
(Ivy)
Vigorous evergreen plant grown
for its large, gold-flushed leaves.
Thrives in most soils and
situations. Cut back if
necessary in spring or
summer. Height 30ft/9m.

7 *Tropaeolum speciosum*
(Scots flame flower)
Herbaceous twining perennial.
Very hardy; allow it to spread
across tall trees and conifers.
Cut down in autumn.
Height 6–10ft/2–3m.

8 *Hedera helix* **'Goldheart'**
(Ivy)
Self-clinging aerial roots and
small, neat, brightly marked
leaves. Good climber and ground
cover. Needs some sun in any soil.
Prune if necessary in spring and
summer. Height 50ft/15m.

CLIMBERS

Climbing plants give the garden a vertical element, lifting the eye above ground level to accentuate—or conceal—particular features. Climbers do not need to be permanent, although with so many large, beautiful perennial climbing plants, it is easy to overlook the annuals.

There are many plants which, in a matter of months, will scramble to a surprising size and flower copiously. They give the gardener a chance to experiment with textures and colours each year, which is not possible with perennials. Most can be grown easily from seed; if a packet describes the climber's habit as "rampant", heed this warning and do not put it where it will overwhelm other plants.

Many annual climbers, with their tousled look of plants in a hurry, suit an informal setting. Climbers, such as *Cobaea scandens* (Cup-and-saucer vine) and *Lathyrus odorata* (Sweet pea), cling to their supports with tendrils, rushing up trellis or poles at astonishing speed. Gentle guidance, tucking in a shoot here and there, will be enough to direct their growth. *Cobaea*, with its cup-shaped purple flowers on green saucers, reaches a height of 12ft/3.6m in a season, *Lathyrus* about 6ft/2m.

Such light plants will not endanger growth and can be allowed to romp over the trunk or stump of a tree or trained over a garden shed without fear of damage. The long stems of the perennial *Aristolochia macrophylla* (Dutchman's pipe) makes it another suitable climber to grow up a tree.

Some perennial climbers behave more like annuals, among them the striking *Tropaeolum speciosum* (Climbing nasturtium), whose slender stems bear scarlet flowers and can reach 15ft/4.5m before dying back

ANNUAL CLIMBERS

- *Ipomoea quamoclit* syn. *Quamoclit pinnata* (Cypress vine)—twining climber, with finely cut bright green leaves and tubular scarlet or orange flowers borne singly in summer or autumn. Height 6–10ft/2–3m.
- *Ipomoea tricolor* 'Heavenly Blue' (Morning glory)—twining climber with glorious, azure blue funnel-shaped flowers in summer; needs a sheltered sunny spot. Height 10ft/3m.
- *Mina lobata*—twining climber, with attractive lobed leaves and shiny racemes of cream and orange-scarlet flowers in summer. Height 8ft/2.4m.

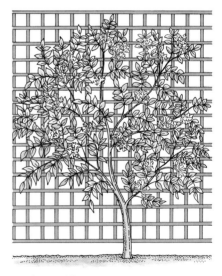

Jasminum nudiflorum (Winter-flowering jasmine), must be tied to a support; a wall trellis makes a good host for this plant.

See also: Supporting climbers Pages 150–151
Planting climbers Pages 156–157

to a root stock in autumn. Other genuinely half hardy climbers like *Thunbergia alata* (Black-eyed Susan) and *Eccremocarpus scaber* (Glory vine), though actually perennial, are best treated as annuals in colder climates and discarded at the end of the growing season.

Most small gardens do not have the facilities for many large, free-growing climbers. Where space is limited, climbers should be confined to arches and pergolas covered with formally trained plants. A superb choice for a sunny pergola is the perennial wisteria, *Wisteria sinensis*, which requires patience; it can take five years or more to flower. The wait will seem worthwhile, however, when the cascade of sweetly scented mauve-blue flowers finally appears.

Other climbers—among many—that are suited to trellises and pergolas are the unusual spring-flowering *Akebia quinata* (Chocolate vine), *Solanum crispum*, *Jasminum officinale affine* (Summer jasmine) and *Clematis*. *Hydrangea petiolaris* and *Trachelospermum jasminoides*, being self-clinging, are best grown against a wall. Ivy, traditionally regarded as a superb evergreen wall covering, can also be most effective as ground cover, especially the golden-leafed *Hedera helix* 'Buttercup'.

Pruning, usually done in late winter, is necessary to control and train perennial climbers and to stimulate growth, and special vigilance is required to prevent vigorous wall climbers from destroying gutters and windowframes and dislodging roof tiles. Binding ties should be regularly checked as stems thicken to ensure they are not too tight and constricting.

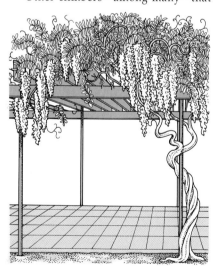

Wisteria twines its stems around the frame of a pergola. This plant is a natural climber, but should initially be tied and trained to the support.

Clematis montana will clamber around the trunk and wind into the branches of a tree, or cover a large fence or garden shed.

Clematis are much loved as climbers, and the Large-flowered varieties especially can make a wonderful show. They need support, and their rather untidy growth should be controlled by correct pruning. They prefer cool, moist conditions around their roots. Some alkalinity in the soil suits their growth, and all benefit from an application of fertilizer in spring and liquid feeding during the season.

1 *Clematis* **'The President'**
Flowers throughout the summer. Large-flowered. Prune in early spring by cutting back the previous season's growth by about 12in/30cm. Shaded roots in loamy, well-drained soil. Height 6–10ft/2–3m.

2 *Clematis macropetala*
Slender-stemmed climber, graceful over low walls and fences. Flowers in spring. Attractive foliage, silky heads that turn grey and fluffy. Lightly trim unwanted shoots immediately after flowering. Will grow in partial shade. Height 10ft/3m.

4 *Clematis montana*
Vigorous, even rampant growth, charming draped over trees, pergolas and walls. Prefers partial shade, cool roots in moist soil. Either leave unpruned or prune lightly immediately after flowering. Height 22–40ft/7–12m.

3 *Clematis viticella*
Profuse blooms on slender stems from mid- to late summer. Sunny spot in well-drained but moist soil. In early spring cut all previous season's growth back to 30in/75cm. Height 6–10ft/2–3m.

5 *Clematis armandii*
Glossy evergreen foliage, with fragrant flowers in spring. Vulnerable to severe winter frost, so plant against a sunny wall. Well-drained soil. Prune lightly immediately after flowering. Height 10–15ft/3–4.5m.

6 *Clematis* **'Perle d'Azur'**
Large-flowered, blooming mid-
to late summer. Vigorous
growth. Well-drained, loamy
soil and shaded roots. Prune as
'The President'. Height 10ft/3m.

7 *Clematis* **'Marie Boisselot'**
Large-flowered. Pure white
blossoms, vigorous and free
flowering from spring to
autumn. Prune as *C. viticella*.
Height 10ft/3m.

8 *Clematis tangutica*
Vigorous, with nodding yellow
flowers midsummer to autumn.
Easily cultivated; train over a
wall or to cover a bank. Prune as
C. viticella. Height 15–20ft/4.5–6m.

9 *Clematis alpina*
Lovely species with silky seed
heads and richly hued blooms
in spring. Train over a small
bush or low wall in partial
shade. Moist, well-drained soil.
Prune as *C. macropetala*.
Height 6–10ft/2–3m.

10 *Clematis* **'Nellie Moser'**
Large-flowered. Tolerates sun
but flowers fade less in a partially
shaded spot. Cool, moist, loamy
soil. Prune as 'The President'.
Height 11ft/3.5m.

11 *Clematis* **'Jackmanii'**
Original Large-flowered hybrid.
Spectacular climber with a profusion
of flowers in late summer and
autumn. Prune as *C. viticella*.
Height 10ft/3m.

CLEMATIS

This lovely plant has been called "the queen of climbers", a tribute to its beauty and adaptability. Colours range from white and yellow through pinks and mauves to a deep wine-purple, and the flowers can be either double or single. In many varieties, even the seed head is a thing of beauty.

All clematis thrive in full sun, but will grow on a shady wall if their flowers can reach up into the sunlight. They prefer to have their roots in cool, moist, slightly alkaline soil, and need plenty of feeding.

When planting, dig a hole wide enough to take the spread of the roots and deep enough to bury the crown 2in/5cm below the surface. Mix organic material and some bonemeal or blood, fish and bone into the soil. Remove the plant carefully, loosen the roots and spread them out in the hole. The stem is fragile, so do not detach the cane that supported the plant in the pot. To keep the roots cool, plant a small bush on the sunny side of the climber or place a large stone on the soil over the roots.

Clematis cling with twining leaf stems to netting, trellises, pergolas, trees and bushes; they climb and tumble without pruning, so it is better to control and train their growth. There are many species and numerous hybrids (most gardeners cultivate Large-flowered Clematis, which are hybrids), which can be divided into three groups for the purposes of pruning.

Group One comprises the evergreens and the early-flowering species, *C. armandii*, *C. alpina*, *C. macropetala*, *C. montana*, which produce their spring blooms on the new stems of the last season's growth. These tend to make tangled growth which can be controlled if old, over-long stems are pruned soon after flowering.

Group Two embraces the early and mid-season single-flowered hybrids and the double and semi-double hybrids. In the early blooming types, flowers are borne on old stems, and pruning is carried out every year in early spring. The previous season's growth is cut back by about 12in/30cm.

Group Three includes the late Large-flowered hybrids and late-flowering species such as *texensis, tangutica* and *viticella*, the *jackmanii* types and the so-called herbaceous types. Blooms are borne on the current season's growth, and the plants will become leggy if they are not pruned hard regularly. Cut back all stems to buds 6–12in/15–30cm from the ground when the plants are dormant.

HERBACEOUS CLEMATIS

Although most clematis are climbers, there are a few hardy herbaceous species that are excellent in the border. They need sunshine and will do well in any ordinary garden soil, but since they flourish in alkaline soil are useful plants for chalky areas. Their loose, floppy habit of growth means that they require support.

C. heracleifolia var. *davidiana*—scented blue tubular flowers in late summer. Height 3ft/1m.

C. integrifolia—deep blue, bell-shaped flowers in midsummer. Height 24–30in/60–75cm.

C. recta—masses of fragrant, star-shaped white blooms in mid-season, followed by silky seed heads. Needs support. Height 3–5ft/1–1.5m.

PRUNING CLEMATIS

Group One Prune the shoots that have carried flowers, cutting back to one or two buds on the main stems. This job should be done soon after flowering is over. The plant then needs to be assiduously watered and fed to ensure vigorous growth in the next season.

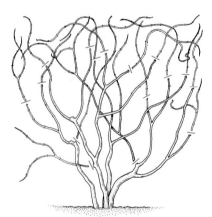

Group Two These flower on the previous season's growth. In early spring, cut back old stems by about 12in/30cm to stong leaf-axil buds.

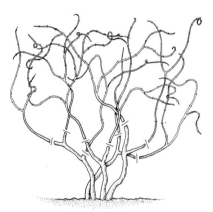

Group Three These flower on current growth. Prune hard in late winter, cutting all stems down to strong buds near the base.

HERBACEOUS PERENNIALS/1

A carefully planned herbaceous border can bring colour to the garden from early spring to late autumn.

Herbaceous perennials can be planted among shrubs, but taller varieties should not be planted too close to hedges or trees which will restrict air and light; they may also need to be staked.

Give thought, too, to the height of the plants so that the smaller lower-growing varieties are not masked by taller, more vigorous growers.

1 *Papaver orientale* **'Turkish Delight'**
(Oriental poppy)
Large flowers with crinkled petals in mid-season, followed by untidy foliage. Cut down flower heads after flowering unless saving the ornamental seed heads; divide every three years. Well-drained soil in full sun.
Height 24–36in/60–90cm.

2 *Aquilegia* **'Olympia'**
(Columbine)
Delicate flowers borne on slender stems. Water well and mulch in late spring. Dead-head regularly. Well-drained soil in sun or partial shade. Height 24–36in/60–90cm.

3 *Geranium* **'Johnson's Blue'**
A hardy perennial, good as ground cover. Flowers in midsummer in any reasonable soil in sun or light shade. Cut down in autumn. Height 18in/45cm.

4 *Euphorbia polychroma*
(syn. *E. epithymoides*)
Will grow in most soils and situations. Sharp yellow flowers early in the season. Height 20in/50cm.

5 *Geum* **'Mrs Bradshaw'**
Brilliant scarlet double blooms in mid-season; fine front-of-border plants. Grows anywhere, but prefers sun and compost-rich soil. Height 12–24in/30–60cm.

6 *Paeonia* **'Festiva Maxima'**
(Peony)
Long-lasting giant double blooms. Needs rich, well-fed soil in a sunny spot. Dead-head regularly and cut down stems in autumn. Height 36in/90cm.

7 *Bergenia cordifolia purpurea*
Purplish leaves in winter, mauve-pink flowers in spring. Grows well in moisture-retentive soil in sun or shade, excellent ground cover. Height 18in/45cm.

12 *Primula florindae*
(Giant yellow cowslip)
Tall stems bear flowers in
mid-season. Prefers a moist
site or bog garden soil rich
in organic material.
Height 24in/60cm.

11 *Heuchera sanguinea*
(Coral flower)
Makes a good edging plant for a
border; pretty evergreen foliage in
mounds, with pink or red flowers
in mid-season. Any reasonable
soil in sun or light shade.
Height 18–30in/45–75cm.

8 *Pulmonaria saccharata*
(Lungwort)
Foliage heavily flecked
with white, and early blue
flowers; popular ground
cover. Grows best in fertile
soil in light or full shade.
Height 12in/30cm.

9 *Helleborus niger*
(Christmas rose)
Thrives in partial shade in
moisture-retentive soil.
Flowers in late winter; untidy,
semi-evergreen foliage.
Height 12–18in/30–45cm.

10 *Omphalodes cappadocica*
Flowers early in the season,
but foliage green nearly all
year. Thrives in shade and
moist fertile soil.
Height 9in/23cm.

THE HERBACEOUS BORDER

Although ready-to-plant herbaceous perennials are comparatively expensive to buy, a well-planted herbaceous border can be the main asset of the garden plan. The expense of the initial investment will, however, prove worth while, for in most instances, after a year or two, these plants can easily be propagated by division or by cuttings.

Most perennials are not unduly fussy and will grow in any reasonable garden soil, but, like most plants, they benefit from mulching in spring after a good rainfall or thorough watering. They also benefit from an open, sunny position and the free circulation of air, so they should not be planted too close to hedges or under overhanging trees.

In general, they need little attention other than dead-heading and, where necessary, staking. To a great extent, weeds can be kept down by the use of ground cover plants or by hand weeding or careful hoeing between the plants.

In late autumn, when most of the plants have finished flowering, the leaves and stems can be cut back and the crowns of the more tender plants covered with a mulch of compost or leaf mould to protect them from winter frost. Some gardeners prefer to leave stems standing as a protection, but this tends to look untidy and is really only an option in larger gardens where the border is not always in view.

With thoughtful planning, and by planting a selection of early, mid-season and late-flowering plants—including perhaps a few small shrubs and bulbous plants—it is possible for the gardener to have a border displaying colour from late February to November.

KEY TO THE PLAN
1 *Bergenia cordifolia purpurea*
2 *Cimicifuga racemosa*
3 *Lilium henryi* (Lily)
4 *Acanthus mollis*
5 *Aconitum napellus* 'Bressingham Spire'
6 *Delphinum* Pacific Hybrids
7 *Digitalis* (Foxglove)
8 *Achillea filipendula* 'Gold Plate'
9 *Paeonia* (Peony)
10 *Leucanthemum superbum* 'Snow Cap' (Shasta daisy)
11 Dahlias

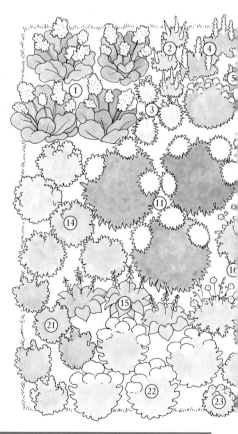

12 *Helenium* 'Copper Spray'
13 *Helleborus orientalis* Hybrids
14 *Euphorbia polychroma*
15 *Hosta* 'Krossa Regal'
16 *Geranium phaeum*
17 *Doronicum plantagineum* 'Harpur Crewe'
18 *Gladiolius* Butterfly varieties
19 *Phlox paniculata* 'Bright Eyes'
20 *Ceratostigma plumbaginoides*
21 *Omphalodes cappadocica*
22 *Sedum spectabile* 'Autumn Joy'
23 *Geranium clarkei* 'Kashmir White'
24 *Lavandula nana alba* (White lavender)

25 *Aster nova belgii* 'Little Pink Beauty'
26 *Hosta sieboldiana elegans*
27 *Geranium himalayense* 'Plenum'
28 *Calamintha nepetoides*
29 *Alyssum saxatile compactum.*

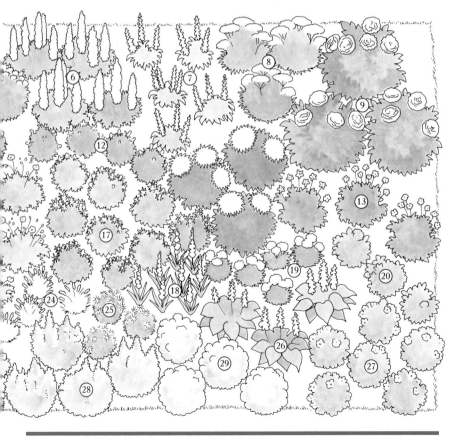

See also: Lifting and overwintering Pages 172–173
Plant lists Pages 210–219

These perennials make a grand display in the garden in midsummer. Many of the taller plants need staking. Dead foliage should be cut down in autumn or late winter and the crowns protected from frost. To maintain vigorous growth, divide clumps every three years or so. With this care and regular feeding, these plants will give a pleasing show for many years.

1 *Astrantia major* **'Rosea'**
(Masterwort)
This species is less showy than the hybrids, yet still pleasing. Good cut flower. Any moisture-retentive soil; prefers partial shade.
Height 24in/60cm.

2 *Delphinium* **'Black Knight'**
These splendid giants need space and staking, sun, shelter and fertile soil. Cut back flowered stems to induce a second, autumn blooming. Height 3-4ft/1–1.2m.

3 *Leucanthemum* x *superbum*
(Shasta daisy)
Good cut flower. Mulch in spring, cut stems down in autumn. Prefers sun and well-drained soil.
Height 24–36in/60–90cm.

4 *Meconopsis grandis*
(Himalayan blue poppy)
Striking coloured flowers. Short-lived, often only biennial. Some acidity in the soil is important.
Height 3ft/1m.

5 *Geranium sanguineum striatum*
(Cranesbill)
Good ground cover and weed-suppressor. Cut back stems in autumn. Needs well-drained soil in sun or partial shade.
Height 12in/30cm.

9 *Astilbe* **'Bressingham Beauty'**
Early foliage is an unusual
coppery colour; copious plumes
of flowers. Prefers rich, moist
soil in light shade.
Height 24–36in/60–90cm.

8 *Lavatera* **'Barnsley'**
(Tree mallow)
Glossy-petalled blooms on
tall stems. Needs staking.
Well-drained soil in a sunny
and protected position.
Height 6ft/2m.

7 *Achillea filipendulina* **'Gold
Plate'**
Delicate, fern-like, pungent
foliage; flowers good cut or
dried. May need staking. Any
reasonable soil in full sun.
Height 4ft/1.2m.

6 *Lupinus* **'Russell hybrids'**
Quick-growing and
popular perennials. Will
grow in sun or partial
shade. Height 3–4ft/1–1.2m.

ORNAMENTAL GRASSES

These extremely useful garden plants, with graceful forms and delicate colours, can mask an awkward space or serve as a focal point, and hard surfaces such as a path can be softened by the arching stems of an ornamental grass.

The tall pampas grass, *Cortaderia selloana*, can form a dramatic focal point in a large garden; it tends to overwhelm a small space. Dwarf bamboo, *Arundinaria variegata* (now known as *Pleioblastus variegatus*), with its sharp green and white foliage, will provide a focus on a smaller site.

The drooping elegance of *Stipa gigantea* or *Briza maxima* (Giant quaking grass) makes a delicate contrast to other foliage. *Pennisetum orientale* and *Hordeum jubatum* (Foxtail barley) have beautiful, soft-textured heads, while *Festuca glauca* (Blue fescue) creates a charming hazy-blue mound.

Most ornamental grasses need well-drained soil, full sun and minimal attention. Clump-forming grasses for damp or bog conditions include *Carex elata* 'Aurea' (Bowles' golden sedge) and *Glyceria maxima* 'Variegata'. Cut down perennials at the beginning of winter; protect the roots of *Pennisetum orientale*, or treat as an annual.

Perennial grasses are usually propagated by division. It is the female form of pampas grass that bears the long silky heads loved by gardeners, so make sure that this is the one that is divided.

Ornamental grasses can be used in dried flower arrangements; Pampas grass, Bamboo, *Coix lachryma-jobi* (Job's tears), *Briza maxima* and *Agrostis nebulosa* are all satisfactory for this purpose.

Briza maxima: bright green foliage with pearly, purple-brown spikelets. Height 20in/50cm.

Cortaderia selloana (Pampas grass): long grey-green leaves, spikes of silvery plumes. Height 9ft/2.7m.

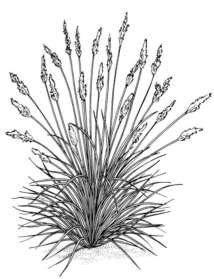

COLOUR SCHEMES

The garden designer Gertrude Jekyll favoured *Elymus arenarius* for its waving grey foliage, but it grows too large for a small garden. *Helictotrichon sempervirens*, with intensely blue-grey leaves, is a better choice. Many grasses and bamboos have green and white leaves; in some, such as *Pleioblastus viridistriatus*, the leaves are yellowish or streaked with yellow. *P. viridistriatus* has, as an added bonus, purple stems. One of the showiest golden-leaved grasses, *Hakonechloa macra* 'Aureola', slowly increases in moisture-retentive soil to form stunning ground cover.

Pleioblastus variegatus (Bamboo): mid-green leaves striped with white. Height 30in/75cm.

Pennisetum orientale: soft greyish leaves, purple-green flowers. Height 24in/60cm.

Festuca glauca: a dainty grass with bluish leaves. Height 10in/25cm.

See also: Propagation by division Pages 22–23
Drying flowers Pages 172–173

Despite the impressive height many perennials attain, do not be tempted to make specimen plants of them. They look better grouped in clumps, which helps them support each other and to obscure the staking most of these plants require. Plant low-growing perennials or annuals at their feet, and provide a green backdrop of a hedge or shrubs to show them off to best advantage.

1 *Thalictrum dipterocarpum* **'Hewitt's Double'** (Meadow rue)
Tall but delicate looking, needs shelter and good soil; place at the back of the border and stake. Height 4ft/1.2m.

2 *Ligularia przewalskii*
Tall spikes of flowers and spreading foliage. Needs moist soil, so mulch in spring and plant in partial shade. Height 5ft/1.5m.

3 *Anemone* x *hybrida* **'Queen Charlotte'** (Japanese anemone)
Popular semi-double variety, flowering late in the season. Forms large clumps in good soil. Plant in sun or partial shade. Height 24in/60cm.

4 *Helenium* **'Golden Youth'** (Sneezewort)
Bright flowers late in the season. Mulch in spring and keep well watered. Staking may be needed. Height 36in/90cm.

5 *Aster* x *frikartii* **'Monch'** (Michaelmas daisy)
The best lavender-blue variety, flowering late summer–autumn. Mulch in late spring, stake the stems and divide every second year. Height 30in/75cm.

6 *Phlox paniculata* **'Eva Cullum'**
Plant in sun or partial shade, mulch in spring and water well as this variety does not like to dry out. Staking needed; cut down after flowering. Wide range of colour in *paniculata* varieties. Height 2–4ft/60cm–1.2m.

7 *Kniphofia* **'Royal Standard'** (Red-hot poker)
Bold spikes late in season; plant in a sunny spot, mulch and water well. Tie up leaves in autumn and protect in cold winter weather. Yellow and white varieties are also available. Height 3–4ft/1–1.2m.

12 *Verbascum olympicum*
(Mullein)
Short-lived perennial with
imposing spikes of yellow
flowers in mid-season,
growing from rosette of felted
grey leaves. Well-drained soil
in full sun. Height 6ft/2m.

8 *Alchemilla mollis*
(Lady's mantle)
Fluffy sprays of flowers over
lovely scalloped foliage in
mid-season. Cut stems back in
autumn. Height 30in/75cm.

9 *Hosta* 'Francie'
(Plantain lily)
Large leaves, bordered with
white; flowers borne on
spikes in mid-season. Plant
in partial shade in any
reasonable garden soil.
Height 18–36in/45–90cm.

**10 *Rudbeckia fulgida*
'Goldsturm'**
(Coneflower)
Hardy, late-flowering, good
cut flower. Plant in sun in any
reasonable soil. Cut back in
autumn. Height 30in/75cm.

11 *Acanthus mollis*
(Bear's breeches)
Large, arching, deeply cut leaves
and long spikes of small purple
and white flowers. Needs plenty
of space, well-drained soil in sun
or partial shade. Height 4ft/1.2m

LIFTING AND OVERWINTERING

Even in the coldest areas some perennial plants are hardy enough to withstand the rigours of winter, but many others cannot survive outdoors. A gardening encyclopedia will tell you whether plants are hardy, and the label on a plant bought from a good nursery will often indicate its status locally. In some ways this will be the more useful information because hardiness is influenced by many factors and the same plant may not be hardy everywhere it is grown.

For instance, some plants that are hardy in North America are not considered so in parts of Britain, where lack of an insulating snow cover and wetter climate (especially in winter), cooler summer temperatures (resulting in less well-ripened growth) and frequency of late spring frosts combine to decrease the hardiness of particular species in comparable climate zones.

Half hardy plants are those that will survive only during the summer in cold areas; they need to be lifted and taken care of during the winter. This means simply that they must not be left in frosty ground; an unheated greenhouse, a cold frame or a dark airy attic or garage, will provide them with adequate protection.

Plants that should be lifted at the end of autumn, potted up and stored indoors include pelargoniums, tuberous begonias and some fuchsias. Chrysanthemums, too, should be dug up, the rootstocks, or stools, trimmed and packed in a compost-filled box for storage. Some bulbous plants, such as gladioli and dahlias, should also be lifted; many people lift lily bulbs, but most will survive in the ground if the crowns are covered with leaf mould or straw.

DRIED FLOWERS

• The simplest method of drying flowers is to cut them just before they are in full bloom. Trim off superfluous foliage, tie stems in loose bunches, then hang the bunches upside down in a warm, dry, dark place such as an airing cupboard. Plants suited to this method are: *Achillea filipendulina* (Yarrow); *Alchemilla mollis* (Lady's mantle); *Anaphalis margaritacea* (Pearly everlasting); *Artemisia*; *Astilbe*; *Cortaderia* (Pampas grass); *Eryngium maritimum* (Sea holly); *Gypsophila paniculata*; *Hydrangea* spp.; *Helichrysum brachteatum*; *Helipterum*; *Lavandula* (Lavender); *Limonium latifolia* (Statice); *Nigella damascena* (Love-in-a-mist).

• Other plants can be dried using silica gel or a drying agent made by mixing white cornflour and borax in a ratio of 10:3; this can be used repeatedly if it is kept dry. Place the flowers upside down in a box and cover the heads with the mix; keep the stems upright and exposed. The silica gel is simply placed in a closed box with the flower stems. Dry the following in this way: *Althaea* (Hollyhock); *Camellia japonica*; *Delphinium* spp.; *Salvia farinacea* and *S. viridis*, *Tagetes* (Erecta hybrids).

• The seed pods of some plants are as attractive as the flowers: *Lunaria annua* (Honesty); *Paeonia* (Peony); *Papaver orientale* (Oriental poppy); *Physalis alkekengi* (Chinese lantern).

Before planting tall varieties, drive a bamboo stake 12in/30cm into the ground and, as the plant grows, tie it loosely to the stake.

In spring, the outer portions of overwintered chrysanthemum stools will grow new roots and leaves, which can be potted up to form new plants.

Alternatively, take 2–3in/5–8cm cuttings from the new growths and set them in shallow compost at 50–60°F/10–15°C; when they have rooted, transfer them to small pots.

Plant out the new plants in early summer in a hole just bigger than the root ball.

See also: Mulching and watering Pages 34–35
Protecting plants Pages 54–55

EARLY-FLOWERING BULBS

The first tremulous and welcome signs of spring are found in the delicate-looking early bulbs. Snowdrops and winter aconites, the first to show—often when there is still snow on the ground—are followed by early crocus and daffodils. These bulbs should be planted in autumn in places that catch the sun in spring, although most will tolerate light shade.

1 *Tulipa* 'Elizabeth Arden'
Single early tulip with large, smooth-petalled, cup-shaped flowers, opening wide. Bulb. Height 8–12in/20–30cm.

2 *Narcissus* 'February Gold'
(Daffodil)
An old favourite with a large trumpet and good scent. Easy to grow and good for naturalizing in grass under trees. Bulb. Height 10–12in/25–30cm.

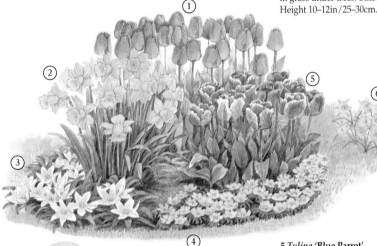

3 *Tulipa tarda*
Hardy species tulip, glossy green leaves with 4–6 flowers to a stem. Grows well in rock gardens, raised beds and pots. Bulb. Height 6in/15cm.

4 *Eranthis hyemalis*
(Winter aconite)
Cup-shaped flowers surrounded by ruffs of bracts in very early spring. Plant in groups in partial shade and rich, well-drained soil. Tuber. Height 2–4in/5–10cm.

5 *Tulipa* 'Blue Parrot'
Large single flowers with frilled, irregular petals in late spring. Bulb. Height 24in/60cm.

6 *Narcissus bulbocodium conspicuus*
(Hoop petticoat daffodil)
Very early; golden-yellow, widely flaring trumpet; looks best naturalized in low grass, preferably on sandy loam. Bulb. Height 3–6in/8–15cm.

13 *Hyacinthoides non-scriptus*
(syn. *Endymion, Scilla*) (Bluebell)
Despite the common name, comes
also in white and pink. Easy to
grow in borders or grass in soil
rich with leaf mould and shaded
in summer; forms clumps. Bulb.
Height 12in/30cm.

12 *Crocus vernus* **'Pickwick'**
Hardy, large-flowered Dutch
hybrid with striped leaves,
suitable also for planting in
grass and in pots indoors.
Corm. Height 5in/13cm.

11 *Narcissus* **'Barrett Browning'**
(Narcissus)
Small-cupped flower, with a
frilled, bright orange-red
trumpet set off by white petals.
Bulb. Height 12–18in/30–45cm.

7 *Narcissus* **'Liberty Bells'**
(Daffodil)
Drooping lemon-yellow flowers with
straight-sided cups and narrow
reflex petals. Slightly scented. Bulb.
Height 12in/30cm.

9 *Hyacinthus orientalis*
'Delft Blue'
(Dutch hyacinth)
Long flowering, with a compact
habit and a dense head of
fragrant flowers. Clump
forming. Add well-rotted
compost to soil when planting.
Bulb. Height 6–10in/15–25cm.

8 *Crocus sieberi*
Hardy, scented species crocus, native
to Greece. Prefers a sunny, protected
position. Corm.
Height 3–6in/8–15cm.

10 *Galanthus* **'S. Arnott'**
(Snowdrop)
Taller than the species, but equally
hardy, sometimes blooming when
snow is on the ground. Bulb.
Height 10–16in/25–40cm.

BULBOUS PLANTS

Bulbs are a great asset in the garden because they can provide colour both very early and very late in the annual cycle. Winter aconites and snowdrops bring relief after the flowerless months of the winter, while autumn cyclamen and colchicums (Meadow saffron) make a last bright splash among the falling leaves and dying annuals.

The term "bulbs" is generally used to cover bulbous plants, comprising bulbs, corms, rhizomes and tubers as well as the true bulbs. But although all store food for the plant, they are botanically quite different.

• A bulb, such as tulip or narcissus, is a specialized shoot, in which the swollen leaves, or scales, are tightly folded over each other; the stem bearing the leaves is reduced to a flat plate at the bottom of the bulb. Other bulbs, such as lilies, have loosely overlapping scales.

• A corm is a solid swollen stem with a bud at the top; crocus, anemone and gladiolus have corms.

• A rhizome is a fleshy stem that creeps horizontally beneath the earth; most irises and lily-of-the-valley have rhizomes.

• A root tuber is yet another type of storage organ, the best-known example of which is the dahlia.

Although bulbs are a delight to grow, since once planted they require little attention yet give a grand display, they can also be quite costly to buy. It is wise to determine which will do best in the soil in different situations in your garden so that you do not waste your money.

Planting bulbs

Most bulbs prefer a sunny site, sheltered from chilly winds, and well-drained,

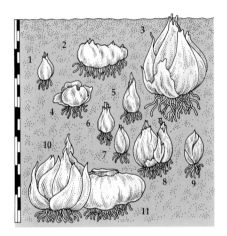

The chart gives the best planting depths for some common types of bulb; the scale shows inches on the left, centimetres on the right. **1** *Puschkinia*; **2** *Cyclamen persicum*; **3** *Lilium candidum*; **4** *Acidanthera bicolor*; **5** *Scilla siberica*; **6** *Galanthus nivalis*; **7** *Iris reticulata*; **8** *Narcissus* 'Trevithian'; **9** *Muscari*; **10** *Lilium auratum*; **11** *Fritillaria imperialis*

LATE-WINTER BULBS

Anemone blanda: star-shaped blue flowers, forming a low carpet.
Chionodoxa luciliae: gentian blue sprays.
Crocus: various, best in groups.
Cyclamen coum: miniature pink or white flowers.
Galanthus (Common snowdrop): many good single or double forms.
Iris histrioides, I. reticulata: blue/purple flowers, best in groups.
Leucojum vernum (Spring snow-flake): graceful white bells.
Narcissus 'Cedric Morris': dwarf daffodil, flower mid- to late winter.

BULBOUS PLANTS

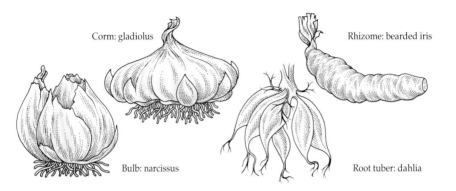

Corm: gladiolus

Rhizome: bearded iris

Bulb: narcissus

Root tuber: dahlia

Daughter bulbs and corms develop from small buds that form at the base of the parent; these should be carefully removed if bulbs or corms are lifted in winter. Root tubers bear buds only at the top of the plant; rhizomes increase by producing underground runners.

loamy soil. The hardy bulbs need adequate moisture during winter and spring, but if there is too much, they will be vulnerable to rot.

If conditions in your garden are not ideal; it is not too difficult to improve the soil.

• Poor soil should have well-rotted manure or compost dug into it, but never fresh animal manure. A special bulb fertilizer can also be added.

• Heavy soil can be lightened with well-rotted manure or compost and the addition of coarse sand or grit. Sand should be packed beneath those bulbs, such as lilies and fritillaries, which are most susceptible to rotting.

• Just before planting, dust sufficient bone meal over the site to whiten the surface of the soil and then fork it in to provide nourishment for the bulbs.

If you are planting a lot of bulbs—in grass for example—a bulb planter is a useful useful tool that can be thrust into the earth to the required depth to remove a plug of turf.

Make sure that the bottom of the bulb sits flat on the earth at the bottom of the hole, and when the bulb has been planted, neatly replace the grass above it. Or use a trowel and check the depth of the hole with a measuring stick.

As a general rule, early-flowering bulbs should be planted in autumn, and mid-season and autumn-flowering bulbs in spring. But follow the nurseryman's or grower's instructions.

Most stocks of bulbs will increase without much attention, but bulbs left in the ground over winter will benefit from a top dressing of bone meal. After three to five years, clumps of most bulbs can be divided when the leaves have died back.

See also: Lifting and overwintering 172–173
Late-flowering bulbs Pages 184–185

MID-SEASON BULBS

High summer brings a display of noble bulbous plants to the garden—the Tall Bearded Irises and grand lilies—as well as the demure arum and bold tropical-looking crocosmia. Most of these plants like moisture-retentive, well-drained soil and sunshine and most are hardy. Left in the ground, after three or four years they will form clumps which can be divided to give new plants.

1 *Iris* **'Headlines',** *left;* **'Peach Frost',** *right.* There are dozens of varieties of Tall Bearded Iris. Stems bear single, often multicoloured flowers with lustrous petals, the falls heavily "bearded" with coloured hairs. Plant in well-drained soil in full sun. Rhizome. Height 30in–5ft/75cm–1.5m.

2 *Agapanthus* **Headbourne Hybrids** Hardier than the species; likes a sunny spot in well-drained soil; protect crowns in winter. Good cut flowers; seed heads can be dried. Fleshy roots. Height 24–40in/60–100cm.

3 *Allium ostrowskianum* This small plant carries its flowers in many-flowered, domed umbels. A good rock-garden plant. Bulb. Height 2–4in/5–10cm.

9 *Lilium candidum*
(Madonna lily)
An old-fashioned favourite;
hardy, with pale green leaves
and up to 20 glistening,
fragrant flowers to a stem.
Prefers soil rich in lime; plant
just below the surface. Bulb.
Height 3–6ft/1–2m

8 *Lilium regale*
(Regal lily)
Hardy, stem-rooting species;
produces many large, strongly
scented trumpet-shaped flowers
in loose clusters. Plant in full
sun in any reasonable soil.
Bulb. Height 4–6ft/1.2–2m.

7 *Crocosmia* **'Canary Bird'**
Stems of brightly coloured
flowers grow from clumps of
stiff, sword-shaped leaves;
good cut flowers. Needs well-
drained soil and sun. In cold
areas, lift in winter. Corm.
Height 36in/90cm.

4 *Arum italicum* **'Pictum'**
(Lords and ladies)
Ornamental leaves in spring
enclose an insignificant flower
spathe which produces bright red
berries in autumn. Needs a rich,
moist soil. Tuber. Height
6–10in/15–25cm.

5 *Fritillaria meleagris*
(Snake's head)
Bell-shaped flowers 1½in/4cm
long, chequered in white or
shades of purple-pink. Needs full
sun and moist conditions;
naturalizes well in grass. Bulb.
Height 12–18in/30–45cm.

6 *Leucojum aestivum*
(Summer snowflake)
White, bell-shaped flowers,
with green-tipped petals,
borne on graceful stems in
May. Likes moist soil and
tolerates partial shade. Bulb.
Height 18in/45cm.

MID-SEASON BULBS

Spring bulbs are often delicate in colour and appearance, but there are some wonderfully dramatic plants among the mid-season bulbous plants. *Agapanthus* give a grand display; and tall bearded irises, with their rich colours and ornate flower heads, enhance the border in early summer, as do the immaculate white spathes and large leaves of *Zantedeschia aethiopica*, the so-called arum lily.

The true lilies are some of the most beautiful of mid-season bulbs. Although initally expensive, once established, lilies can be easily be propagated by dividing clumps, by planting scales taken from mature bulbs and by removing and planting up the bulbils (tiny bulbs) that form on the stems of some species. They can also be grown from seed; this requires patience, however, since with some species there can be a five-year wait between sowing the seeds and flowering.

Lilies are eminently suited to container cultivation, for, planted in this way, they can be given pride of place on a patio or terrace, where their perfect flowers and perfume can be fully appreciated. Tulips, too, are rewarding plants to grow in pots and tubs, and it is easy, when they have flowered, to lift the bulbs for storage during the summer. If it is more convenient, many varieties, particularly the species tulips, can be left in the ground.

The vast choice of tulips can bewilder and intimidate inexperienced gardeners; they are all classified into one of 15 divisions, depending on the type and on flowering time, and within the divisions there are many varieties and species. The tulips illustrated here reveal some of the different flower shapes available.

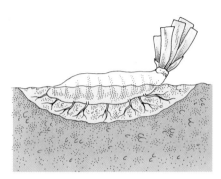

Before planting the bearded iris, cut back the leaves to 6in/15cm. Dig a shallow oblong hole, lay the rhizome in it and spread out the roots. Do not cover the top of the rhizome with soil, but press soil down around the roots, and bank it up when the roots become exposed.

Think carefully what colour, height and blooming time will suit your garden scheme before tackling the catalogues—it is easy to be carried away by the huge and tempting range of tulips they offer.

As with other bulbs, tulips will succeed in most garden soils which are reasonably moisture retentive but not waterlogged. When planting bulbs in containers, ensure effective drainage by putting broken crocks with a covering of spaghnum moss into the bottom of the pot.

Irises belong to another complex genus, some of which, including the Dutch, English and Spanish irises commonly found in gardens, are bulbs. The bearded iris and waterside irises, such as *I. ensata* (syn. *I. kaempferi*) and *I. laevigata*, have rhizomes and are propagated by division of the rhizome. In general, these irises are hardy and easily grown, but the different types must be given the right growing conditions and be planted correctly.

See also: Planting lilies Pages 20–21
Dividing plants Pages 22–23

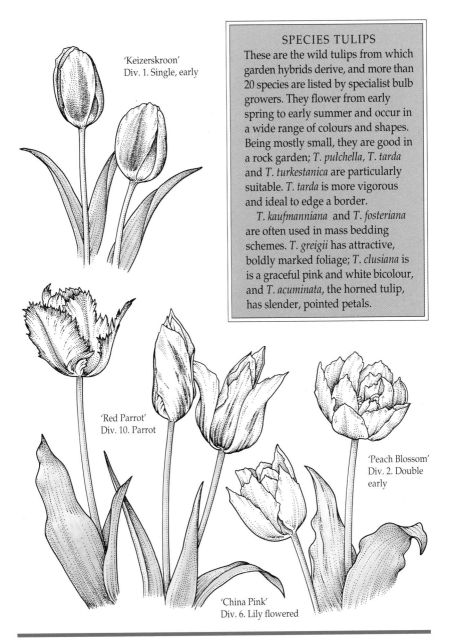

'Keizerskroon'
Div. 1. Single, early

SPECIES TULIPS

These are the wild tulips from which garden hybrids derive, and more than 20 species are listed by specialist bulb growers. They flower from early spring to early summer and occur in a wide range of colours and shapes. Being mostly small, they are good in a rock garden; *T. pulchella*, *T. tarda* and *T. turkestanica* are particularly suitable. *T. tarda* is more vigorous and ideal to edge a border.

T. kaufmanniana and *T. fosteriana* are often used in mass bedding schemes. *T. greigii* has attractive, boldly marked foliage; *T. clusiana* is is a graceful pink and white bicolour, and *T. acuminata*, the horned tulip, has slender, pointed petals.

'Red Parrot'
Div. 10. Parrot

'Peach Blossom'
Div. 2. Double
early

'China Pink'
Div. 6. Lily flowered

LATE-FLOWERING BULBS

With thoughtful planning, the garden can present an almost year-round colourful picture, to which, even in late summer and autumn, bulbs can make an important contribution. Once established, most of these late-flowering varieties look after themselves and increase readily. The true autumn-flowering species generally prefer a good summer baking, so are best planted at the foot of a warm, sunny wall; an exception is *Schizostylis*, which prefers plenty of moisture as well as sun.

1 *Lilium* **'Star Gazer'**
An excellent hybrid; flower is red with pale margins to the petals. Needs rich, moist, but free-draining, soil. Bulb. Height 4ft/1.2m.

3 *Iris unguicularis* (= *stylosa*) (Algerian iris)
Beardless iris forming a large clump of grass-like evergreen foliage; flowers from autumn through to early spring. Thrives in a dry, sunny, sheltered site; tolerates lime. Rhizome. Height 12in/30cm.

2 *Colchicum autumnale roseum plenum* (Autumn crocus, Meadow saffron)
Produces double, goblet-shaped flowers on stems some 6–8in/15–20cm long, followed by strap-shaped leaves in spring. Corm. Height of leaves 8–10in/20–25cm.

4 *Cyclamen hederifolium* (= *neapolitanum*)
Hardy, flowering from late summer to early winter; dark green leaves laced with silver follow the flowers and last until early the following summer. Will grow in shade. Tuber. Height 4–6in/10–15cm.

8 *Crinum x powellii*
Long, strap-shaped leaves form a
large untidy clump; loose bunches
of fragrant, funnel-shaped flowers
borne on tall stems well into the
autumn. Likes a sunny, protected
site and rich, well-drained soil.
Bulb. Height 18in/45cm.

9 *Lilium speciosum*
A Japanese turk's cap lily that
produces up to 12 richly scented
flowers. Prefers neutral or acid
humus-rich soil and a sheltered
site. Bulb. Height 4–6ft/1.2–2m.

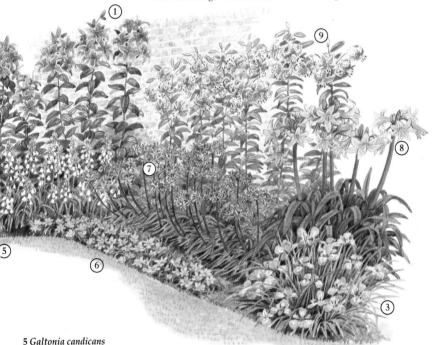

5 *Galtonia candicans*
(Summer hyacinth)
Clumps of grey-green strap-
shaped leaves and long flower
spikes with some 20 bell-shaped
blooms Needs moist, well-
drained soil and a sunny,
sheltered site. Bulb.
Height 3–4ft/1–1.2m.

6 *Sternbergia lutea*
Coming from the Middle East,
this crocus-like plant needs
well-drained soil, full sun and
plenty of summer heat to flower
well. Possibly the biblical "lily
of the field". Bulb.
Height 6in/15cm.

7 *Nerine bowdenii*
Hardy except in severe winter
conditions, but needs well-
drained soil and a hot, dry spell
to encourage production of its
showy flowers, which grow in
an umbel on a leafless stem.
Bulb. Height 18–24in/45–60cm.

LATE-FLOWERING BULBS

As summer drifts into autumn, and autumn turns to winter, the garden begins to lose much of its vitality; but it is now that the late bulbous plants come into their own, bringing colour and life to the fading beds and borders.

If a range of these bulbs is planted in late spring, there can be something in flower from late summer right through to December. *Gladiolus* hybrids produce their tall, colourful spikes of blooms late in the season, complementing lilies such as *Lilium speciosum* and *L. henryi*, which also flower late. (Such heavy-headed lilies may need staking to prevent their stems being snapped by strong autumn winds.)

The decorative, but dainty, *Cyclamen coum* shows its pink, white and red flowers in mid-winter, *C. hederifolium* in autumn. The sweet-scented, but frost-tender, *Freesia* and the common snowdrop, *Galanthus nivalis*, both bloom from late winter into early spring, as do *Eranthis hyemalis* (Winter aconite) and *Iris reticulata* (Dwarf iris).

> ### MAIL-ORDER BULBS
> Buying bulbs through mail order has several advantages. Gardeners need not be hurried into making a choice and unusual bulbs can be acquired from specialist growers, many of whom publish useful, informative catalogues.
>
> Place orders so that the bulbs arrive in good time for planting. Check them for signs of desiccation, damage or disease, particularly rot. Reputable nurseries will usually accept returns of substandard bulbs if a complaint is made soon after receipt.

But while some of the bulbous plants actually flourish during the coldest months, and few need to be lifted during the winter, others must be protected from the worst of the weather. In severe cold, *Nerine* and *Schizostylis* are best covered with a good layer of straw or bracken, and

Lift dahlia tubers with a fork when the foliage dies back. Trim the stems down to about 6in/15cm and

turn the tubers upside down to dry, then wrap each plant in several sheets of newspaper.

half hardy *Gladiolus* hybrids should be lifted before the first frosts, when the leaves begin to turn brown.

It is better to use a fork to lift the plants, and care should be taken not to damage the corms. Cut back the stems to about ½in/1cm above the corms and clean off any earth sticking to them. Put them in an airy place, such as a shed or garage, for 10 days or so, until they are quite dry; then look them over carefully.

Break off and throw away old, withered corms, take off the hard outer skin of large corms, and remove any small corms for future propagation, before storing them in a frost-free place.

Another plant that usually needs to be lifted in autumn is the tuberous-rooted border dahlia. As soon as the foliage has been blackened by the first frost, cut it down to about 6in/15cm and, using a fork, gently lift the tubers, taking care not to spear them. Store them in dry, frost-free conditions until late spring or early summer, when they can be replanted.

When the spring- and summer-flowering bulbs—daffodils and tulips, for example—have finished blooming, their dying foliage looks unsightly among the bedding and border plants and the temptation is to cut back their leaves for aesthetic reasons. It must be resisted, however, for the leaves fuel the bulbs' food reserves, enabling them to produce strong blooms in the following flowering season.

Where daffodils have been naturalized in grass, they need only be left for 6–8 weeks before the leaves can be cut off or mown. The bulbs themselves are hardy and can remain in the ground.

The leaves of hybrid tulips need to left longer and, if their appearance cannot be tolerated, it is better to dig up the bulbs and plant them elsewhere in the garden until the foliage has died back. The bulbs should then be lifted and kept in a shed or greenhouse until they are dry, when stems and leaves, roots and any clinging soil should be removed, ready for planting again in autumn.

Put each wrapped plant in a paper bag, leaving the top open. Stand the bags in a fairly deep box and

store them in a cool, dry, frost-free place such as a loft, shed or garage.

See also: Staking perennials Pages 50–51
Protecting plants Pages 54–55

Annuals and biennials—the mainstay of cheerful bedding displays—are one of the delights of summer. Their flowers, among the brightest sources of colour in the garden, are often produced with a vigour and abundance which belies their size. Most gardeners will want to grow some of these generous and versatile plants, many of which are fine for cutting.

1 *Tagetes erecta* **'Doubloon'**
Sturdy plants which do not need staking; excellent flowering all through summer. Like reasonable garden soil in full sun. Height 12–36in/30–90cm.

2 *Nicotiana* **'Lime Green'**
(Tobacco plant)
A newer variety, of sturdy growth and medium height. Bears unusual trumpet-shaped greenish, night-scented flowers all through summer. Plant in sun or shade in well-drained soil. Height 24in/60cm.

3 *Gazania* **'Splendens'**
A good border and rockery plant; suited to seaside gardens, but happy in a sunny spot in any reasonable soil. Flowers, ranging through cream to orange to salmon pink, close at night; silvery foliage. Height 15in/38cm.

4 *Gaillardia* **spp.**
Fairly hardy, short-lived perennial or annual of slightly untidy growth needing a sunny, well-drained site. Showy flowers bloom all summer. Excellent cut flower. Height 18in/45cm.

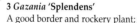

11 *Calendula officinalis*
(Pot marigold)
Bushy, fast-growing plant,
easy enough for a child to
grow. Pale green leaves and
cheerful single or double
flowers throughout the
season. Any well-drained
soil in sun or partial shade.
Height 12–24in/30–60cm.

10 *Helianthus annuus* **'Autumn
Beauty'** (Sunflower)
Newer varieties of the giant sunflower
have a wide range of bronze and gold
shades and a more modest height
that suits beds and borders. Large,
coarse leaves and flowers late in the
season. Height 2–10ft/60cm–3m.

9 *Dimorphotheca calendulacea*
(African daisy)
Dark green, wavy-toothed leaves
and large, daisy-like flowers; good
in a dense display in a border or
container. Needs a sunny site, since
flowers do not open in shade or on
a dull day. Height 12in/30cm.

8 *Limnanthes douglasii*
(Poached egg flower)
Erect, fast-growing annual with
shiny, finely cut leaves and masses
of scented, cup-shaped flowers all
summer. Prefers full sun in any
reasonable soil. Height 6in/15cm.

7 *Lobularia maritima* **'Snow
Carpet'** (syn. *Alyssum maritimum*)
Fast-growing, carpeting annual,
with grey-green leaves and
rounded heads of tiny honey-
scented flowers all summer.
Likes sun and fertile well-
drained soil. Height 6in/15cm.

6 *Zinnia* **'Persian Carpet'**
Upright, bushy growth, with stiff
hairy leaves and small flat flower
heads in a range of jewel-like colours
in late summer. A small, front-of-the-
border variety, good for cut flowers.
Height 15in/38cm.

5 *Mesembryanthemum criniflorum*
(syn. *Dorotheanthus bellidiformis*)
(Livingstone daisy)
Succulent of low, spreading habit,
with almost cylindrical, glistening
leaves and daisy-like flowers that
only open in the sun Prefers poor,
dry soil and must have full sun; good
for hot, dry spots. Height 6in/15cm.

187

BEDDING SCHEMES FOR ANNUALS

Annuals provide ample opportunity for the gardener to experiment with colour schemes, happy in the knowledge that the arrangements are not permanent and can be changed from year to year. But do not let yourself be so carried away by the fun of planning bedding schemes that you forget the needs of the plants. Consider which varieties will succeed best in rich soil or partial shade, for instance, and think, too, of flowering periods, so there will be a continuous display of colour.

Hardy annuals, such as *Eschscholzia californica* (Californian poppy), *Calendula officinalis* (Pot marigold), *Godetia*, *Centaurea cyanus* (Cornflower), *Nigella* (Love-in-a-mist) and a host of others, can be sown *in situ* in late summer to bloom early the following season.

The half hardy annuals, such as *Petunia* and *Antirrhinum*, must be sown in spring in seed trays, raised under protection, pricked out and hardened off before they are planted in the garden bed. They are, therefore, considerably later in blooming.

A number of tender perennial plants, such as *Fuchsia* and *Pelargonium*, have long been used in bedding schemes, but gardeners should look out for exciting new varieties. *Argyranthemum* (Marguerite daisy bush), *Canna*, *Osteospermum* and *Diascia*, grown as annuals or overwintered as plants or cuttings, can provide a novel variety of flower shapes and colours.

The introduction of biodegradable pots, in which seedlings can be grown and then planted directly in the bed, is advantageous for the well-being of the plants and for ease of planting. When planting out annuals, do not crowd them, but give them room to spread as they grow.

KEY TO PLANTING PLAN FOR INFORMAL BED

Informal planting in shades of yellow, orange, bright rose pink, deep and mid blue and white for a bed in full sun.

1 *Iberis* (Candytuft)
2 *Nicotiana* 'Sensation'
3 *Calendula officinalis* (Pot marigold)
4 *Lychnis coronaria*
5 *Petunia* 'Recoverer' Series (white)
6 *Centaurea cyanus* (Cornflower)
7 *Myosotis* (Forget-me-not)
8 *Reseda* (Mignonette)

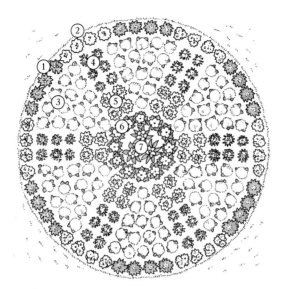

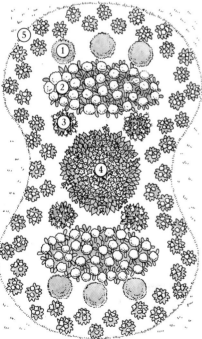

KEY TO PLAN FOR FORMAL CIRCULAR BED
This bed in shades of white, pink and blue is
also designed for full sun.
1 *Tanacetum parthenium* 'Aureum' (Golden
feverfew), groups of four, alternating with
2 *Echeveria* (succulent foliage), groups of four
3 *Ageratum* 'Blue Mink', wedge-shaped blocks
4 *Lobelia erinus* 'Crystal Palace Compacta',
three rows
5 *Begonia semperflorens* (pink), two rows
6 *Lavatera trimestris* 'Mont Blanc'
7 *Canna* x *generalis* (white)

KEY TO PLAN FOR FORMAL FIGURE-OF-
EIGHT-SHAPED BED
A bed in white, yellow and blue for light shade.
1 *Kochia scoparia* f *trichophylla*
2 *Tagetes erecta* x *T. patula* 'Legal Gold' (Afro-
French marigold, F_1 hybrid, yellow)
3 *Fuchsia* 'Ting-a-ling' or 'White Spider'
4 *Campanula pyramidalis* (blue)
5 *Impatiens* 'Tom Thumb' (white)

See also: Propagation from seed Pages 14–15
Pricking out, hardening off Pages 16–17

189

When planning displays of summer colour, it is worth remembering that a carefully chosen annual or biennial, planted in small groups of the same colour, can make an effective addition to the mixed border or to large containers such as windowboxes. The popular annual varieties shown here are the mainstay of traditional summer colour displays. Easily grown in sunny spots, they provide tremendous value as bedding plants or, in many instances, as cut flowers.

2 *Nigella damascena* **'Miss Jekyll'**
(Love-in-a-mist)
Upright, fast-growing, with feathery leaves and large blue or white flowers good for cutting; seed pods may be dried. Likes fertile, well-drained soil and sun. Height 24in/60cm.

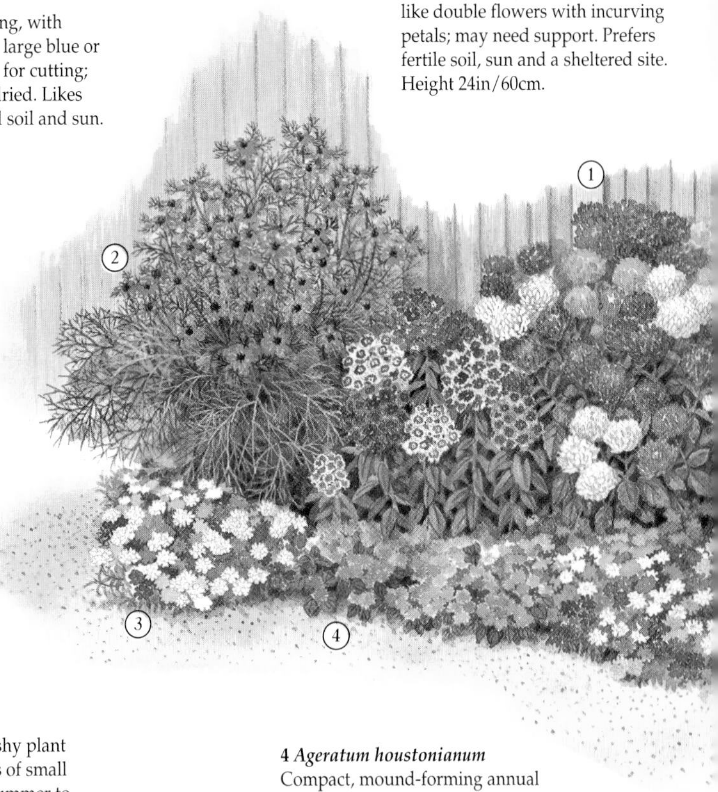

1 *Callistephus chinensis*
'Duchesse' (China aster)
Compact, ideal for formal bedding schemes. Heavy, chrysanthemum-like double flowers with incurving petals; may need support. Prefers fertile soil, sun and a sheltered site. Height 24in/60cm.

3 *Iberis umbellata*
(Candytuft)
Quick-growing bushy plant with copious heads of small flowers from midsummer to early autumn. Best planted in groups in ordinary well-drained soil. Tolerant of urban pollution. Height 6–12in/15–30cm.

4 *Ageratum houstonianum*
Compact, mound-forming annual with powder-puff flower heads from early summer to autumn. Good edging plant. Likes moist, well-drained soil and sun. Height 6–12in/15–30cm.

10 *Centaurea cyanus*
(Cornflower)
A good erect plant in bedding
schemes in any well-drained
soil. Sprays of blue and, more
recently, pink and white flowers
in mid-season, and pleasing
grey-green foliage; tall and
dwarf varieties available.
Height 12–36in/30–90cm.

9 *Clarkia elegans*
Flowers borne from mid-summer.
Grow in clumps in a sunny spot and
support upright stems with twigs.
Height 24in/60cm.

8 *Dianthus barbatus*
(Sweet william)
Short-lived perennial grown as a
hardy biennial. Flat heads of
densely packed, sweetly scented
flowers in midsummer. Grows in
well-drained soil in a sunny spot.
Height 12–24in/30–60cm.

7 *Salvia splendens*
Half hardy perennial grown as an
annual in any reasonable soil in
full sun. Scarlet tubular flowers
and bracts in midsummer; pinch
out tips of seedlings for best
effect. Height 9–15in/23–38cm.

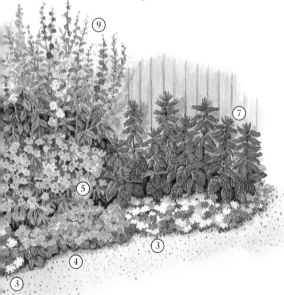

5 *Godetia grandiflora*
(now *Clarkia amoena*)
Hardy annual with bushy
growth and single or double
flowers in mid-season. Needs
sun and light, not over-rich
soil. Good border plants.
Height 12–15in/30–38cm.

6 *Lavatera trimestris*
'Silver Cup'
Hardy, fast-growing annual
with bushy habit. Large
glossy flowers in summer
and early autumn. Needs
well-drained soil and sun.
Height 24in/60cm.

SWEET PEAS

The cultivation of sweet peas (*Lathyrus odoratus*) may seem complicated when undertaken by the specialist grower, but by following a few simple rules most gardeners will have few problems in growing these lovely flowers. They are well worth the effort, for the mass of blooms, in attractive, toning colours and with an appealing fragrance, makes a grand display in the garden. They are also excellent cut flowers.

Choice of site is important. Sweet peas will not grow under trees or in the shade of buildings but need a sunny, airy spot in the garden. The plants should, however, be protected from excessive wind, so if your garden is exposed, it may be necessary to construct some kind of windbreak.

Planting sweet peas
• The soil should be rich in humus, well drained and well dug.
• Allow about 24in/60cm width for each row of plants, or a circle of the same diameter if you grow them in clumps.
• In autumn, prepare the site by digging in well-rotted farmyard manure to a depth of 18–24in/45–60cm; mix it in well.
• Add two big handfuls of bonemeal to every square yard/metre; mix it in well.

Sweet peas may be raised in several different ways. The seeds may be sown in pots in autumn and overwintered in a cold frame or cool greenhouse, or they may be sown directly into the ground in autumn or late spring. Other gardeners prefer to sow the seed in pots in early spring, giving them some protection.

Except in very cold areas, where spring sowing under protection is the best option, the most satisfactory method is to sow in pots in autumn.

In early autumn, sow seeds, two to a 3-in/8-cm pot, in a soil-based, not a peat-based compost. Water, cover with newspaper and put in a cold frame; protect if necessary with slug bait and a mousetrap.

OLD-FASHIONED BEDDING PLANTS
Try planting some of the old-fashioned annuals and bedding plants that are currently regaining their popularity through new or improved forms.
Clarkia, Princess strain
Consolida (Larkspur) Imperial strain
Dianthus barbatus (Sweet william)
Dianthus chinensis (Chinese pink)
Digitalis purpurea (Foxglove) pink shades.
Matthiola Brompton Series (Stock)
Nigella 'Persian Jewels' (Love-in-a-mist)
Papaver nudicaule (Iceland poppy)
Papaver rhoeas Shirley Series
Salvia horminum Art Shades Series
Schizanthus (Poor man's orchid)
Silene coeli-rosa

When the seedlings emerge, remove the newspaper and insert small stakes into the pot. To harden them off, open the cold frame in all but exceptionally cold and wet weather.

To encourage bushy growth, pinch out the top of each seedling when two or three pairs of leaves have formed. Plant out the seedlings in late spring, when weather and soil have warmed up.

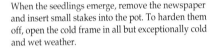

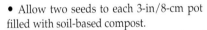

• Allow two seeds to each 3-in/8-cm pot filled with soil-based compost.
• To speed germination, nick seeds of hard-coated varieties with the point of a sharp knife on the side opposite the eye, or soak them in water for 12 hours.
• Push the seeds about ½in/1cm below the surface of the compost.
• Water, then cover the pots with newspaper and place them in a cold frame.
• When the seedlings emerge, remove the newspaper and leave the frame open in all but severely cold or wet weather.
• Pinch out the tops of seedlings when they have two or three pairs of leaves.
• Plant seedlings out in late spring, spacing them 8in/20cm apart.

Supporting the plants

The ordinary tall variety of sweet pea is a climber which needs support, so provide each plant with a cane or length of twine when growing them in rows, or a light framework of canes on either side of the row. If sweet peas are grown in clumps, provide them with a wigwam of canes or twiggy branches about 8ft/2.4m high. Plants must be tied to canes, but they will cling to twine or twigs with their leaf tendrils. To maintain vigorous growth:
• Do not allow the plants to dry out; watering and mulching with leaf mould when the first flower buds form will help.
• Cut flowers and dead-head regularly to prevent the plants setting seed; this will prolong the flowering season.

Breeders have now introduced miniature sweet peas, eliminating the problems of support. As their name, *Lathyrus odoratus* 'Dwarf Patio Mixed', suggests, they are a mere 12in/30cm high and can be used in pots and hanging baskets or to edge a border. Hybridization has extended the colour range to include bright red, but many gardeners still prefer the old-style, pastel shades and the challenge of growing sweet peas in the traditional way.

See also: Supporting plants Pages 48–49

ANNUALS FOR CONTAINERS

For the gardener with only a tiny site to cultivate, containers are a delightful way of extending planting space and by arranging containers of different sizes and shapes, additional interest and different perspectives can be introduced.

While most annuals bloom in the summer, if you plan ahead—bringing on some plants while others are already in bloom—and incorporate some biennials or "cool season" plants, such as polyanthus and pansies, in your planting schemes, it is possible to have a colourful display from early in the season until the first autumn frosts cut these plants back.

3 *Verbena* 'Peaches and Cream'
Perennial, grown as an annual; to promote bushy growth, pinch out leading shoots. This new and unusually coloured variety produces heads of small, sweet-scented flowers from midsummer to mid-autumn. Height 6–12in/15–30cm.

1 *Viola* x *wittrockiana* 'Ullswater'
(Pansy)
Hardy perennial usually grown as an annual or biennial. The richly coloured, velvety flowers which appear throughout summer make this an excellent container plant. Dead-head regularly to maintain flowering. Height 6–8in/15–20cm.

2 *Begonia semperflorens*
Bushy perennial, grown as an annual, with glossy green or bronze leaves and white, pink, red or white flowers. Light, moist, but well-drained soil in partial shade. Height 6–9in/15–23cm.

4 *Schizanthus*
(Butterfly flower, Poor man's orchid)
Upright, bushy annual with feathery green leaves and showy pink, purple and yellow flowers, some striped and spotted. Plant in a sheltered, sunny site and stake taller varieties with twigs. Height 12–18in/30–45cm.

5 *Petunia* x *hybrida* 'Resisto' Series
Bushy perennial usually grown as an annual. Showy trumpet-shaped flowers with spicy perfume from midsummer to the first frosts. Likes light, rich soil in a sheltered, sunny spot; needs regular dead-heading. Height 6–12in/15–30cm.

10 *Nemesia strumosa* 'Carnival' Series
Easily grown, bushy, half-hardy
annual. Lance-shaped, pale green
leaves and small, funnel-shaped
flowers in a wide range of colours
all summer. Fertile, well-drained
soil in sun or light shade. Plants
need to be pinched out when young
and trimmed after flowering.
Height 9in/23cm.

9 *Brachycome iberidifolia*
(Swan River daisy)
Half hardy annual. Masses of daisy-
like flowers and fine, ferny foliage
from midsummer to early autumn.
Happy in good garden soil in a sunny
sheltered site. Ideal for container
growing. Height 15–18in/38–45cm.

8 *Cheiranthus chieri*
(Wallflower)
Hardy perennial grown as a biennial
for its brightly coloured, scented
flowers borne in dense spikes from
late spring to midsummer. Plant in
autumn in a sunny spot with lime in
the soil. Excellent for windowboxes
and tubs. Height 8–24in/20–60cm.

7 *Lobelia erinus* 'Crystal Palace'
Half hardy perennial with sprawling
habit, grown as an annual. Small
bronze leaves and dark blue flowers
throughout summer make it an
excellent filler in hanging baskets
and pots. Likes rich, moist soil in sun
or partial shade. Height 4–9in/10–23cm.

**6 *Impatiens balsamina* 'Tom Thumb'
Series** (Busy lizzie)
Compact, bushy perennial grown
as an annual. Original species used
to be an indoor plant, but new F_1
hybrids can be planted outdoors.
Masses of bright spurred flowers
produced from spring to autumn.
Height 8–12in/20–30cm.

GROWING ANNUALS IN CONTAINERS

Although it is tempting to buy colourful annuals for use in containers ready grown, even in flower, this is an expensive way to garden and there is considerable satisfaction in producing your own choice of seedlings and seeing them flourish.

Drainage is the first consideration when growing annuals in containers; all need a layer of drainage material at the bottom.

• Large pots need fine gravel, expanded clay or pebbles.

• In small pots, use a layer of crocks or a filter sheet, obtainable from garden centres.

• Lay a filter sheet over drainage material in large pots to stop compost seeping out.

The best general-purpose potting compost is John Innes No 2 with some peat or fine humus added to it, rather than purely peat-based compost which can quickly become either very dry or waterlogged.

The display of annuals in containers must be planned so that there is a continuous show of colour and foliage. A half-functioning tub or pot, with a few blooms surrounded by dull foliage or empty spaces is a depressing sight.

In a windowbox, avoid plants that will grow too tall, blocking the light and the outlook. Choose flowers that vary but complement each other in colour, growth habit and flower shape: the small flowers of nemesia will stand a little above the larger, softer petals of petunia; the opulent heads of tuberous begonia can be offset by an under-sprinkling of low-growing blue lobelia. Set a trailing geranium or verbena to spill its blooms over the edge of a pot.

Plants in containers, especially those in hanging baskets, must be watered at least daily in warm weather, and because this

By using evergreens, perennials and some bulbs, it is possible to have a decorative windowbox all through the winter. Dwarf conifers and trailing ivy provide foliage interest, while winter pansies and early crocus give colour. The arangement is enlivened in early spring by *Pulsatilla vulgaris*, (Pasque flower), with its purple, or reddish flowers, which are succeeded by feathery seed heads.

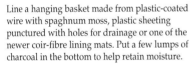

Line a hanging basket made from plastic-coated wire with spaghnum moss, plastic sheeting punctured with holes for drainage or one of the newer coir-fibre lining mats. Put a few lumps of charcoal in the bottom to help retain moisture.

Half-fill the basket with potting compost and insert some trailing plants through the sides. Top up with compost, finish planting and water well. Keep the basket in a sheltered spot until the plants have settled down.

leaches the nutrients out of the soil, they should be given a liquid feed at least once a week.

Hanging baskets, already planted up, are available from most nurseries, but they can be costly, and it is not difficult to set up your own. Ensure that the bracket from which you hang the basket is sturdy, since baskets become very heavy when they are filled with plants and wet compost.

A hanging basket should contain a selection of plants that will flower all through summer, without the need to remove any or to add more. Alyssum, lobelia, dwarf petunia and verbena fulfill these conditions and are available in colours that complement each other. *Bidens*

ferruginea and *Helichrysum petiolatum* will provide a non-stop cascade of flowers and foliage respectively, and small climbing plants such as *Manettia bicolor* can be used to twine around the chains of the basket.

Annuals are the mainstay of containers for summer colour, but perennials such as pelargonium and fuchsia will give height, substance and variety of foliage to the planting. Variegated *Glechoma* and ivies and, in warmer areas, *Ficus pumila* (Creeping fig), with bright green leaves, which can be trained up the chains of a basket, will also provide foliage interest.

Containers planted up with evergreens, winter pansies and early-flowering bulbs will give colour and interest in the winter.

See also: Annual climbers Pages 156–157

POND PLANTS AND MARGINALS

Even in the smaller garden, a pond appropriately sited and attractively planted with a colourful and varied range of aquatic and marginal plants can make an appealing focal point. Modern developments in plastics have made ponds easier and cheaper to install. And the wildlife that lives in water or is attracted by it adds liveliness and interest to the garden.

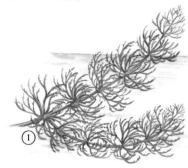

1 *Ceratophyllum demersum*
(Hornwort)
Submerged water plant with masses of horny leaves; excellent oxygenator suited to cool water ponds. Prefers an open sunny pond.

2 *Iris ensata* 'Mandarin'
(syn. *I. kaempferi*) (Bog iris)
A beardless species which prefers moist conditions, close to water. Bears sumptuous flowers of blue, purple, lavender and white or mixtures of these colours in midsummer. Rhizome. Height 2–3ft/60–90cm.

3 *Cyperus involucratus*
(Umbrella sedge)
Tender evergreen with unusual spiky bracts forming a circle beneath greenish flower heads. Prefers to stand in about 6in/15cm of water. Height 2–5ft/60cm–1.5m.

5 *Caltha palustris*
(Marsh marigold, Kingcup)
Popular waterside plant with large, lovely dark green leaves and bold clusters of cup-shaped flowers in late spring. Prefers water 4–6in/10–15cm deep. Height 12–18in/30–45cm.

4 *Iris laevigata* 'Colchesteri'
A beardless Japanese iris, similar to *I. ensata*. Elegant flowers mostly in shades of blue and white in early summer. Easily grown in very moist sites. Height 24–36in/60–90cm.

6 *Sagittaria sagittifolia*
(Common arrowhead)
Arrow-shaped aerial leaves reach well above the water; produces three-petalled white flowers in summer. Water depth from margin to 10in/25cm. Height 18in/45cm.

7 *Nymphaea pygmaea* 'Helvola'
(Water-lily)
Compact, moderately hardy water-lily with small floating leaves, mottled brownish-purple, and waxy, star-shaped, semi-double blooms in midsummer. Needs water 4–12in/10–30cm deep.

12 *Lobelia cardinalis*
(Cardinal flower)
Impressive half hardy perennial
suited to moist or boggy sites.
Eye-catching spikes of dramatic
scarlet–crimson flowers in midsummer; foliage sometimes red-
bronze. Height 30–36in/75–90cm.

11 *Myriophyllum verticillatum*
(Water milfoil)
Submerged water plant with
vivid green foliage in whorls
around the stem which offers
shelter to aquatic creatures.
Efficient oxygenator, but a
vigorous spreader suited to
larger pools.

10 *Nymphaea marliacea* 'Carnea'
(Water-lily)
Moderately vigorous perennial
with large, dark green leaves and
semi-double star-shaped flowers
6–10in/15–25cm across; fragrant.
Water depth 8–24in/20–60cm.

8 *Alisma plantago-aquatica*
(Water plantain)
Erect, bright green, oval leaves
and small gypsophila-like white
flowers borne in tall, loose heads
in summer. Margin to a water depth
of 6in/15cm. Height 30in/75cm.

9 *Nymphaea* 'Escarboucle'
(Water-lily)
Vigorous, free-flowering
perennial, with fragrant, cup-
shaped semi-double flowers
and large floating leaves. One
of the finest of all water-lilies.
Water depth 8–24in/20–60cm.

GARDEN PONDS

Ponds fall into the same category as rockeries—both need careful siting and good design if they are to enhance the garden and not look artificial or intrusive.

Practical considerations must, however, go hand in hand with aesthetics, and you first need to consider whether your garden has an appropriate place for a pond before deciding on the style you want—formal or natural-looking—and the size. The minimum size to sustain animal and plant life and to give a depth that will not freeze solid in winter (to the detriment of plants and fish) is about 6 x 3 x 1ft/ 2 x 1 x 0.3m.

• Choose an open site, for sunlight is essential to the health of surface-living aquatic plants; not many will survive in even partial shade.

• Do not site a pond under large deciduous trees. Falling leaves in autumn will clog it up and if left in the water will use up oxygen at a time when oxygenating plants cannot replace it; tree roots may also crack it.

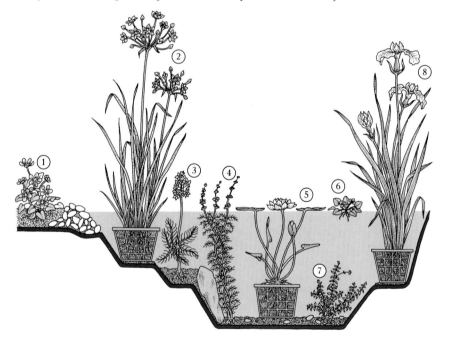

This cross-section of a pond shows marginals planted straight into the soil and also in baskets, for ease of handling. Water-lilies are set in baskets; other plants are planted in soil at the bottom of the pond. Floating plants need water deep enough to accommodate their trailing roots.

1 *Caltha palustris* (Marsh marigold); 2 *Butomus umbellatus* (Flowering rush); 3 *Hottonia palustris* (Water violet); 4 *Myriophyllum spicatum* (Water milfoil); 5 *Nymphaea* spp. (Water-lily); 6 *Stratiotes aloides* (Water soldier); 7 *Elodea canadensis* (Canadian pondweed); 8 *Iris laevigata* (Bog iris).

• Do not site a pond at the bottom of a slope unless you wish also to create a bog garden; excess water will drain down the slope, causing the pond to overflow so that the ground around it is constantly sodden.

Making a pond
Ponds were traditionally built of puddled clay—clay beaten with a spade or mallet until it is thick and smooth—lined with a mixture of straw, lime and clay. Concrete replaced these traditional materials, but it was not entirely satisfactory, for it needed waterproofing and often developed cracks.

Modern materials make construction easy. Today most ponds, other than the pre-formed fibre glass type, some of which can be rather ugly, are made by lining an excavated shape with a toughened plastic or butyl rubber sheet.

When excavating for an informal pond, round the corners and slope the sides outward, leaving a few shallow planting ledges for marginal plants. Line the hole with about 2in/5cm of sand, lay the sheet in it (this should be big enough to overlap the edges by about twice the depth of the pond) and anchor it around the edge with heavy stones. When the pond is filled, the sheet will stretch with the weight of the water and take up the shape. Soil or turf will conceal the edge of the sheeting.

Start preparations in the autumn; this will allow time to complete the pond and to choose plants (they may have to be ordered from a specialist nursery) ready for planting in spring.

Planting methods
As with land plants, most aquatics need some earth to anchor their roots, but planting methods are necessarily different.

• Line a plastic basket with fine nylon mesh and fill it with soil. Never use leaf mould, manure or organic compost; these rot in the water, depleting it of oxygen.

• Dip the plant in a weak solution of permanganate of potash as a precaution against infection of other plants with any pests or diseases.

• Set the plant in the soil. Spread out the roots, but do not entirely cover the crown.

• Spread a layer of gravel over the surface to prevent fish stirring up the soil and making the water murky.

• Position the basket at the recommended depth for the particular plant. Water-lilies should be lowered only gradually to the bottom of the pond or they may not flower in their first season.

PLANTS FOR PONDS

A pond needs different types of plants to keep it healthy and attractive; some examples are given below:

• **Submerged oxygenators**—*Elodea canadensis* (Canadian pondweed); *Hottonia palustris* (Water violet); *Myriophyllum spicatum* (Water milfoil); *Ceratophyllum demersum* (Hornwort).

• **Floating plants**—*Hydrocharis morsus-ranae* (Frogbit); *Stratiotes aloides* (Water soldier).

• **Pond plants**—*Nymphaea* spp. (Water-lily); *Sagittaria natans* (Arrowhead); *Aponogeton distachyum* (Water hawthorn).

• **Marginal plants**—*Menyanthes trifoliata* (Bog bean); *Alisma plantago aquatica* (Water plantain); *Caltha palustris* (Marsh marigold); *Acorus calamus variegata* (Sweet flag).

See also: Pond plants and marginals Pages 198–199
Plant lists Pages 210–219

ROCK GARDEN PLANTS

Most of the plants shown here fall into the category of "alpines", although not all originate in mountain areas. However, most need gritty, free-draining soil and plenty of sunshine, and all share the ability to withstand considerable changes of temperature. These requirements often prompt gardeners to construct special rocky beds for them, where their miniature beauty, raised above ground level, can be better appreciated .

1 *Gentiana septemfida*
(Gentian)
Evergreen perennial, easily grown but preferring humus-rich soil. Trumpet-shaped flowers appear in mid- to late summer. Height 6–8in/15–20cm.

2 *Dianthus deltoides*
(Maiden pink)
Perennial, forming evergreen mound of grey-green leaves; flowers in white, pink or cerise all through summer. Trim after flowering. Height 6–8in/15–20cm.

3 *Lychnis alpina*
(Alpine catchfly)
Perennial with dense tufts of dark green leaves; heads of flowers on sticky stems in summer. Height 4in/10cm.

4 *Lewisia* **Cotyledon Hybrids**
Evergreen perennial with large thick leaves forming flat rosette; showy clusters of yellow, pink to purple flowers in early summer. Good for walls, rock crevices, but needs perfect drainage. Height 12in/30cm.

5 *Sedum spathulifolium*
Mat-forming evergreen with rosettes of grey-green fleshy leaves and clusters of small flowers in midsummer. Height 2–4in/5–10cm.

6 *Saxifraga oppositifolia*
(Purple mountain saxifrage)
Forms a spreading mat of dark green leaves flecked with white; large cup-shaped flowers in spring. Prefers some shade, adequate moisture and peaty soil. Height 2in/5cm.

14 *Saxifraga moschata* **'Dartington Double'**
Forms a moss-like clump of tiny, dense leaves; short stems of double flowers in loose heads in early summer. Prefers a moist, lightly shaded site. Height 4in/10cm.

13 *Primula auricula*
Hardy perennial forming clumps of pale green leaves; umbels of fragrant yellow flowers in late spring. Height 6–9in/15–23cm.

12 *Saxifraga cochlearis* **'Minor'**
Small rosettes of green leaves with white-encrusted edges and heads of red-spotted white flowers in early summer. Needs well-drained alkaline soil. Height 8in/20cm.

11 *Campanula cochleariifolia*
Spreading perennial with wiry stems bearing clusters of small pale blue, white or pink bell-shaped flowers in summer. Height 4–6in/10–15cm.

8 *Aubrieta* **'Gurgedyke'**
Evergreen, mat-forming perennial, good for walls and banks. Compact spreader flowering profusely from spring to early summer; trim after flowering. Thrives in chalky soil. Height 3in/8cm.

9 *Oxalis adenophylla*
Mat-forming, tuberous perennial which produces a rosette of grey-green leaves that die down in winter. Flowers in early summer. Height 3in/8cm.

7 *Armeria maritima*
(Thrift, Sea pink)
Hardy, clump-forming evergreen with grey-green leaves. Stiff stems bear many-flowered heads in summer. Height 4–12in/10–30cm.

10 *Viola* x *wittrockiana* **'Irish Molly'**
Hardy perennial; one of the tufted pansies propagated by division or cuttings. Flowers throughout the season if dead-headed and well watered. Upright habit. Height 4–6in/10–15cm.

ROCK GARDENS AND ALPINES

M any small gardens do not have a natural focal point, but all gardens need something to draw the eye and to provide a change of visual pace and perspective. A well-designed rockery will do just that. It will also enable you to grow interesting and beautiful plants which may not thrive or be shown to advantage elsewhere in the garden.

If it is to look really pleasing, a rockery must fit in with the scale of the garden and look as if the stones belong there. Aim for a natural look by utilizing any existing slope of the land; if the site is flat, build the earth up gradually toward the stones. A garden wall can be used to retain the earth on one side and difficult areas can be disguised by plants, such as *Aubrieta*, which form spreading mats of colour.

Building a rockery
The choice of stone for a rockery is critical; where possible, use local stone. Make sure the stones are big enough—a few well-placed, larger rocks are better than many small ones. Set them in a roughly layered fashion (make sure the graining, or stratification, runs in the same direction) to form a natural-looking outcrop. When you are satisfied you have found the correct position, mix coarse gravel with the soil and pack it under and around the rocks.

It is essential for the health of alpines that the drainage is good, that they have plenty of sunshine and that their leaves and roots are not subject to constantly damp conditions. It follows, therefore, that an alpine bed or rockery should never be sited under trees with their dripping foliage and that the soil mix should contain plenty of grit or fine gravel.

Rocks and water go naturally together; try to combine a rockery with an informal pool or even, where there is sufficient slope and space, with a small cascade. A submersible electric pump in the lowest pool will return the water to the top.

Raised beds
If a rockery is inappropriate in your garden, but you wish to have some genuine alpines, it is possible to grow them in other ways. A raised bed can be constructed from brick or the walls can be made from logs or old railway sleepers.

Filled with hardcore at the bottom for good drainage, a layer of peat mixed with soil and grit in a ratio of 3:1 and a thin top layer of gravel, such a bed will provide alpines with good growing conditions. As

Clothe a bare wall by planting hardy dwarf species *Dianthus* to form a mat on the top and inserting *Lewisia* into a pocket of rich, well-drained soil between the stones.

In a small garden, where there is no space for a conventional rockery, alpines and rock plants can be shown to advantage by planting them in the crevices between paving slabs. Choose a sunny, well-drained part of the garden, where the plants are not in constant danger of being trodden on.

a bonus, the small plants can more easily be seen and appreciated when they are raised off the ground. Do not use heavy compost or manure and be sure that the soil does not contain lumps of chalk; top up the peat and gravel in the bed yearly.

Another attractive way of growing alpines is to plant them in the crevices between the paving of pathways and patios. A paved corner in which alpines, such as sempervivums, phlox and saxifrages, can flourish makes an interesting feature in a garden.

The slabs, whether concrete or stone, should be large and not laid in a tight mosaic. Gaps between them need not be great but should be big enough to allow the plants to root securely. The area must be well drained and enjoy sunshine or a little light shade, and plenty of peat and grit should be mixed with the soil.

Planting alpines

Alpines should be planted in the same way as perennials: dust a little bonemeal into the hole and pack a little peat around the roots as they are planted. Then spread a handful of coarse grit around the plants and under the leaves to prevent them becoming sodden. Those plants that cannot stand damp winter conditions can be protected with a glass cloche during the worst of the weather.

See also: Planting Pages 20–21
Protecting plants Pages 54–55

HERBS AND ORNAMENTAL VEGETABLES

Herbs were once an essential part of the domestic garden, since they were used for medicinal and cosmetic purposes as well as cooking. Still popular for culinary use, they have recently assumed a renewed importance as healing agents. And decorative vegetables, such as ornamental cabbage and crimson chard, have renewed a fashion for the old French *potager*, or ornamental kitchen garden.

1 *Foeniculum vulgare*
(Fennel)
Self-seeding perennial usually treated as an annual; light feathery foliage with a slight aniseed flavour used in fish dishes; also in soap and confectionery. Height 5–6ft/1.5–2m.

2 *Borago officinalis*
(Borage)
Annual with attractive flowers, usually electric blue, used to decorate summer punches and in salads and pickles. Height 24in/60cm.

3 *Ocimum basilicum*
(Sweet basil)
Half hardy, heat-loving annual. Aromatic, used extensively in stews, salads and fish dishes. When grown in the house is supposed to keep flies away. Height 18in/45cm.

4 *Mentha* x *piperita*
(Peppermint)
Perennial which likes moisture-retentive soil and spreads by runners; control growth or grow in a tub. Used in salads and drinks. Height 12–18in/30–45cm.

5 *Thymus* x *citriodorus* 'Silver Queen' (Variegated lemon thyme) Small, hardy, evergreen shrub, with tiny, highly aromatic silvery leaves and pink flowers. Widely used in cooking. Height 10in/25cm.

6 *Artemisia dracunculus*
(French tarragon)
Bushy, slightly spreading perennial needing a sunny, well-drained site. Add the strongly flavoured leaves to fish dishes, sauces and vinegar. Height 18–24in/45–60cm.

12 *Brassica oleracea*
(Ornamental cabbage)
Biennial grown as an annual. Large
round head of curly pink, white
and/or green leaves; inedible but
decorative in herb garden or border.
Height 10–18in/25–45cm.

11 *Laurus nobilis*
(Sweet bay)
Evergreen bush or small tree. Keep
trimmed or grow in a container; foliage
may be scorched by frost or cold wind.
Tough, elongated leaves, used in stews,
are believed to act as a digestive.
Height 10–18ft/3–5.5m.

10 *Rosmarinus officinalis*
(Rosemary)
Evergreen shrub; keep trimmed.
Small, highly aromatic dark
green leaves are delicious added
to many foods. Used also to
counter high blood pressure
and as a hair tonic.
Height 3–6ft/1–2m.

7 *Petroselinum crispum*
'Neapolitanum'
(Large-leaved parsley)
Biennial, usually grown as an
annual; curled leaves used to
flavour sauces and salads and as
a garnish; high vitamin A and C
content. Height 10–12in/25–30cm.

8 *Allium schoenoprasum*
(Chives)
Hardy perennial bulb, with
round heads of pink flowers in
summer. Mild onion-flavoured
leaves used in salads, sauces,
egg and cheese dishes. Height
10–12in/25–30cm.

9 *Salvia officinalis*
(Sage)
Semi-evergreen, spreading
bushy shrub; propagate by
cuttings or seeds. Strong-
flavoured grey-green leaves
good with pork or duck; use as
an infusion as a gargle for sore
throats. Height 24in/60cm.

THE HERB GARDEN

Herbs for cooking and medicinal purposes have traditionally been grown in beds, in a decorative formal scheme, and this is still the most suitable way to plant them where there is sufficient space. In a small garden it may not be possible to find room for a separate herb garden, but that is no reason to be without these plants. Rosemary and lavender, for example, are attractive enough to be used as hedges or, with fennel, as ornamental shrubs in the border; other herbs, such as basil and parsley, will do well in containers on a patio or even a window ledge.

Ideally, a herb garden should be sited on a slope facing the sun, and the soil should be well drained, light and rich in humus, although most herbs will tolerate any reasonable garden soil. Some, mint for example, enjoy moist conditions, and thyme will flourish in dry chalky soil.

Beds should be small enough for easy access and, where a bed is shared by several different herbs, it is important to place the taller ones at the back so that they do not prevent lower-growing plants getting their share of the sunshine.

Before planting, the beds should be dug over and plenty of organic material—well-rotted manure or compost—mixed with the soil. Thereafter, herbs demand little care. A spring feed of blood, fish and bone meal will benefit them, but since many of these plants originate in the comparatively dry Mediterranean region, most can survive without heavy watering.

Annuals, such as borage, coriander and dill, can be grown from seed; but others, including sage and thyme, are easily grown from cuttings. The mints can be propagated by division.

The plan for the herb garden illustrated here shows box and rosemary used as low hedges to define the design. The herbs include those commonly used in the kitchen, such as parsley, bay and basil, and less well-known varieties of the familiar mint and thyme.

Herbs grown outdoors can be picked during the summer to be used fresh, or dried for winter use. Bunch them and hang them in a warm, airy place; when the leaves are brittle, take them off the stems and store them in airtight containers. Herbs with soft leaves, such as chervil, can also be freeze dried. Blanch the leaves in boiling water for a minute; cover with cold water; when quite cold, drain them, place in plastic containers, and freeze at once.

KEY TO THE PLANTING PLAN
1 *Mentha spicata* (Spearmint); **2** *Mentha suaveolens* 'Variegata' (Variegated applemint); **3** *Mentha x piperita* 'Citrata' (Eau de Cologne mint); **4** *Mentha x piperita* (Black peppermint); **5** *Petroselinum crispum* (Parsley—compact); **6** *Allium schoenoprasum* (Chives); **7** *Origanum vulgare* 'Aureum' (Golden marjoram); **8** *Melissa officinalis* 'Aurea' (Golden balm); **9** *Allium fistulosum* (Welsh onion); **10** *Helichrysum angustifolium* (Curry plant); **11** *Calendula officinalis* (Pot marigold); **12** *Petroselinum crispum* 'Neapolitanum' (Parsley—large leaved); **13** *Coriandrum sativum* (Coriander); **14** *Tanacetum parthenium* 'Aureum' (Golden feverfew); **15** *Salvia officinalis* 'Purpurascens' (Purple sage); **16** *Salvia officinalis* 'Tricolor' (Variegated sage); **17** *Ocimum basilicum* (Basil); **18** *Laurus nobilis* (Sweet bay); **19** *Borago officinalis* (Borage); **20** *Artemisia dracunculus* (French tarragon); **21** *Thymus vulgaris* (Common thyme); **22** *Thymus x citriodorus* (Lemon thyme); **23** *Rosmarinus officinalis* (Rosemary); **24** *Buxus microphylla* (Box).

V See also: Preparing the ground Pages 10–11
Planting out Pages 20–21

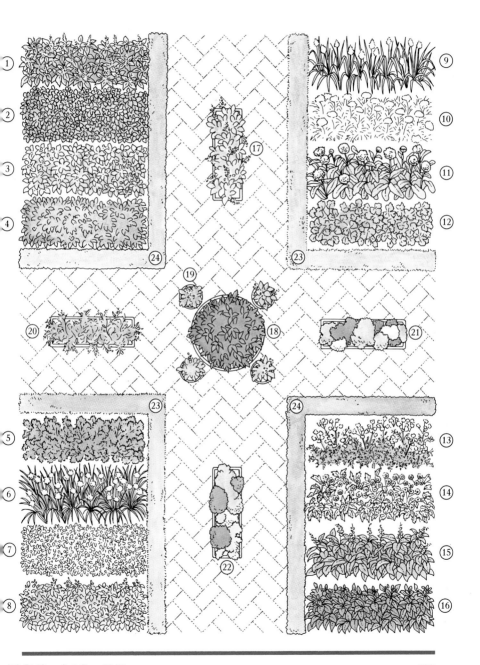

PLANTS FOR SPECIAL PLACES/1

HERBACEOUS PLANTS (INCLUDING GRASSES) FOR HOT, DRY CONDITIONS

Acaena
Acanthus
Achillea
Agave
Aloe
Alyssum
Antennaria
Anthemis
Arabis
Armeria
Artemisia
Asphodelus
Aubrieta
Ballota
Calamintha
Centaurea
Centranthus
Cerastium
Chamaemelum
Cheiranthus
Cichorium
Cirsium
Cistus
Convolvulus
Coreopsis
Cotula
Crambe

Crepis
Crinum
Cynoglossum
Dianthus
Cynara
Diascia
Echinops
Elymus
Erodium
Eryngium
Erysimum
Euphorbia (most)
Festuca
Foeniculum
Geranium (some)
Glaucium
Gypsophila
Helianthemum
Helictotrichon
Holcus mollis
Hypericum
Iberis
Incarvillea arguta
Linaria
Linum
Lupinus
Lychnis

Mandragora
Nepeta
Oenothera
Onopordum
Osteospermum
Pennisetum
Penstemon
Perovskia
Phlomis
Potentilla (some)
Romneya
Salvia argentea
Santolina
Saponaria
Scabiosa
Sedum
Sempervivum
Senecio
Silene maritima
Stachys
Stipa
Thymus
Verbascum
Zauschneria

BULBOUS PLANTS FOR HOT, DRY CONDITIONS

Agapanthus
Allium
Alstroemeria
Amaryllis belladonna
Aristea
Crinum
Crocosmia

Crocus (some)
Eucomis
Hermodactylis
Ipheion
Iris (bearded)
Muscari
Nerine

Ornithogalum
Pancratium
Sternbergia
Tigridia
Triteleia laxa
Tulipa (some)
Watsonia

HERBACEOUS PLANTS (INCLUDING GRASSES) FOR MOIST SHADE

Aconitum
Actaea
Ajuga
Alchemilla mollis
Aquilegia
Arum
Aruncus
Asarum
Astilbe
Astrantia
Bamboos (most)
Bergenia
Brunnera
Carex
Cimicifuga
Deinanthe
Deschampsia
Dicentra
Epilobium

Epimedium
Ferns (almost all)
Filipendula
Hakonechloa
Helleborus
Hepatica
Heucherella
Holcus
Hosta
Jeffersonia
Kirengashoma
Ligularia
Liriope
Luzula
Lysimachia
Mentha
Mertensia virginica
Milium
Miscanthus

Molinia
Omphalodes
Pachysandra
Paeonia (some)
Petasites
Phlox (some)
Polygonatum
Primula (most)
Pulmonaria
Rancunculus (some)
Rheum
Rodgersia
Scrophularia
Thalictrum
Tiarella
Trillium
Vancouveria
Viola
Waldsteinia

BULBOUS PLANTS FOR MOIST SHADE

Anemone (some)
Asarum
Camassia
Convallaria

Erythronium
Fritillaria (some)
Galanthus
Leucojum

Lilium (some)
Narcissus (some)
Tricyrtis

HERBACEOUS PLANTS FOR DRY SHADE

Alchemilla
Arum
Bergenia
Brunnera
Digitalis
Epimedium
Euphorbia robbiae

Galeobdolon argenteum
Helleborus
Heuchera
Iris foetidissima
Lamium
Liriope
Omphalodes

Pachysandra
Pulmonaria
Rubus
Symphytum
Tellima grandiflora
Vinca
Viola labradorica

PLANTS FOR SPECIAL PLACES/2

SHRUBS FOR SHADE

Arctostaphylos
Aucuba
Buxus
Camellia
Cornus canadensis
Daphne
Elaeagnus
Euonymus
Fatsia
Gaultheria

Hypericum calycinum
Ilex
Kalmia
Leucothöe
Ligustrum
Lonicera
Mahonia
Neillia
Pieris formosa
Prunus laurocerasus

Rhododendron (not azalea)
Ribes (some)
Ruscus
Sarcococca
Skimmia
Symphoricarpos
Taxus
Vaccinium
Viburnum (some)
Vinca

HERBACEOUS PLANTS FOR WET SITES

Acorus
Astilbe
Caltha
Cardamine
Carex
Decodon
Filipendula
Glyceria
Gunnera
Hemerocallis
Houttuynia

Inula
Iris (some)
Ligularia
Luzula
Lysichiton
Lysimachia
Lythrum
Matteuccia
Mimulus
Miscanthus
Parnassia

Peltiphyllum
Persicaria
Polygonum (some)
Pontederia
Primula (many)
Rodgersia
Trollius
Zantedeschia

TREES AND SHRUBS FOR WET SITES

Alnus
Amelanchier
Betula (some)
Clethra
Cornus
Crataegus (some)
Gaultheria
Ilex
Lyonia

Mespilus
Metasequoia
  glyptostroboides
Myrica
Photinia
Physocarpus
Populus
Pyrus
Salix

Sambucus
Sorbaria
Sorbus aucuparia
Spiraea
Symphoricarpos
Taxodium
Vaccinium
Viburnum (some)

HERBACEOUS PLANTS (INCLUDING GRASSES) FOR CLAY SOILS

Acanthus
Alchemilla
Aruncus
Bergenia
Caltha
Carex
Cimicifuga
Deschampsia
Epimedium

Euphorbia robbiae
Euryops
Filipendula
Helleborus
Hemerocallis
Hosta
Lamium
Molinia
Panicum

Polygonatum
Potentilla (some)
Primula (many)
Prunella
Rheum
Rodgersia
Symphytum
Trollius
Viola

TREES AND SHRUBS FOR CLAY SOILS

Acer
Aesculus
Alnus
Amelanchier
Aralia
Aucuba
Berberis
Betula
Carpinus
Chaenomeles
Chamaecyparis
Choisya
Colutea
Cornus
Corylus
Cotinus
Cotoneaster
Crataegus
Cryptomeria
Deutzia

Drimys
Escallonia
Eucalyptus
Forsythia
Fraxinus
Genista
Hamamelis
Hibiscus
Hypericum
Ilex
Juglans
Juniperus
Laburnum
Lonicera
Mahonia
Magnolia
Malus
Philadelphus
Pinus (some)
Populus

Potentilla
Pterocarya
Prunus
Pyrancantha
Quercus (some)
Rhododendron (some)
Ribes
Rosa
Salix
Sambucus
Senecio
Skimmia
Sorbus
Spiraea
Taxus
Thuja
Tilia
Viburnum
Weigela

PLANTS FOR SPECIAL PLACES/3

HERBACEOUS AND BULBOUS PLANTS
FOR SEASIDE GARDENS

Achillea	Crocosmia	Nerine
Agapanthus	Dianthus	Oenothera
Allium	Echinops	Origanum
Alstroemeria	Erigeron	Penstemon
Amaryllis	Erodium	Phygelius
Anemone	Eryngium	Pulsatilla
Anthemis	Euphorbia	Ruta
Artemisia	Geranium	Salvia
Aster	Heuchera	Santolina
Bergenia	Iris (some)	Scabiosa
Campanula	Kniphofia	Schizostylis
Catananche	Limonium	Sedum
Centaurea	Linaria	Stachys
Crambe	Melissa	Veronica

TREES AND SHRUBS FOR SEASIDE GARDENS

Acer pseudoplatanus	Griselinia	Pittosporum
Arbutus	Hebe	Podocarpus
Castanea	Helianthemum	Populus
Choisya	Helichrysum	Prunus
Colutea	Hippophae	Pyracantha
Cordyline	Hydrangea	Quercus
Corokia	Ilex	Rhamnus
Cotoneaster	Juniperus	Rosa
Crataegus	Laurus	Rosmarinus
Cupressus	Lavandula	Salix
Cytisus	Lavatera	Sambucus
Elaeagnus	Leycesteria	Santolina
Erica	Ligustrum	Senecio
Escallonia	Lonicera	Sorbus
Eucalyptus	Myrica	Spartium
Euonymus	Olearia	Spiraea
Euphorbia	Parahebe	Tamarix
Fraxinus	Phlomis	Ulex
Fuchsia	Phormium	Viburnum
Garrya	Pinus (some)	Yucca

ANNUALS AND BEDDING PLANTS FOR SEASIDE GARDENS

Antirrhinum	Gilia	Matthiola
Arctotis	Helichrysum	Mesembryanthemum
Calendula officinalis	Helipterum	Myosotis
Chrysanthemum	Iberis	Papaver
Clarkia	Impatiens (Novette Series)	Pelargonium
Coreopsis	Kochia	Penstemon
Cynoglossum	Limnanthes	Portulaca
Dahlia	Limonium	Salvia
Dimorphotheca	Linaria	Sedum
Eschscholzia	Lobelia	Tagetes

HERBACEOUS PLANTS FOR ACID SOILS (LIME HATING)

Carex pendula	Glaucidium	Primula (several)
Celmisia	Lewisia	Smilacina
Dicentra (some)	Lilium (some)	Tricyrtis
Fritillaria (some)	Lithodora	Trillium
Gentiana sino-ornata	Osmunda	Uvularia

TREES AND SHRUBS FOR ACID SOILS (LIME HATING)

Abies (some)	Disanthus	Lomatia
Acacia (some)	Embothrium	Magnolia (some)
Andromeda	Empetrum	Myrica
Arctostaphylos	Enkianthus	Nyssa
Calluna	Erica	Pernettya
Camellia	Eucryphia	Phyllodoce
Cassiope	Fothergilla	Picea (most)
Chamaedaphne	Gaultheria	Pinus (some)
Clethra	Kalmia	Pieris
Cornus (some)	Halesia	Rhododendron
Corylopsis	Hamamelis	Rhodothamnus
Crinodendron	Ledum	Stewartia
Daboecia	Leucothöe	Styrax
Desfontainea	Liquidambar	Vaccinium
Diapensia	Loiseleuria	Zenobia

HERBACEOUS PERENNIALS FOR ALKALINE SOIL

Acanthus	Erysimum	Penstemon
Achillea	Euphorbia	Phlox
Alchemilla	Filipendula	Physostegia
Allium	Gaillardia	Polemonium
Althaea	Gazania	Polygala
Alyssum	Geranium	Polygonum
Anaphalis	Geum	Potentilla
Anchusa	Gypsophila	Primula (some)
Anthemis	Helenium	Pulmonaria
Aquilegia	Helianthus	Pulsatilla
Aubrieta	Helichrysum	Pyrethrum
Bellis	Helleborus	Rudbeckia
Bergenia	Hemerocallis	Salvia (some)
Campanula	Hesperis	Sanguisorba
Catananche	Heucherella	Saponaria
Centaurea	Hosta	Saxifraga (some)
Centranthus	Hypericum	Scabiosa
Cheiranthus	Iberis	Sedum
Clematis	Iris (some)	Sempervivum
Convolvulus	Kniphofia	Sidalcea
Coreopsis	Linaria	Silene
Dahlia	Linum	Solidago
Delphinium	Lobelia	Stachys
Dianthus	Lunaria	Thalictrum
Dicentra (some)	Lupinus	Tradescantia
Dimorphotheca	Matthiola	Trollius
Doronicum	Myosotis	Verbascum
Echium	Nepeta	Verbena
Erigeron	Origanum	Veronica
Erinus	Paeonia	Viola
Eryngium (some)	Papaver	

TREES AND SHRUBS FOR ALKALINE SOILS

Acer (many)	Buddleia	Ceanothus
Aesculus	Buxus	Cercis
Aucuba	Caragana	Choisya
Berberis	Carpinus	Cistus

Colutea	Hypericum	Rhus
Cotoneaster	Juniperus	Rosa
Crataegus	Laurus	Rosmarinus
Cytisus	Ligustrum	Sambucus
Deutzia	Lonicera	Sarcococca
Elaeagnus	Mahonia	Senecio
Euonymus	Malus	Spartium
Fagus	Olearia	Spiraea
Forsythia	Philadelphus	Symphoricarpos
Fraxinus	Phillyrea	Syringa
Fuchsia	Photinia	Taxus
Genista	Pinus	Thuja
Hebe	Potentilla	Vinca
Hibiscus	Prunus (some)	Weigela

TREES FOR WINDY, EXPOSED SITES

Acer	Chaemacyparis (some)	Laurus
Alnus	Cupressus (some)	Melia
Araucaria	Elaeagnus commutata	Pinus (some)
Arbutus	Eucalpytus	Salix
Cedrus	Fraxinus	Sorbus
Celtis	Ilex	

TREES AND SHRUBS FOR SMALL GARDENS

Acer*	Cotoneaster	Hydrangea*
Arbutus	Crataegus*	Hypericum
Berberis	Cytisus	Ilex*
Betula	Daphne	Juniperus*
Buxus*	Deutzia	Kerria
Calluna*	Erica*	Laburnum
Camellia*	Escallonia	Laurus*
Ceanothus	Euonymus	Lavandula*
Chaenomeles	Fuchsia*	Lonicera
Choisya	Genista	Magnolia*
Cistus	Gleditsia	Mahonia
Cornus	Hamamelis	Malus*
Cotinus	Hebe*	Myrtus*

PLANTS FOR SPECIAL PLACES/5

Osmanthus
Philadelphus
Phlomis
Potentilla
Prunus* (various)
Pyrus
Rhododendron*
Ribes

Robinia
Rosa*
Rhus
Santolina*
Senecio
Skimmia
Sorbus*
Spiraea*

Syringa
Thuja*
Trachycarpus*
Viburnum*
Weigela

suitable for containers.

CLIMBERS FOR COOL, SHADED WALLS

Akebia
Celastrus
Clematis (some)

Hedera
Hydrangea
Lonicera

Muehlenbeckia
Parthenocissus
Schizophragma

PLANTS FOR PAVING, WALL CREVICES AND ROCKERIES

Acaena
Achillea
Ageratum
Alyssum
Arabis
Armeria
Arenaria
Artemisia
Aubrieta
Calceolaria
Calluna
Campanula
Cerastium
Cheiranthus
Chionodoxa
Corydalis
Cyananthus
Cyclamen (some)
Dianthus
Draba
Dryas
Erica

Erigeron
Erinus
Erodium
Genista (some)
Gentiana
Geranium (some)
Geum
Gypsophila repens
Helichrysum
Helianthemum
Houstonia
Hepatica
Hypericum (some)
Iberis
Inula (some)
Iris (some)
Lampranthus
Leontopodium
Lewisia
Limnanthes
Linaria
Linum

Lithodora
Lobelia
Lobularia
Lychnis
Malcolmia
Morisia
Muscari
Myosotis
Nemophila
Nierembergia
Omphalodes
Origanum
Papaver (some)
Parahebe
Penstemon (some)
Phlox (some)
Ramonda
Saxifraga
Scilla sibirica
Sedum
Thymus
Viola

PLANTS FOR GROUND COVER

Acaena
Ajuga*
Arctostaphylos
Asperula odorata*
Aubrieta
Bergenia*
Brunnera
Calluna
Campanula
Ceanothus
Ceratostigma
Cornus canadensis*
Cotoneaster
Dianthus
Dryas
Duchesnea*
Epimedium*
Erica
Euonymus*
Euphorbia*
Galeobdolon*
Gaultheria*
Geranium

Hebe (some)
Hedera
Helianthemum
Helxine*
Hosta*
Hypericum*
Juniperus
Lamium*
Leucothöe*
Loiseleuria
Lysimachia*
Mahonia (some)
Oxalis*
Osteospermum
Pachysandra*
Picea abies
Pernettya
Phlomis
Polygonum (some)
Portulaca
Potentilla
Pulmonaria*
Rheum

Rosa (some)
Rosmarinus
Rubus (some)*
Ruscus*
Salix
Sarcococca
Saponaria
Saxifraga*
Sedum
Stachys
Stephanandra
Tellima*
Thymus
Tiarella*
Tolmiea*
Vaccinium
Veronica (some)
Vinca*
Waldsteinia*

* *suitable for shade*

PLANTS FOR POND MARGINS AND BOG GARDENS

Acorus
Alisma
Astilbe
Butomus
Calla
Caltha
Carex
Dodecatheon
Filipendula
Geum
Glyceria
Gunnera

Hosta (some)
Houttuynia
Iris (some)
Lysimachia
Lysichiton
Lythrum
Matteuccia
Menyanthes
Mimulus
Myosotis
Myrica
Osmunda

Polygonum
Pontederia
Primula (various)
Ranunculus
Rodgersia
Sagittaria
Scirpus
Symphytum
Trollius
Typha
Veronica
Zantedeschia

INDEX

Page numbers in **bold** type indicate major references, including illustrations; page numbers in *italic* indicate captions.

ACKNOWLEDGEMENTS

Illustration credits

Eileen Batterberry Pages 72/3
Patricia Capon Pages 37, 62
Lynn Chadwick Pages 98–9, 102–3,
  106–7, 110–11, 114–15, 118–19, 122–3,
  126–7, 130–1, 134–5, 138–9, 142–3,
  146–7, 150–1, 154–5, 162–3, 166–7,
  170–1, 186–7, 190–1, 194–5, 198–9
Coral Mula Pages 1, 2, 3, 14, 15, 17, 19,

20, 21/2, 23, 24/5, 26-7, 30/1, 33,
  34/5, 38, 40, 42, 44, 46, 48/9, 50/1,
  54/5, 56/7, 59, 60/1, 78/9, 90/1,
  92/3, 94/5, 108, 124–5, 156/7,
  164–5, 168/9, 188/9, 204/5, 209
Gillie Newman Pages 74–5
Liz Pepperell Endpapers
Sandra Pond & **Will Giles** Pages 6, 8,
  10–11, 13, 52, 63, 65, 66, 68, 71, 76/7,
  80/1, 82/3, 85, 86/7, 88–9, 96,

100/1, 104/5, 113, 117, 136, 141, 149,
  152/3, 161 173, 181, 184/5, 200
Gill Tomblin Pages 206–7
Ann Winterbotham Pages 174–5,
  178–9, 182–3, 202–3
John Woodcock Pages 116,120–1, 129,
  133, 144/5, 176/7, 180, 192/3, 196/7

Index Valerie Chandler